Cybercrime

**Recent Titles in
Crime, Media, and Popular Culture**

Cybercrime

Criminal Threats from Cyberspace

Susan W. Brenner

Crime, Media, and Popular Culture
Frankie Y. Bailey and Steven Chermak, Series Editors

 PRAEGER

AN IMPRINT OF ABC-CLIO, LLC
Santa Barbara, California • Denver, Colorado • Oxford, England

Library of Congress Cataloging-in-Publication Data

Brenner, Susan W., 1947–
    Cybercrime : criminal threats from cyberspace / Susan W. Brenner.
        p. cm. — (Crime, media, and popular culture)
    Includes bibliographical references and index.
    ISBN 978–0–313–36546–1 (hard copy : alk. paper) — ISBN 978–0–313–36547–8 (ebook)
1. Computer crimes. 2. Computer networks—Law and legislation. I. Title.
HV6773.B75   2010
364.16′8—dc22 2009048693

ISBN: 978–0–313–36546–1
EISBN: 978–0–313–36547–8

14 13 12 11 10   1 2 3 4 5

This book is also available on the World Wide Web as an eBook.
Visit www.abc-clio.com for details.

Praeger
An Imprint of ABC-CLIO, LLC

ABC-CLIO, LLC
130 Cremona Drive, P.O. Box 1911
Santa Barbara, California 93116-1911

This book is printed on acid-free paper ∞

Manufactured in the United States of America

Contents

Series Foreword

This book is an outstanding contribution to the interdisciplinary series on *Crime, Media, and Popular Culture* from Praeger Publishers. Because of the pervasiveness of media in our lives and the salience of crime and criminal justice issues, we feel it is especially important to provide a home for scholars who are engaged in innovative and thoughtful research on important crime and mass media issues. It seemed essential to include a book in the series that examined the dynamic nature of cybercrime.

Many of us have a limited knowledge of the crimes that occur in the world of computers and the Internet, known as "cybercrimes" because they occur in "cyberspace." These crimes run the gambit from scams and fraud to stalking and even terrorism. These crimes have the potential for extraordinary impact on the lives of individuals and on society as a whole. Although many people fear street crimes involving face-to-face interactions with violent strangers, they are unaware of the predatory possibilities of an e-mail solicitation.

Cybercrime is not an altogether new breed of crime. As Professor Brenner explains in this book, the crimes carried out by this new breed of criminal often reflect emotions as old as humankind. These emotions include greed, obsession, or a desire for revenge. What is new is the space in which the crimes are played out. The cybercriminal and his or her victim may be only miles apart or a world away from each other. Scam artists on another continent can seduce those inclined to avarice into parting with their money. An obsessed acquaintance can go into cyberspace and stalk the object of his or her desire. Another can seek revenge by assuming the identity of the victim to post photos on a porn site or leave angry or embarrassing messages about the victim on a another site. And it can all be done while the cybercriminal sits at his or her computer.

Cybercrime raises issues of privacy, or rather, the increasing loss of privacy. The use of the computer for legitimate activities—from banking and social networking to searches for employment—is a commonplace, almost taken-for-granted aspect of modern life. However, the information that we send into cyberspace makes us vulnerable to cybercrime. The details of our identities and our activities, once shared online, become accessible to those who would steal and misuse the information.

From the beginning, as Professor Brenner discusses, cyberspace attracted "hackers," a breed of outlaw computer whizzes who attacked sites, such as federal agencies, to prove that it could be done. These young outlaws sometimes were recruited to develop ways of protecting the sites they had penetrated. In recent years, for professional criminals who hack into sites, it has been done for the money that can be made from crimes such as corporate extortion. The lack of a sufficient number of law enforcement and security experts trained in detecting and eradicating cybercrime means that organizations and agencies remain at risk from cyberattacks.

The goal for agencies such as the Federal Bureau of Investigation (FBI) is to reduce, if not eliminate, this risk by capturing the criminals. However, the techniques that have been developed to prevent computer intrusions frequently lag behind the ability of cybercriminals to develop a new virus or to carry on their activities beyond the reach of the U.S. government. The increased risk post-9/11 of a terrorist attack launched in cyberspace is no longer the stuff of science fiction.

At the same time, there are some issues, such as invasion of privacy of suspects or the censorship of free speech concerns, with which we must deal. At what point would such concerns be suspended in pursuit of the cybercriminal?

In this book, Professor Brenner provides an accessible and informative exploration of the history of cybercrime, the various categories of cybercrime, and the law enforcement response. Drawing on true cases of cybercrime and fictional depictions in popular culture, Professor Brenner tells us what we need to know about the new world created by the expansion of computer technology. As she illustrates, although there are reasons for concern about cyberspace, we can only go forward into this brave new world. As the technology evolves, the responses of both citizens and the criminal justice system must also evolve.

Frankie Y. Bailey and Steven Chermak,
Series Editors

Twenty-First Century *Twilight Zone*: Stalking a Town

INTRODUCTION

In the *Twilight Zone* episode "The Monsters Are Due on Maple Street," aliens from another planet manipulate the residents of a sleepy Midwestern suburb into turning on each other in what becomes an orgy of violence.[1] The aliens do this by turning the suburbanites' technology against them on a summer evening. They begin by shutting off phone and electric service to the suburb.

As the residents gather in the street to speculate about what is happening, one of them named Pete leaves, saying he will walk to the next suburb and find out what "is going on." Those left behind speculate about the outages and the odd things that preceded them: a flash of light, something passing overhead, and a loud roar. A man named Les tries unsuccessfully to start his car. As he walks away from the vehicle, the aliens start it remotely, with no one inside. This causes the other, already unnerved residents to think Les must be "in on" whatever is happening to them. They begin to interrogate Les about why he spends nights in his backyard, looking up at the sky. A boy who reads science fiction says the mysterious events are part of an invasion by "space aliens," some of whom would have infiltrated the suburb disguised as humans. By now, night has fallen, and the residents still have no electricity, no transportation, and no communication.

Les says he is an insomniac and goes to the backyard when he cannot sleep. As he tries to explain his behavior, the lights go on in his home and loud music blares from inside. The others become even more suspicious. A neighbor named Steve tries to defend Les, which makes the crowd also suspect him of being involved in whatever is happening to them. Charlie, a loud and aggressive resident, begins cross-examining Steve about a mysterious radio he claims to be building but no one has seen. At that point, the terrified crowd sees a silhouetted figure—maybe a "space monster"—walking toward them. Frightened, like the others, Charlie grabs a shotgun and shoots at the figure, killing Pete, who had walked to the next suburb to find out what was going on.

As Charlie claims it was self-defense, the lights come on in his house, and the crowd turns on him. He runs for home, with the others chasing him and throwing stones. After being hit by a stone, he stops and tries to deflect the crowd by blaming the boy who told them an invasion was coming. ("How did he know?")As the crowd turns on the boy, lights and telephones start going on and off in other houses, and cars and lawn mowers begin to start and stop for no apparent reason. The residents of Maple Street descend into madness, smashing windows and attacking each other.

The scene shifts to a hillside overlooking the suburb. Two aliens stand by their spaceship, watching the riot on Maple Street. One of them notes how easy it is to turn humans against each other by tinkering with the technology on which they rely.

When this *Twilight Zone* episode aired in 1960, the only entities that could have implemented the scenario it depicts were the utility companies . . . and, perhaps, space aliens. That is no longer true. As we will see in this chapter and in succeeding chapters, our ability to use cyberspace alters the fabric of our lives in fundamental and irreversible ways. The most significant aspect of cyberspace for our purposes is that our access to it erodes the monopolization of power by governments and corporations.

In 1960, only the electric company would have been able to turn the power on and off on Maple Street, and only the telephone company could have done the same with the phone service. Back then, utility companies (and government agencies, banks, and other private entities) were the masters of their respective domains. Someone bent on harassing the residents of Maple Street could have shut off the phone or electric service by cutting cables but would not have been able to tinker with the services, turning them on and off selectively. In 1960, the world revolved around tangible assets and resources; utility companies and other public and private entities could secure their assets and their processes behind walls, fences, and doors. They could screen and limit those who had access to the premises and the assets they protected. They could, in sum, keep the rest of us, including "the bad guys," out.

Almost 50 years later, that has changed. Walls, fences, and doors still keep people from physically invading protected places, but physical access is no longer the only option. Today, people with sophisticated computer expertise—commonly known as "hackers"—could replicate the tactics the aliens used on Maple Street except, perhaps, for remotely turning cars and lawn mowers on and off. As we will see in later chapters, cyberspace makes what used to be physically secured areas accessible to anyone with the requisite, often minimal, level of computer expertise. As a result, we effectively live in a world with four dimensions (five if you include time): the height, length, and width of real space plus virtual space. Virtual space lets those of us who are law-abiding citizens do marvelous things. Unfortunately, as we shall see, it also lets those of us who are less law-abiding break rules and wreak havoc in various ways.

Perhaps no case better illustrates the power cyberspace gives us to wreak havoc in new and terrifying ways than a 1999 incident in which a man effectively replicated the aliens' manipulation of the hapless residents of Maple Street.

STALKING A TOWN

Townsend is a small town in northern Massachusetts, located about 55 miles from Boston. Townsend was incorporated in 1732 and had 9,501 citizens by 2000. It has four schools: a high school, a middle school, an elementary school, and a preschool. The middle school—Hawthorne Brooke—has approximately 600 students in grades six through eight and 60 faculty and staff members.

In the fall of 1999, some Hawthorne Brooke eighth-graders were spending time after school in an online chat room for Limp Bizkit fans.[2] They used the room to talk about personal things, as well as the band. At one point, a new personwho said he was a Hawthorne Brooke student began hanging out in the chat room. Because he was from Hawthorne Brooke, the others invited him to join them in their private chat room. He did and soon was always there, ready to talk to the others and hear about how their days had gone, what was happening at home, whom they liked, and whom they didn't . . . all the things children of that age talk about.

The new person began to say and do strange things. He said he was a serial rapist and would be coming for them. And he sent them to child pornography that was posted online, which included horrific images of a five-year-old girl being raped. When the others pressed him to tell them who he was, he said he was an eighth-grader they talked about in the chat room. The others retaliated by harassing the innocent boy at school.

By October, the students were beginning to wonder if he really was a Hawthorne Brooke eighth-grader, both because of his increasing erratic behavior and because he was making mistakes when he talked about the school. Some of them finally told him they didn't believe he was a student at their school, which seemed to infuriate him. He said he was going to blow up their school because they didn't believe him.

On October 19, he sent them a link to a Web site with photos posted on it. One was an image of Hawthorne Brooke Middle School with the cross hairs of a rifle scope superimposed on it. Another was a photograph of the school principal, altered to make it look as if he was bleeding from bullet holes in his head and chest. The site also lauded the high-school students who had carried out the Columbine school shootings five months earlier. On October 20, the mystery person added a "hit list" to the site. It listed the first names of 24 Hawthorne Brooke students and the last names of three teachers. Under the list was this sentence: "You lucky individuals will go home with more holes in your body than you came with."

The students were terrified. When they told their parents what was going on and showed them the site, the parents were terrified, too. No one knew what to do, and no one knew whom to trust. It was clear that the mysterious person in the chat room was a local because he knew so much about what had gone on in the school from day to day—who wore what, who sat with whom at lunch, who was mad at whom, and so on.

Police and school officials held a meeting with the parents of the students whose names were on the "hit list," but no one really knew what to do about the person who posted it. Panic set in as the community realized they were at the apparent mercy of an unknown psychopath. As a member of the community noted later, their tormentor made it seem that violence was imminent, and in a post-Columbine world, everyone—students, teachers, and parents—was terrified and suspicious of each other. Everyone knew the person responsible *had* to be someone affiliated with the school; otherwise, how could he know so much about it? So students suspected their teachers, the staff at the school, and each other; parents suspected teachers, staff members, and every child but their own; and teachers and staff members suspected each other and their students. The climate must have been unimaginable.

The morning after the meeting, police used bomb-sniffing dogs to search the halls and classrooms at Hawthorne Brooke. They found nothing. They assigned an officer to the school, to be on the lookout for . . . whatever. As students arrived, teachers searched their book bags, looking for weapons or anything suspicious—anything that might identify the person who was responsible for all of this. Many parents simply refused to send their children to school, and some teachers quit.

At that point, their mysterious tormentor took things offline and into the real world. The mother of a girl who was on the "hit list" was a secretary at Hawthorne Brooke. When she answered a call to the school, all she heard was music. Police later identified it as a song linked to the Columbine shootings. When the woman got home, the same music had been left on the family's answering machine. Her husband was so upset he went to his brother to borrow a gun to protect his family from the person who was terrorizing their town. His brother talked him out of it.

When it seemed as if disaster would strike at any minute, the police got a break. Working with the state police, Townsend officers traced the mysterious person's Internet activity to the Maple Woods Community College in Missouri. They later traced the calls to the school and the family's answering machine to a pay phone at the same college. At that point, the police assumed the perpetrator was in Townsend and was working with someone in Missouri to make it seem that the online activity and calls were coming from there.

As the Massachusetts officers worked with their Missouri counterparts, it began to become apparent that their perpetrator was not, and had never been, in Townsend. The mysterious figure who terrorized a town and turned neighbor against neighbor was a 19-year-old paraplegic from Smithville, Missouri: Christian Hunold.[3]

Hunold's mother was the chief financial officer for a local school district; his father was a retired high-school teacher. Until he was 15 years old, Hunold was an honor-roll student who played soccer and participated in his school band. When he was 15, he took a ride with a friend who had just gotten his driver's license. They were on their way to a mall when the driver lost control of the car, and it smashed into a tree. Hunold was badly injured. He eventually regained the use of his arms and some use of his hands, but he would never walk again.

As the years passed and Hunold graduated from high school, his parents and friends all thought he had put the accident behind him, but he had not. He resented being physically dependent on his parents; and he seethed about the unfairness of having lost everything—sports, music, the ability to lead a regular life—while the person who was responsible for the accident, the driver, walked away essentially unharmed.

Isolated at home in his wheelchair, Hunold discovered he was good at computer programming and Web design, and he decided to study computer science at a community college. As he spent hours on the family computer, he discovered something else: He could be a different person—a strong, whole person—in cyberspace. By the time he found his way into the Limp Bizkit chat room and met the Hawthorne Brooke students, he was spending eight hours a day online, escaping the life he hated.

As Hunold got to know the Hawthorne Brooke students, he found he hated their childish obsessions and complaints, and he decided to give them a taste of "the real world." He later told investigators he was able to pass as a Hawthorne Brooke student for so long because he spent a lot of time listening to the students talk to each other and talking to them individually. When he chatted with students, Hunold would ask about their families, their houses, their pets, and who they hung out with at lunch and other times. Thus, he acquired the information he used to convince them he was one of their classmates. As Hunold grew adept, he could chat knowledgeably about who lived where or wore what or had a dog (and what the dog's name was) He could even chat about who sat with whom at lunch and what someone wore to school that day. One thing that made his pretense so successful was that he dealt with children, who tend to be more gullible than adults.

Hunold said he began threatening the Hawthorne Brooke students when he began to lose control of the charade—when they began to doubt that he was a student at their school. When interviewed at his home in Missouri by two Massachusetts officers, Hunold seems to have vacillated between expressing remorse and dismissing the affair as a joke. He told the officers he never had any intention of going to Townsend to carry out the threats he made and probably would not have been physically able to do so, in any event.

Perhaps the most chilling thing that came out of the officers' visit to the Hunold home was a discovery they made when they searched the computer he used to terrorize the people of Townsend. On it, they found evidence they believed indicated that he was preparing to stalk another school—in Georgia, this time. If he not been caught when he was, Hunold might have gone on to stalk the Georgia school and other schools in other states. If he had continued, he probably would have been much better, more believable, and more terrifying the second time and with each succeeding iteration.[4]

If Hunold had been more sophisticated in his use of cyberspace, his career as a stalker of schools might not have been interrupted, at least not until after he terrorized more communities. If he had hidden his tracks—if he had made it appear he was using a computer in Massachusetts or Ohio or California—he probably would not have been caught, especially in 1999.

Cybercrime was a very new phenomenon then, and few law enforcement agencies were adept at investigating it. The Massachusetts investigators were able to track Hunold because the state had a computer crimes unit and because he apparently made no effort to hide his tracks, either when he was online or when he called the school.

The Hunold case is old news now. Cybercriminals have moved far beyond the relatively simple tactics he used to carry out his crime. But what Hunold did still perfectly exemplifies the distinctive aspects of cybercrime: A crippled boy was able to manipulate and terrorize people in a town 1,000 miles away. His use of virtual space gave him abilities no one has in the real world, where we are subject to the laws of gravity and the rules of physics. In the next four chapters, we will see how these virtual-space abilities create new crimes and alter traditional crimes. In Chapters 8 through 10, we will see how they create major challenges for law enforcement officers and, in so doing, erode the likelihood that clever cybercriminals will be caught and punished.

From Mainframes to Metaverse:
The Origins and Evolution
of Cybercrime

In this chapter, we trace the evolution of modern cybercrime as a new type of criminal activity. We will touch on the legal issues cybercrime raises but will examine them in detail in Chapters 3 through 5.

WHAT IS CYBERCRIME?

Before we can trace the evolution of cybercrime, we need to define what it is. More precisely, we need to distinguish "cybercrime" from "crime."[1]

"Crime" consists of engaging in conduct that has been outlawed by a society because it threatens the society's ability to maintain order. Order cannot exist without rules that proscribe certain "harmful" activities and institutions that enforce these rules. These rules constitute a society's criminal law. Criminal law is designed to prevent the members of a society from preying on each other in ways that undermine order. It does this by defining certain types of behavior as intolerable as "crimes."

Crimes take many forms because each targets a specific "harm." Crimes target harming individuals (murder, rape), property (arson, theft), government (obstructing justice, treason), and morality (obscenity, gambling).

Because societies have dealt with crime for millennia, they have developed standardized definitions of real-world crimes.

"Cybercrime" also consists of engaging in conduct that is outlawed because it threatens order. Cybercrime differs from crime primarily in the way it is committed: Criminals use guns, whereas cybercriminals use computer technology. Most of the cybercrime we see today simply represents the migration of real-world crime into cyberspace. Cyberspace becomes the tool criminals use to commit old crimes in new ways.

THE EMERGENCE OF CYBERCRIME (1950–1990)

This section traces cybercrime from its origins in the era of mainframe computers to 1990, when the Internet and personal computers were becoming more sophisticated and more pervasive. The next section outlines its evolution from 1990 to the present.

Mainframes and the Rise of Hacking

The first published reports of computers being used to commit crimes appeared in the 1960s, when computers were large mainframe systems.[2] The history of modern computing dates back to the nineteenth century, but the development of the mainframe business computer did not begin until after World War II.[3] In 1946, several companies began working on a commercial mainframe, and by 1951, the UNIVAC (UNIVersal Automatic Computer), created by the company of the same name, was being used by the Census Bureau.[4] In 1951, CBS used a UNIVAC to predict the outcome of the presidential election, which helped to popularize the new technology.[5] By 1960, 5,000 mainframes were in use in the United States; by 1970, almost 80,000 were in use in the United States and another 50,000 were in use abroad.[6] Given the tremendous increase in the number of computers, it is not surprising that computer crime began to become an issue in the 1960s.[7]

Computer crime in the 1960s and 1970s differed from the cybercrime we deal with today. There was no Internet; mainframes were not networked to other computers. In 1960, a typical IBM mainframe cost several million dollars, needed an entire room to house it, and needed a special air-conditioning system to ensure that its vacuum tubes would not overheat and fry the data in the computer.[8] A mainframe needed a group of specialist technicians to ensure that "its innards wouldn't melt" if the air conditioning went off and to generally keep it up and running.[9] Only a select group of researchers were allowed to use a mainframe. To access a mainframe, a researcher gave the data he or she wanted the computer to analyze to a keypunch operator, who used a machine to punch holes in manila cards.[10] The holes encoded the research-er's data into a form the machine could read. The cards were then given to another operator, who fed the cards into a machine that transmitted the information to the mainframe. At some point, the researcher would receive a printout showing the machine's analysis of his or her data.

Because mainframes were not networked with other computers, and because the only way to access a mainframe was by using this cumbersome process, only a few people were in a position to commit computer crime. They were the "insiders"—people whose employment gave them access to a mainframe computer.[11] That influenced the kind of computer crimes that were committed in this era. Insiders sometimes spied on other employees by reading their confidential files; and they might sabotage a computer or the data it contained as retaliation for being fired or disciplined.[12] These crimes occurred, but the most common type of computer crime in this era was financial; insiders used their access to a mainframe computer to enrich themselves.

In the mid-1960s, for example, "Val Smith" (an alias) was an accountant for a company in his hometown.[13] He also used a "small UNIVAC" he owned to provide the company with computing services. Over time, Smith became convinced the company was abusing him and cheating him out of money he had earned. Smith decided to use his control over the company's accounts and computing system to recoup "his share of the profits." He set up dummy companies to provide imaginary services to his employer and billed the company for their nonexistent efforts. Smith used the computer to automate the billing process; he also used it reduce the amount of the company's reported profits and took "his" money from the unreported excess. He was so successful that within a year or so, he was making $250,000 a year, an astonishing income for a 1960s-era accountant in a small town. Smith later said it was easy to conceal the embezzlement from his bosses because they believed any figures that came from a computer were infallible.

After six years, Smith had accumulated a million dollars and decided to quit. He did so by making a deliberate error that was discovered and led to his being charged with several crimes. Smith pled guilty because he believed he would only get 18 months in jail, and he thought 18 months was a fair exchange for the million dollars he still had. Unfortunately for him, the judge sentenced Smith to serve 10 years; while in prison, he earned a college degree and taught courses to other prisoners, all of which resulted in his being paroled after 5-1/2 years. He came out of prison a free man with a million, tax-free dollars at his disposal and never had to work again.[14]

The outcome of Smith's story—getting away with a million dollars—is unique, but his crimes were not. Many computer embezzlement cases came to light during this era, even though companies often did not report the crimes to the police.[15] In a California case, a teller used his access to the bank's computer to embezzle more than $100,000 from his employer. Instead of turning him in to the police, his employer promoted him to a higher-paying position, on the condition he never explain what he did to other tellers.[16] As Senator Abraham Ribicoff noted, banks that would call the police if a gunman robbed them would "say nothing" to police when an insider used a computer to steal: "They would rather absorb the loss than call in the police. They are fearful of bad publicity."[17] As we will see, businesses are still reluctant to report cybercrime for fear of bad publicity.

Bank employees were not the only insiders committing computer crimes in the 1960s. In 1964, executives of Equity Funding Corporation of America, an insurance company, began a 10-year scheme in which they used the company's computers to inflate its earnings.[18] At the beginning, they simply entered false commission income—eventually totaling $85 million—into the computerized accounting system. Because blatant false entries were relatively risky, they later moved to a different approach: showing that the company had sold more policies than it actually had. When the scheme collapsed in 1973, the Equity computers showed that the company had sold 97,000 insurance policies; it had actually sold fewer than 33,000. Federal investigators said two-thirds, or $2 billion dollars' worth, of the insurance the company claimed to have written was fraudulent.[19] After the fraud was discovered, Equity went bankrupt—in what was then the second largest bankruptcy ever—and 22 of its officers and employees were convicted of federal criminal charges.[20]

While embezzlement and fraud were the most common crimes, employees found other ways to profit from their access to a mainframe. Some stole information and sold it; they usually took trade secrets, but in one case, employees of the Drug Administration Association stole the names of informants and information about pending investigations and sold it to drug dealers.[21] Other employees had the company computer issue phony payroll checks to nonexistent employees, which they, of course, cashed.[22] Another less common tactic was to misappropriate company data and hold it for ransom.[23]

The crimes committed in this era all had one thing in common: The victims were a company or a government agency because large entities were the only ones who used mainframe computers. Furthermore, mainframes were generally incapable of inflicting "harm" on an individual. It might have been possible for an insider to manipulate mainframe data to fire someone improperly, but that would have been a very risky crime. The victim would probably complain, triggering an inquiry that could lead to the unraveling of this scheme and any others in which the perpetrator was involved. Using computers to "harm" individuals did not become a problem until the 1980s, when the "personal computer" appeared.

Because only insiders could commit mainframe crime, it consisted of committing old crimes a new way. And because mainframe crime was purely internal, it did not empower criminals the way cyberspace empowered Christian Hunold. That was the product of developments we examine in the next sections.

Phone Phreaking

The term "phone phreaking" is based on a *portmanteau*—a word created by blending other words.[24] "Phone" and "freak" were blended to create "phreaking" and "phreak" (as in "phone phreak"). Phone phreaking consists of using various devices to experiment with and manipulate a phone system.

The origins of phone phreaking are murky. Most accounts trace its beginnings to 1957, when an eight-year-old blind boy named Joe Engressia learned that whistling a particular tone (the E above middle C) into a telephone gave him access to the system.[25] Engressia was the first civilian to discover the 2600-Hz frequency, which the telephone company used to take control of its trunk lines; with control of a trunk line, he could make free calls to anyone, anywhere in the world. As he grew older, Engressia learned more about how to manipulate the phone system and shared his knowledge with others.[26]

Because Engressia had perfect pitch, he could create a 2600 tone by whistling. Others could not. They had to come up with devices to create the tone. At first, they used electronic organs or synthesizers, recording the tone and playing it back to activate a trunk line. In the late 1960s, someone realized that the toy whistle included as a prize in boxes of Cap'n Crunch cereal produced a perfect 2600 tone. As a sort of homage, John Draper, who became a legendary phone phreak, began using the alias "Captain Crunch" (his spelling) to hide his identity.[27] By 1970, the whistle had been superseded by devices—"blue boxes"—that generated the 2600 tone.[28]

Phone phreaks did not consider their activity to be illegal, even though they were stealing services from the telephone company; theft of services is a crime in most, if not all, states.[29] Phreaks thought of themselves as researchers, not criminals. In a 1971 *Esquire* interview, Joe Engressia said he phreaked for "the pleasure of pure knowledge. There's something beautiful about the system when you know it intimately."[30]

Unfortunately for the phreaks, the *Esquire* article brought law enforcement down on them: Soon after the article appeared, police broke into Engressia's apartment in Memphis and arrested him for theft of services.[31] The charges were reduced and the jail sentence he received upon being convicted was suspended . . . on the condition that he never phreak again.[32] Engressia, who had an I.Q of 172, did menial work for the phone company until 1988, when he chose to be five years old for the rest of his life. He died in 2007, having spent his last years living on disability payments in an apartment full of toys and stuffed animals.[33] The blind security analyst—"Whistler"—in the 1992 hacker movie *Sneakers* was apparently based on Engressia.[34]

The *Esquire* article also caused trouble for other phreaks, including Captain Crunch. He was arrested on federal wire fraud charges, convicted, and sentenced to five years of probation. It was the first of three arrests, convictions, and sentenced he would receive. He seemed unable to resist phreaking until he discovered computers in the early 1980s. Draper spent years working as a software programmer and computer security consultant, but his career fell into decline with the beginning of the twenty-first century.[35] Like Draper, other phone phreaks became interested in the technology, and many became hackers, as we will see in the next section. Traditional phone phreaking was dead by the 1990s, a casualty of the shift to digital call switching.[36]

Hacking

The term "hacker," and much of what would become hacker culture, emerged from the Massachusetts Institute of Technology's Artificial Intelligence Laboratory in the late 1950s.[37] Some MIT students were interested in computers and programming, but they had a problem: The only computers were mainframes, and only faculty and other "important" users were authorized to use the MIT mainframes. A sympathetic computer technician eventually let the students use a special mainframe on loan to MIT, where they could interact with this computer instead of having to use the punch card-reader process. By working with the computer, the students learned how to program it to make it "do" things. In other words, they learned to "hack," but "hacking" did not have the destructive, illegal connotation it has today. At MIT, a "hacker" was "someone who does . . . interesting and creative work at a high intensity level."[38]

An MIT "hack" was a clever practical joke, similar to elevator hacking: The buttons on an elevator were rewired, so that pushing the button for the second floor sent the person to the twentieth floor.[39] The "Cookie Monster" was a popular MIT computer hack in the 1970s: As someone worked at a computer terminal, the machine would begin to flash "Give me a cookie" and similar messages, making the person think their work had been lost.[40] The program would eventually flash "I didn't want a cookie anyway" and disappear, leaving the work unharmed. If the victim typed "cookie" when the attack began, the screen would display "thank you," and the attack would end.[41]

A culture of hacking grew up at MIT and spread to other centers of academic computing. It was based on an informal ethos, which held that access to computers "should be unlimited and total."[42] Hackers freely explored computer systems; they shared what they learned and created. When a hacker created a program, he (they were almost always male at this time) would distribute it to others, to be used and improved. Of course, this ethos evolved at a time when computers were closed systems and software had not become a commercial product.[43]

That began to change in 1969 when the ARPANET—Advanced Research Projects Agency Network, the first packet-switching network—went online.[44] It linked mainframes in hundreds of universities, research laboratories, and defense contracting companies. It also linked hackers, transforming them into "a networked tribe."[45] This second-stage hacker culture evolved over the next decade. Because ARPANET could link a maximum of 256 computers,[46] hacker culture was limited to a relatively small group until the 1980s, when the personal computer brought it to a much wider audience.

The popularization of hacking was the result of two innovations: the Internet and the personal computer. Three personal computers—the Apple II, the PET 2001, and the TRS-80—hit the market in 1979; "over half a million . . . were sold," and computing ceased to be a niche activity reserved for specialists.[47] The era of the *War Games* hacker had begun.

As the *New York Times* noted in 1983, the number of "young people roaming without authorization through" the country's computer systems was in the thousands and growing "hand-in-hand with the boom in personal computers."[48] The *Times* article was one of many stories about hackers that appeared in 1983, most prompted by the FBI arresting a group of Milwaukee hackers known as the 414s (after the local area code).[49]

The 414s were six boys between the ages of 16 and 22 who met in an Explorer Scouts group. Using personal computers and dial-up modems, they hacked into more than 60 computer systems, including the Memorial Sloan-Kettering Cancer Center, Los Alamos National Laboratory, and Security Pacific Bank in Los Angeles. They destroyed data in at least two of the systems they hacked. The 414s were caught because they came back to the same computers over and over. A system administrator figured out what was happening and called the FBI. The FBI used wiretaps to track the 414s to their homes in Milwaukee. Only two were prosecuted (for making harassing phone calls); the other four agreed to stop hacking and pay restitution for the damage they had caused. The two who were prosecuted pled guilty and were sentenced to probation.

When he testified before Congress, one of the 414 hackers said the group was inspired by the movie *War Games*. In 1984, four teenagers suspected of hacking into the NASA Marshall Space Flight Center reportedly told police they used techniques they learned from the same film.[50] These were not the only instances in which life imitated art. Markus Hess, a German hacker recruited by the KGB to spy on U.S. military systems, was inspired by *War Games*. He vowed that he, similar to the movie's protagonist David Lightman, would hack NORAD, the North American Aerospace Defense Command in Colorado.[51] Hess was not able to hack NORAD, but he hacked 400 U.S. military computers, including a Pentagon database.[52]

In addition to accurately depicting how a hacker accessed a remote system, *War Games* romanticized hackers.[53] As *Wired* noted 25 years later, it was the "geek-geist classic that legitimized hacker culture" and "minted the nerd hero."[54] *War Games* brought the concepts of "hacking" and "hackers" to the attention of American society. It initially popularized the image of hackers as creative but benign, but that image rather quickly began to change. The arrests of the 414s and others engaged in similar activity indicated hackers were anything but benign. The image of hackers was further tarnished by a wave of publicity about FBI efforts to deal with hackers' online depredations.[55] In 1984, a hacker-turned-FBI informant estimated hackers stole $100 million a year in long-distance service, pirated the same amount of software, and were responsible for $200 million a year in credit card fraud.[56] In the mid-1980s, news stories reported that hacking had become "an epidemic" among high-school students.[57]

The essentially innocent image of *War Games'* David Lightman hacking a system to find a new game morphed into the image of a hacker as a criminal. Both images survive. "Hacker" has come to have two distinct meanings: hacker as a brilliant programmer, and hacker as a computer criminal. To differentiate the two, hacker jargon divides hackers into two categories. "Black hat" hackers use their computer skills to commit crimes, whereas "white hat" hackers use theirs for "altruistic or at least non-malicious reasons."[58] As is probably obvious, the categories "derive from the dress code of formulaic Westerns, in which bad guys wore black hats and good guys white ones."[59]

In the post-*War Games* 1980s, a number of hacker groups arose to exploit the opportunities available in what was now known as "cyberspace," a term introduced in William Gibson's novel *Neuromancer*.[60] A juvenile known as Lex Luthor created the Legion of Doom (LOD) in 1984.[61] Some LOD members were white hats driven by intellectual curiosity; others were black-hats pursuing "for-profit computer crime."[62] In 1989, LOD member Phiber Optik was expelled for reasons that are still unclear.[63] What is clear is that Phiber Optik (a high-school student, like most of the others), Acid Phreak, Scorpion, Corrupt, and Outlaw decided LOD had "outlived its reputation" and created a new group: the Masters of Deception (MOD). As one source notes, the name "perfectly suited" the group, which used "artful deception" of various types to attain "new heights" in understanding computer systems.[64]

The MOD and the LOD became infamous when they fought the Great Hacker War in 1990–1991. The first flare-up came when LOD accused a MOD member of using information from a LOD bulletin board to start a security company. The war began when MOD members joining a conference call intended to settle things heard LOD members using racial epithets to describe members of MOD.[65] At first, they played phone pranks (e.g., shutting off service, arranging for phones to ring continuously) on each other. Things escalated when a LOD member used a computer program to translate "The History of MOD" into racist jive. As things escalated, MOD members began to cross the line into serious criminal activity. They hacked phone systems to obtain free services; they also hacked information services such as TRW to obtain personal information that they sold or used to harass their rivals and others. In 1991, five members of MOD were indicted on federal criminal charges, including conspiracy, wire fraud, computer fraud, computer tampering, and wiretapping.[66] All of them pled guilty, and all were given some time in jail.[67] No LOD members were charged; the LOD seems to have dissolved after apparently losing the war.

As the 1980s turned into the 1990s, hacking was changing. Personal computers and software—including the software being developed specifically to facilitate hacking—were much more common. So were targets. In the 1970s and most of the 1980s, it was a challenge "just to find a system to hack"; by the 1990s, the Internet was starting to link everything, which meant hackers had thousands, and eventually millions, of targets.[68] Because most organizations did not realize the need to secure their computers, most targets were wide-open, easy pickings for hackers. But hackers had to deal with a new phenomenon: law enforcement, which was becoming aggressive in pursing notorious hackers, such as Los Angeles' "Dark Dante."

Kevin Poulsen—also known as Dark Dante—began phreaking when he was in his early teens,[69] and moved on to hacking after his parents bought him a TRS-80 computer and modem for this sixteenth birthday.[70] In 1982, Poulsen left high school after the eleventh grade and became Dark Dante. He and another hacker broke into computer systems, preferably ones owned by the U.S. Department of Defense. In August 1983, they hacked several think tanks that worked on classified military projecs. In September, police arrested Poulsen's hacker comrade, who was 19 and could be tried as an adult; he was convicted of "malicious access" to computers and spent less than two months in jail.[71]

Because Poulsen was 17, he could not be tried as an adult; no charges were ever brought against him for this episode. Instead, Poulsen was hired by one of his victims. SRI International, which conducted classified research for the military, hired him to teach the military how to safeguard its computers.[72] Poulsen had a security clearance, a more than adequate salary, and a condo near his job in northern California; he worked on a variety of projects, including the Strategic Air Command's computer systems.

Things begin to fall apart in February 1988, when the owner of a storage rental facility entered a unit because its rent had not been paid.[73] He found what he thought was stolen property and called the police. The police recognized it as phreaking paraphernalia, including stolen Pacific Bell manuals and fake IDs. The police linked Poulsen to the storage unit and called him in for questioning; he denied doing anything illegal. When FBI agents searched Poulsen's home, they found evidence linking him to hacking but thought something more sinister was afoot. The FBI suspected Poulsen was hacking classified systems and violating national security. More precisely, they thought he had been selling U.S. secrets to other countries.[74]

In November 1989 a grand jury indicted Poulsen and two co-defendants on 18 counts of computer and telecommunications fraud. The others surrendered, but Poulsen fled before FBI agents could arrest him and then called the FBI to taunt them for letting him escape.

While hiding in Los Angeles, Poulsen used his phreaker and hacker talents in a money-making scheme. A radio station was giving away $50,000 Porsches, one a week to the 102nd person to call after a DJ played three songs in sequence.[75] Poulsen hacked the phone company's computers and diverted the radio station's incoming calls to a line he controlled. When a DJ played the songs, Poulsen counted calls that had come in, intervening when it reached 60. Then he took over the station's phone line and counted down as the number approached 102. When it was close, Poulsen and a confederate known as "Agent Steal" began calling to ensure theirs was the 102nd call. They used this system to win two Porsches from the first radio station; they also used it to win $20,000 in cash from another radio station and two trips to Hawaii plus $2,000 in cash from a third radio station.[76] Poulsen sold one Porsche and used the money for living expenses.

Frustrated by their inability to catch him, the FBI arranged for the television show *Unsolved Mysteries* to air a segment on Dark Dante.[77] When Poulsen heard about the show, he sent the program a letter, saying it would slander him.[78] A few hours before the show aired, an *Unsolved Mysteries* secretary took a call she found odd: Instead of leaving a tip, the caller wanted the toll-free number people called to provide tips. She found that odd because the number was displayed on the screen when the program was on the air.[79]

The Dark Dante segment was scheduled for October 10, 1990. When *Unsolved Mysteries* aired that evening, its phones went dead before the show got to its segment on Poulsen. No one could reach *Unsolved Mysteries* to submit tips about Dark Dante. Many think Poulsen shut down the phone lines; such a feat would presumably not have been beyond such a talented hacker and phone phreak.[80]

Poulsen was finally captured six months later, on April 11, 1991. He was caught after the FBI got a tip he had been at a grocery store in Van Nuys. When agents showed his photo to store employees, they identified Poulsen as a man who had been there but had not come in for several weeks. An agent staked out the store after the FBI heard he had been back. On April 11, Poulsen came to the store and was arrested.[81]

On June 14, 1994, Poulsen pled guilty to computer fraud, mail fraud, money laundering, wiretapping, and obstructing justice. On February 9, 1995, Poulsen was sentenced to serve 51 months in prison and pay almost $58,000 in restitution for the radio station scams.[82] It was, at the time, the "longest prison sentence ever received by a hacker."[83] Poulsen was released from prison on June 4, 1996, because he was given credit for time he served while awaiting trial and sentencing. In all, he spent more than five years in prison, the "longest any computer hacker" had served to that point.[84]

One journalist called Poulsen "the last hacker," because Poulsen's career began when hacking was still seen as a playful intellectual exercise and ended when it was morphing into something much darker: cybercrime.[85] The term appeared around the time Poulsen pled guilty[86] and was used with increasing frequency as Americans began to realize online crime was a real, and potentially serious, threat.[87] By the end of the 1990s, Attorney General Janet Reno was calling for a multilateral "crackdown on cybercrime."[88] "Hacker" became synonymous with "cybercriminal," and the notion of white-hat hackers slipped into obscurity, where it remains.

Kevin Poulsen exemplifies the shift from hacker as prankster to hacker as criminal. None of his intrusions into computer systems were done for personal gain; they were inspired by the intellectual curiosity that produced the hacker code. But the world had changed. Instead of exploring a closed system to which he had legitimate access, Poulsen rummaged through networked systems without the permission of their owners. That would be trespass in the real world; as we will see in Chapter 4, it became a crime in the digital world. Although hackers such as Poulsen may not have intended to "harm" the systems they invaded, they could (their conduct might inadvertently delete or alter data) and did (their presence compromised the privacy of proprietary or classified information) cause such "harm." We will return to that "harm" in Chapter 4.

Malware

Malware is another *portmanteau*, a term that blends "malicious" and "software."[89] It denotes software that is designed to infiltrate and/or damage a computer without the owner's knowledge and consent. There are many types of malware,[90] but most people are familiar with only two: viruses and worms.

A computer virus is a program that can copy itself and infect computers, much as a biological virus infects people.[91] Similar to biological viruses, computer viruses need a host to spread to other computers; computer viruses use computer code as their host. They infect program code in one system and use that host—plus their capacity for replication—to infect other systems.[92]

Viruses are far from new: In 1975, John Walker created Pervading Animal, a virus that infected UNIVAC mainframes through files transferred between systems on magnetic tape.[93] In 1982, a Pittsburgh ninth-grader named Rich Skrenta created the first virus to infect personal computers. His Elk Cloner virus, which was spread by infected disks, targeted Apple II computers. (Infected computers shut down or performed a "trick" every fifth time they booted up, and they displayed a poem every fiftieth time.) In 1984, computer scientist Fred Cohen was the first to use "virus" to refer to self-propagating code. In 1986, Amjad Farooq Alvi and Basit Farooq Alvi, two

Pakistani brothers, released the first virus to infect IBM personal computers. (It caused computers to flash an advertisement for their business: Brain Computer Services of Lahore.)

Since then, the number of viruses has grown almost exponentially: About 200 viruses were in circulation by the end of 1990. By 2003, the number had jumped to 70,000,[94] and by 2008, it was more than one million.[95]

Similar to a virus, a computer worm is a self-replicating computer program. Unlike a virus, it does not need to attach itself to a host to spread to other systems. A worm uses a network to send copies of itself to other nodes on the network. Worms can replicate on their own, without the assistance of any activity from a computer user.[96]

The term "worm" comes from a 1975 science-fiction novel, John Brunner's *The Shockwave Rider*.[97] It is set in a "dystopian early 21st century America dominated by computer networks." The hero is a fugitive from a sinister government think tank. At one point, he uses a "computer tapeworm" to disable the programs the government uses to lock down its network and ensure its nefarious activities remain secret.

In the early 1980s, computer scientists at the Xerox Palo Alto Research Center began experimenting with benign worm programs, such as the "vampire" worm that put computers to work at night, when they would otherwise be idle.[98] This research ended when it became apparent that worms could be dangerous. A worm developed at Xerox malfunctioned one evening and repeatedly crashed computers at the research center.

In 1988, Robert Morris was a graduate student in computer science at Cornell University.[99] He developed a worm either to gauge the size of the Internet or to test the level of security on the Internet. Whatever Morris' motive was for creating the worm, he clearly did not mean for it to cause "harm." He designed the worm to spread through the Internet once it was released; it was not supposed to impair the computers it infected. To prevent the worm from reinfecting computers—which would make it easier to detect, as well as cause computers to crash—he programmed it to "ask" a computer if it had been infected. If it said "yes," the worm would not reinstall itself. Had he stopped there, no one might ever have heard of the Morris worm. But he went a step further. To ensure programmers could not defeat the worm by programming computers to falsely answer "yes" when asked if they were infected, Morris set the worm to duplicate itself every seventh time it received a "yes." In other words, he ensured a 14 percent replication rate.

Morris released the worm "into the wild" at 5:00 p.m. on November 2, 1988, and it quickly became apparent he had made a terrible error. The 14 percent replication rate proved disastrous, as the worm raced through computers, reinfecting them every seventh time it received a "yes" to its query about infection. It took less than 90 minutes for the worm to shut down a computer system.[100] It infected an estimated 6,000 computer systems,[101] 10 percent of the Internet host computers at the time. The cost of dealing with the worm at each infection site was estimated as ranging from $200 to more than $53,000.

When Morris realized what was happening, he consulted a friend. They sent an anonymous e-mail telling programmers how to kill the worm and prevent reinfection.[102] Because the worm had clogged the Internet, the message did not reach programmers until it was too late. Programmers across the country spent the next two days cleaning up after the worm and reviving their systems.[103]

Blame became the issue in the worm's aftermath. Many demanded that Morris be prosecuted for what he had done, but there was a problem. It was clear he had not intended for the worm to cause damage, and it had not destroyed or altered data in the systems it attacked. But it had caused damage. Programmers spent 50 or 60 hours disabling the virus and getting their systems back up and running, and universities (and taxpayers) lost research time worth millions of dollars.[104] The difficulty lay in quantifying the damage. The Computer Virus Industry Association estimated it cost "nearly $100 million in lost computer time and manpower to eradicate the worm and restore" the victimized systems.[105] Other estimates were lower but still in the millions of dollars.

It was inevitable that Morris would face criminal charges. In July 1989, a grand jury in Syracuse, New York, indicted him on one count of gaining unauthorized access to university and military computers.[106] Morris was the first person charged under the new Computer Fraud and Abuse Act, which we will examine in Chapter 4. He faced five years in prison and a $250,000 fine. Morris pled not guilty, went to trial, and was convicted.[107] He was sentenced on May 5, 1990. After noting that prison "did not fit the crime," the federal judge sentenced him to pay a $10,000 fine, spend three years on probation, and do 400 hours of community service.[108] Morris served his sentence, received a PhD from Harvard in 1999, and became a professor at MIT.[109]

The Morris worm and the viruses described earlier revealed what no one realized in the early years of the Internet: When computers are linked to a network, they become vulnerable to hostile programs and programmers in ways that were not possible when computers were freestanding mainframes. In the 1990s and the early years of the twenty-first century, it became increasingly apparent how serious, and intractable, this threat is.

CYBERCRIME INCREASES IN INCIDENCE AND COMPLEXITY (1990–2009)

In the early stages of computing, cybercrime essentially consisted of hacking. In this era, hacking was a matter of overcoming an intellectual challenge. Hackers might interfere with the operation of the systems they invaded, but that tended to be a by-product of the hack instead of its purpose. In the 1990s, this changed. Personal computers and the Internet were becoming increasingly sophisticated, and a new type of criminal emerged to exploit the opportunities and vulnerabilities both offered.

Hacking Evolves

The most notorious hacker of the 1990s was another Kevin: Kevin Mitnick. Like Kevin Poulsen, Kevin Mitnick grew up in Southern California and was a phone phreak.[110] His favorite movie was *Three Days of the Condor*, released in 1975. In this movie, Robert Redford's portrayal of a CIA agent who uses his knowledge of the telephone system to avoid being captured by sinister government forces made quite an impression on Mitnick. Later, his hacker name would be "Condor."

Mitnick hung around with a group of phone phreaks at school but began hacking after he started studying computers. He got into trouble in high school for hacking into the Los Angeles Unified School District's computers. His first brush with the law came in 1981, when he was 17. He was prosecuted as a juvenile for stealing computer manuals from a Pacific Bell telephone-switching center, convicted, and put on probation. In 1982, while on probation, Mitnick was arrested for breaking into computers at the University of Southern California. He spent six months in a juvenile institution for violating probation and was released at the end of 1983.

For the next five years, Mitnick held various jobs, attended college and a computer school, and kept hacking. In 1987, police charged him with unauthorized access to a computer; he bargained the charge down to a misdemeanor and was again put on probation. In 1988, Mitnick hacked a computer at the NASA Jet Propulsion Laboratory and was expelled from Pierce College for illegally copying school software. That same year, FBI agents arrested Mitnick for hacking the Digital Equipment Corporation and stealing prototype operating system software valued at $1 million. The company claimed it spent $4 million tracking Mitnick's intrusions into their systems. Mitnick was convicted and served one year at a minimum-security federal prison, followed by three years of probation. As a condition of his probation, he was prohibited from touching a computer or a modem.

In 1992, FBI agents showed up at the private investigation firm where Mitnick was working to arrest him for violating that condition of his probation. He eluded them and went into hiding. In 1993, the California Department of Motor Vehicles issued a warrant for Mitnick's arrest. It claimed he wiretapped calls from FBI agents and used law enforcement access codes he obtained by eavesdropping to illegally access the driver's license database for the state.

Mitnick would remain a fugitive until 1995. As a fugitive, he moved from town to town, using various aliases. News stories called him a "computer terrorist" and "the most wanted hacker in the world." The Secret Service thought they had him in 1994, when agents raided a Seattle apartment rented to "Brian Merrill," one of his aliases. But Mitnick was working on his resume at a Kinko's and listening to the raid on his police scanner.[111]

Mitnick made a fatal error on Christmas Day of 1994 when he hacked a computer at the San Diego home of Tsutomu Shimomura, a physicist who worked for the San Diego Supercomputer Center. Mitnick stole thousands of files stored on the computer, all of which dealt with hacking. Shimomura's computer logged every detail of the hack and sent the log file to an Internet site. A month later, Shimomura heard his files were on The WELL, a San Francisco-based online community. Mitnick had apparently been using The WELL for various purposes. Shimomura and a team of experts used an office in The WELL's headquarters to set traps and wait for the so far unidentified hacker to return. When they heard someone using similar techniques had hacked the San Jose Netcom On-Line Communication Services and copied 20,000 credit cards, they moved to Silicon Valley and monitored the intruder as he stole data from Apple and other companies.[112]

In this era, computer connections were made over telephone lines, so they were relatively easy to trace. A federal prosecutor working with Shimomura sent subpoenas to the phone companies and, on February 11, 1995, received records that showed the intruder was dialing in from Raleigh, North Carolina. Because Shimomura and his team had found cellular telephone-control software in the intruder's files on The WELL, they believed he was using a cell phone to connect to the Internet. Shimomura went to Raleigh, where he and a Sprint technician used cell-frequency direction-finding equipment to key in on an apartment complex near the airport. Then FBI agents took over, identifying the apartment where the cell phone was located and obtaining a search warrant. When they executed the warrant on February 15, 1995, they found and arrested Mitnick.

Mitnick was held without bail for 4-1/2 years, while the government was preparing for trial. He spent eight months in solitary confinement. In

2000, he pled guilty to seven counts of computer and wire fraud and was sentenced to five years in prison. Because he was given credit for the time he had served, he was out of prison in six months but was still on probation. One of the conditions of his probation was that he could not use a computer or a phone connected to the Internet until 2003.

Although he began hacking when he was an adolescent, Kevin Mitnick's career as a hacker lasted well into adulthood. He was 31 when he was arrested in Raleigh. And while none of his hacks seem to have been committed for financial gain—there is no indication he ever used the credit card numbers he stole or tried to sell the proprietary software he copied—they were perceived as being far more serious than those of Kevin Poulsen and the other, essentially juvenile hackers we examined in the previous section.

Kevin Mitnick committed crimes. He went where he had no right to be and took data he had no right to have. But instead of simply reporting on what he did, the press demonized him. Some reporters said he hacked into the NORAD computers and inspired the movie *War Games*. He did neither. He was described as a "digital desperado," a "dark side" hacker who broke into computers to "carry out bizarre vendettas" and cause "havoc."[113] *Time* magazine reported that the judge in one of Mitnick's cases discovered that "files at a credit-information service had been mysteriously altered to downgrade the judge's credit rating."[114] Like so many of the Mitnick stories, this one was not true.

Authorities were so frightened of the "mayhem" Mitnick could unleash that when he was arrested in 1988, the federal judge said he could not have access to a telephone "for fear of the damage he might cause."[115] A Los Angeles detective said he was "forced to go into hiding" while he was investigating Mitnick because " [i]f he targets you, he can make your life miserable."[116]

The paranoia about Mitnick continued after he was arrested. In a 2005 interview, he said he spent eight months in solitary confinement because the judge in his case was told "Mitnick could start a nuclear war by calling up NORAD on a payphone and whistling modern tones into the receiver."[117] That, of course, was not true. Mitnick said the guards took his radio because they were afraid he could turn it into a cell phone (not true), and they put him in handcuffs for using an electric typewriter in the prison library.[118]

Why did Kevin Mitnick, who was not a "dangerous" hacker, become so feared? He was not at all terrifying in person; he resembles a mild-mannered computer scientist or an accountant. He seems to have become a symbol of the new, almost mystical threat posed by those who had the power to control computers and computer networks. Kevin Mitnick became the poster boy for America's realization that computers could be used to commit crimes in new and quite incomprehensible ways. Most of the public probably did not understand what it was that made Kevin Mitnick so dangerous, but they knew they should be frightened. Their fear may have been exacerbated by the portrayal of hackers in movies such as *War Games* (a hacker nearly causes thermonuclear war) and *The Net*. In *The Net*, which came out five months after Mitnick became a fugitive, Sandra Bullock plays a software engineer whose life is almost destroyed by a gang of cyberterrorists who want to seize control of U.S. government and military computer systems.[119]

The paranoia about Mitnick was probably also exacerbated by attacks on U.S. government computers in the 1990s. Perhaps the most egregious attack came in 1994 when the Rome Air Development Center at Griffiss Air Force Base in upstate New York—the "premier command and control research facility in the United States"—was attacked by two hackers.[120] They installed password sniffers—programs to capture passwords—on seven of the Rome Center's computers. The hackers also used the Rome Center's network to launch attacks on other sensitive networks, including NASA, NATO, Wright-Patterson Air Force Base, the Korean Atomic Research Institute, and five defense contractors. They copied all of the data on the Korean Atomic Research Institute's computers and cached it on the Rome Center's network. The attack on the Korean Institute was of particular concern because Air Force personnel initially thought it was in North Korea; fortunately, it turned out to be in South Korea. As one Air Force officer noted at the time, because the attack on the Korean Institute seemed to come from an Air Force installation, it could have been perceived as an "aggressive act of war" by North Korean authorities.

The hackers—who used the names "Datastream Cowboy" and Kuji—broke into the Rome Center computers more than 150 times over a period of 26 days. Air Force investigators could not trace them because they used systems in South Africa, Mexico, and Europe to disguise the origins of their attacks. When the investigators were about to give up, they got a break: They had informants who surfed the Internet, looking for tips. One of the informants found out that Datastream Cowboy liked to hang out and chat on a Seattle Web site. Datastream Cowboy proved to be both chatty and naïve. He told the informant he lived in the United Kingdom and provided his phone number. Air Force investigators worked with Scotland Yard to trace the number to a house in a London suburb. Air Force officers flew to London and staked out the house, along with British police officers. On May 12, 1994, the America and British officers knocked on the door. When a man opened it, they swept through the house and upstairs, where they found 16-year-old Richard Pryce—also known as Datastream Cowboy—collapsed on the floor in tears.

Pryce was arrested and questioned about Kuji. He denied knowing who Kuji was, and the investigators were unable to find any evidence identifying him. In June 1995, Pryce was charged with 12 counts of violating the United Kingdom's Computer Misuse Act. He pled guilty in March 1997 and was sentenced to pay a fine, pay court costs, and forfeit his computer equipment. It was not until June 1996 that investigators identified Kuji, almost by accident. As they reexamined Pryce's hard drive, they found a phone number that led them to Kuji. He turned out to be Matthew Bevan, a 19-year-old who worked with computers and whose father was a police officer. Bevan successfully contested the charges against him. After a series of hearings, prosecutors conceded they could not prove their case, and Bevan was acquitted.

The Rome Center case contributed to the paranoia about hackers. In 1996, the Senate Armed Services Committee was told that Datastream Cowboy had "caused more harm than the KGB and was the 'No. 1 threat to U.S. security.'"[121] Actually, both Pryce and Bevan were old-style, *War Games*-style hackers. Pryce said that for him, hacking "was a game, a challenge." Neither Pryce nor Bevan was a superspy, a computer saboteur, or a cyber-terrorist. They were "sport hackers." Sport hackers, who are usually juveniles, are not interested in doing anything except getting into a computer system and analyzing its structure and contents.[122] They still exist, but, as we will see in subsequent chapters, they have been eclipsed by a new phenomenon: adult, professional hackers who hack either for profit or for ideological reasons.

The investigation also revealed that the hack was not as sophisticated as it once seemed. Pryce and Bevan would never have been able to access the Rome Center computers had it not been for a ferret named Carmen. Air Force officers with access to the system were supposed to use complex passwords that combined numerals and letters, but one officer used his ferret's name—"Carmen"—as his password.[123] The password-cracking program Pryce ran on the Rome Center system had no difficulty identifying the "Carmen" password,[124] and that gave Pryce access to the system. Had the officer followed orders and used a more complex password, the program would not have succeeded, and Pryce would have moved on to other, presumably more innocuous, targets.

There were other *War Games*-style hacks during the 1990s, but the decade saw the beginning of a new trend: Hacking for profit began to replace hacking for fun.

The SMAK case illustrates the onset of this trend. On March 28, 1997, computer technicians doing routine maintenance on servers used by an Internet service provider (ISP) discovered someone had hacked into one of the servers.[125] As the technicians investigated, they realized the intruder had installed a "packet sniffer" on the server and was using it to capture user names and passwords of the ISP's customers.[126] They also realized their intruder was still logged into the server and was deleting data to cover his tracks. To prevent further damage and preserve evidence, the technicians took the server offline. The next day, one of the ISP's customers—whom law enforcement files identify only as "CW" for "cooperating witness"—contacted the ISP's owner. CW said that when he was online the previous day, he had chatted with "SMAK," the hacker who attacked the ISP's server. According to CW, SMAK bragged about how easy it was to hack the server and said he had copied credit card numbers from one of the sites hosted by the server. SMAK offered to sell CW those credit card numbers plus others he had obtained from other servers—a total of 60,000 in all.

The ISP's owner called the FBI, which began investigating. FBI agents traced the Internet connection SMAK used to hack the ISP to the University of California at San Francisco (UCSF), but the trail ended there. Agents concluded that SMAK had hacked into and used the Internet account of an innocent UCSF student. The FBI turned to CW, who became an informant. On May 2, CW began an e-mail correspondence with SMAK. When CW said he was interested in buying some of the stolen credit card numbers, SMAK said that was doable.[127] CW and SMAK negotiated the sale of 710 stolen credit card numbers for $710; it was styled as a test purchase, so CW could see what SMAK had to offer. CW sent the money to SMAK anonymously, via a Western Union wire transfer. When FBI agents checked out the card numbers SMAK had sold, they found they were all valid numbers that had credit limits ranging from $5,000 to $12,000.

CW made a second small buy on May 13 and then negotiated an agreement to buy a large quantity of credit card numbers for $260,000. On May 21, 1997, CW and SMAK met in the American Airlines Terminal at the San Francisco Airport. SMAK—who turned out to be 36-year-old Carlos Felipe Salgado Jr.[128]—was arrested after he gave CW a CD containing more than 100,000 stolen credit card numbers. On June 6, he was indicted on three counts of federal computer crime and two counts of trafficking in stolen credit cards.[129] On August 25, Salgado pled guilty to four of the five counts and was sentenced to serve 2-1/2 years in prison and spend five years on probation. While on probation, he was forbidden to use computers.[130]

The SMAK/Salgado case illustrates how hacking evolved over the next decade. Hackers tended to be adults. and hacking ceased to be an end in itself and became a tool used to commit crimes, usually financial crimes. A Willie Sutton phenomenon began to emerge: In the 1930s and 1940s, Willie Sutton was a notorious bank robber, who was eventually captured. According to legend, when a reporter asked Sutton why he robbed banks, he said "that's where the money is."[131] As the 1990s ended and the new century began, criminals realized the Internet was increasingly where the money was and went after it. We will review some examples of that trend in the remainder of this chapter and examine it in detail in Chapters 4 through 6.

There is one respect in which Salgado does not exemplify the evolved hackers of the twenty-first century. He was an American citizen who operated within the territory of the United States. That changed over the next decade, as computer crime increasingly became transnational, and Americans found themselves being attacked by perpetrators in Asia, Europe, and elsewhere. We will examine this development in Chapter 10.

Twenty-First-Century Phone Phreaking

As we have seen, traditional phone phreaking declined in the late 1980s and early 1990s and ended when phone companies moved from multifrequency to digital call switching in the 1990s. A variation still crops up on occasion, though.

It differs from traditional phreaking in two ways. The first is that twenty-first-century phone phreaking is usually a product of hacking. Phreaks access a computer system without authorization and modify settings to obtain free telephone service. Because it relies on compromising a computer system, this type of phreaking is sometimes called "telephone hacking." The other way it differs from traditional phreaking is the Willie Sutton effect: Unlike traditional phone phreaks, who saw phreaking essentially as an intellectual exercise, twenty-first-century phone phreaks (or telephone hackers) often sell pirated phone service to people who want to make free calls, especially overseas calls.

In 2006, for example, federal agents arrested two men who were accused of using hacking to steal phone service and resell it for a profit. One of them, Edwin Pena, created two companies to sell discounted telephone service. He hired Robert Moore to hack the networks of 15 telecommunications providers and "hundreds of businesses" and steal the phone service Pena sold.[132] According to a federal prosecutor, Pena netted more than a million dollars from the scheme; he paid Moore $20,000.[133] In March 2007, Philippine police arrested seven hackers who compromised 2,500 telephone networks in various countries and used them to sell cheap phone service. One of the victims, AT&T, said it had lost approximately $38 million to the scheme.[134]

Businesses are not the only victims of phone hacking and phreaking: In August 2008, a hacker (or hackers) broke into the Federal Emergency Management Agency (FEMA) voice mail system and "racked up about $12,000 in calls to the Middle East and Asia."[135] The phone hack occurred on a weekend. During that weekend, the compromised system was used to make more than 400 calls to countries including Afghanistan, India, Saudi Arabia, and Yemen. The hacker(s)/phreaker(s) would probably have made many more calls, but Sprint employees discovered the system had been compromised and shut down long-distance service to that part of the FEMA network. It is possible, but unlikely, that the intruder(s) made all of those calls for personal reasons or as a prank. It is more likely that he, she, or they sold the calls and made a modest profit.

Malware Evolves

Robert Morris's worm demonstrated the destructive potential of malicious code, but it was a different kind of malware—viruses—that would realize this potential in the years after 1990. The history of destructive network viruses really began in 1995, when the Concept virus appeared.

It was the first macro virus.[136] A macro virus is written in the language used in software applications such as word processors or spreadsheets. When a macro virus infects a computer system, it replaces the normal command macros in a program such as Word or Excel. The macro virus activates when someone using an infected computer selects a command and infects the documents, templates, and other files created on the system. The user may not realize the system has been infected until the virus begins to cause problems.

Because macro viruses are hidden in program or data files, they can spread via e-mail, unlike the more primitive viruses we have already examined, which spread when users shared infected disks. The proliferation of early macro viruses such as Concept was usually the result of one person e-mailing an infected file to another. As they became more sophisticated, viruses developed the ability to spread by other means, as we will see.

The Concept virus demonstrated how rapidly a macro virus could spread. It emerged in July 1995 and took "less than a month to spread around the world."[137] One victim said there was "hardly a Microsoft Word user" who had not "been hit by the Concept virus."[138] Unlike the viruses to come, Concept was more aggravating than destructive. When someone used Word to open an infected file, Concept would infect Word on that system and modify it so files could be saved only in template form. When an uninfected user opened one of these template files, Concept loaded itself on that copy of Word, with the same effect and consequences. Some believed Concept was merely a prank—a way of warning users how insidious macro viruses could be. They based this belief on two aspects of the Concept virus: It did not destroy data or cause any other real harm, and its anonymous author included the phrase "That's enough to prove my point" in the virus code.[139]

A few obscure viruses followed Concept, but it was not until 1999 that a truly destructive item of malware appeared.[140] It is usually known as the "Melissa virus," but it actually combined the characteristics of a virus and a worm. As we saw earlier, worms, unlike viruses, do not have to attach themselves to a host to spread to other systems. A worm can copy itself and use a network to send the copies to other systems linked to the network. Similar to Concept, Melissa was a macro virus that targeted Microsoft Word; however, unlike Concept and other earlier viruses, Melissa was able to spread on its own.

Melissa appeared on March 16, 1999. It came in an e-mail with the subject line "An important message from (name)." The (name) in the subject line was the name of the person whose computer sent the e-mail; the message itself consisted of a single statement: "Here is that document you asked for ...don't show anyone else. ;-)" A Word document was attached to the e-mail. When the recipient opened the Word document, the virus located the computer's Outlook or Outlook Express e-mail address book and immediately used it to send copies of the message and attachment to the first 50 names in the address book. Melissa repeated this process with each recipient of the e-mail. The infected attachment was a list of pornographic Websites. Melissa's creator apparently assumed, correctly, that those who opened the attachment would pause for a moment, trying to figure out why (name) had sent them such a list.[141] That pause gave the virus the time it needed to find the address book and e-mail copies of itself to other victims.

Although Melissa may seem annoying but not destructive, it had a devastating effect on networks around the world. E-mail generated by the virus "proliferated rapidly and exponentially," overwhelming networks and forcing companies such as Lucent Technologies, Lockheed Martin, Merrill Lynch, and Microsoft to shut down their e-mail systems.[142] It also overwhelmed systems at NATO headquarters in Brussels and in the Washington offices of the Marine Corps and Veterans Administration.[143] Melissa "moved in Internet time, crippling tens of thousands of messaging servers worldwide in a few hours."[144] It was, as many noted, another demonstration of the evolving destructiveness of malware.

Amazingly, law enforcement officers apprehended the author of the Melissa virus less than a week after it appeared. On April 1, 1999, New Jersey police arrested David L. Smith of Aberdeen Township, New Jersey. Smith, who apparently named the virus after a topless dancer, was caught so quickly because he had been sloppy. As soon as Melissa appeared, virus experts began dissecting its code. They soon discovered the names of people who had modified it, including one who went by the alias of VicodinES. Experts from an antivirus company in Reston, Virginia, linked VicodinES, who was well known for posting messages about viruses in Internet chat groups, to Smith.[145]

Smith was charged with computer crimes under both federal and state law. In December 1999, as part of a plea bargain, he pled guilty to one count of second-degree computer theft in violation of New Jersey law and one count of spreading a computer virus in violation of federal law.[146] Under the plea bargain, the New Jersey prosecutors agreed to recommend a sentence of 10 years in prison and a fine of up to $150,000; on the federal charges, Smith faced up to five years in prison and a fine of up to $250,000. The plea bargain specified that the state and federal sentences were to be "concurrent and coterminous," which meant that they would be served simultaneously (instead of consecutively) and would end at the same time.[147]

At the plea hearing, Smith told the judge he did not "anticipate the amount of damage that's occurred. When I posted the virus, I expected . . . financial injury would be minor."[148] Prosecutors pointed out that Melissa affected more than a million computers around the world and caused an estimated $80 million in "losses"; the losses were a function of lost computer time and the time and resources needed to restore the infected systems. The state Attorney General noted that the crimes Smith committed were "not victimless crimes. . . . This paralyzed worldwide communications." The federal prosecutor—the U.S. Attorney for the District of New Jersey—emphasized the significance of what Smith had done: "The Melissa virus demonstrated the danger that business, government, and personal computer users everywhere face in our technological society. . . . Far from being a mere nuisance, Melissa . . . disabled computer networks" around the globe.[149]

On May 2, 2002, a federal judge sentenced David Smith to 20 months in prison, a $5,000 fine, and 100 hours of community service.[150] Prosecutors had asked the judge to impose a lenient sentence because Smith had cooperated with law enforcement on investigations into other viruses.[151] (This also explains why he was not sentenced until almost 2-1/2 years after his guilty plea.) Two days later, Smith was sentenced on the state count, but this was little more than a formality. Because the state sentence was served simultaneously with, and ended at the same time as, his federal sentence, it did not add any prison time, although the state judge did impose an additional $2,500 fine. Smith's total prison term was 20 months, which he served in a federal prison. He was released in December 2004, after serving 19 months.[152]

At Smith's sentencing on the federal charge, his attorney unsuccessfully tried to convince the judge that Smith did not deserve jail time because his virus was much less destructive than one that appeared two years earlier. On May 4, 2000, computer users around the world began receiving e-mail that had ILOVEYOU in the subject line and an attachment entitled LOVE-LETTER-FOR-YOU.TXT.vbs.[153] When someone opened the attachment, the virus embedded in it e-mailed itself to everyone in the person's address book; thus, when this "Love Bug" virus struck a large corporation or government agency, it caused chaos. Thousands of computers began e-mailing the virus to each other.[154]

That was not all the Love Bug did. It installed keys in the Windows registry so the virus would start when a computer booted up, and it searched the drives connected to an infected computer and replaced files with .doc, .jpg, .css, .jpeg, .vbs, .js, .jse, .sct, and .hta extensions with copies of itself. This destroyed the original data. The Love Bug also turned .mp3 or .mp2 files into hidden files and copied itself with the same file name, but these files could be recovered.[155] Finally, the Love Bug tried to steal passwords. Once active, the Love Bug connected an infected computer's browser to a Web site in the Philippines, where it downloaded an executable file onto the computer. After installing itself, that file tried to steal passwords stored in the computer's memory cache and send them to an email address in the Philippines.[156]

While the Love Bug was superficially similar to Melissa, it was at once more virulent and more destructive. Between May 4 and 10, the Love Bug infected 45 million computers in at least 20 countries and caused $8–$10 billion in damage.[157] It spread faster than Melissa because it e-mailed itself to every e-mail address in a victim's address book, instead of only 50. As a result, the Love Bug raced around the globe in hours. It was also cleverly designed to overcome computer users' hesitance to open e-mail from an unknown source. As one observer noted, the genius of the Love Bug virus lay "not in its technical power but in its emotional impact."[158] Millions were disarmed by the phrase "I love you" and did what they would not if the subject line of the virus-carrying e-mail had been a pitch for money-making opportunities or pornography. The Love Bug was also extraordinarily destructive—three times more so than Melissa.[159] It surpassed Melissa in this regard for two reasons: The Love Bug infected more computers; and unlike Melissa, the Love Bug not only clogged networks, it destroyed and altered data.

The Love Bug also differed from Melissa in another respect: No one was ever prosecuted for the Love Bug and the damage it caused. The FBI quickly began investigating the origins of the virus, with the assistance of a number of virus experts. The investigation soon focused on the Philippines. As we saw, the Love Bug went to a Philippines Web site to download the password-stealing file it installed on infected machines, and it sent the passwords it captured to an e-mail address in the Philippines. FBI agents flew to Manila, where they worked with agents from the Philippine National Bureau of Investigation. The investigators linked the virus to a phone line connected to a Manila apartment; one of its occupants had graduated from a Manila computer college, and students from the college visited her.[160] One of the most frequent visitors was her brother, Onel de Guzman.

The investigators linked de Guzman and another student at the college to the Love Bug. Similar to David Smith, the author(s) of the Love Bug had embedded their online pseudonyms in the virus code. A number of pseudonyms were embedded in the Love Bug, one of which apparently belonged to de Guzman. With this and other evidence, the investigators eventually got a warrant and searched the apartment from which the virus had been released. They did not find a computer, but they did seize computer disks and other items. At the time, many believed the delay in obtaining the warrant coupled with the intense publicity surrounding the investigation had given the suspect(s) time to dispose of evidence, including the computer used to create the Love Bug.

However, that was not the only problem the investigators faced. In 2000, the Philippines had not made creating and spreading a computer virus a crime. Indeed, it had no laws criminalizing hacking or any other type of computer crime. This was not unusual because many countries, and many U.S. states, had not yet recognized the need for such laws.[161] The lack of computer crime laws was a major problem for the Love Bug investigators. With what could they charge de Guzman? Philippine authorities finally charged him with theft (based on the virus stealing passwords) and credit card fraud (based on the theory that de Guzman used stolen passwords fraudulently to connect to a Manila ISP).

Two months later, prosecutors at the Philippine Department of Justice dismissed the charges because they concluded neither charge actually applied to what de Guzman had done. Both crimes were written to encompass activity in the real, physical world, not the play of bits and bytes in the cyberworld. As we will see in later chapters, this has been a problem in other countries, as well as the Philippines. Criminal laws have had to be expanded and revised to encompass digital crime. The Philippines quickly remedied the deficiencies in their law. In June 2000, Philippine President Estrada signed legislation adding a number of computer crimes, including the dissemination of a computer virus, to the Philippine criminal code. But because the new law could not be applied retroactively, Onel de Guzman was never charged for whatever role he played in the spread of the Love Bug. In interviews he gave in 2001, de Guzman admitted playing a role in creating the virus but always maintained he did not release it into the wild. He tended to suggest either that someone else released it or that it was released by accident.[162]

The Love Bug signaled the onset of several disturbing malware trends: Viruses became more common and more destructive. In 2001, the Code Red worm and Nimda virus caused billions of dollars in damage.[163] In 2003, the first flash worm, Slammer, was released. A flash worm is an extremely fast worm that infects all vulnerable computers in 15 minutes or less.[164] Slammer infected 90 percent of vulnerable computers within 10 minutes of being released.[165] It infected hundreds of thousands of computers worldwide and shut down a variety of systems, including 911 systems, ATMs, and an airline booking system. It also infected computers at a nuclear power plant in Ohio,which was not operational at the time.[166] In 2004, the Sasser worm appeared and shut down up to one million computer systems around the world, including business and government systems.[167]

The proliferation of malware continued. As noted earlier, by 2008, experts estimated there were more than a million viruses and worms in circulation worldwide. They also noted that the authors of malware had changed: In the 1990s and early 2000s, malware tended to be written by adolescent or post-adolescent hackers who were bent on doing "mischief" or building their reputation as code writers. By 2007, the Willie Sutton effect was in full swing: Malware had become the domain of professionals who use it to make money by stealing proprietary information and other resources from victims, by extorting money from victims (usually businesses), and by encrypting data and holding it for ransom.[168] Because they are professionals, these malware writers are adept at avoiding law enforcement. We will return to this issue in Chapter 4.

The authors of malware also changed tactics. Instead of sending viruses or worms out to infect users' computers, they began embedding malware in otherwise innocent Web sites. Those who visited the sites would, quite unknowingly, have their computers infected by whatever had been posted on them. In 2008, the antivirus company Sophos said its employees were finding a new infected Web site every 14 seconds of every hour of every day of each year.[169]

In 2008, that malware migrated to the next frontier. In August, NASA confirmed that a virus known as Gammima.AG had made it to the International Space Station. The virus had not infected the space station's computers; instead, it infected laptops used to "run nutritional programs" and send email to Earth via a NASA system. (The space station is not linked to the Internet.) Similar to the Love Bug, Gammima.AG is a password-stealing program. It lurks on infected computers and, when the opportunity arises, steals login names and passwords for several online games. Once it captures them, the virus tries to send the data to a remote server.[170] Although NASA would not discuss how Gammima.AG infected the laptops or what NASA was doing to deal with it, a NASA spokesperson dismissed the virus as a "nuisance." Others pointed out that while this particular virus posed no threat to the space station or to the astronauts it houses, "the fact . . . it got on board" raises concerns about vulnerable the space station is to malware.[171]

Malware in space is not likely to become a significant problem, but it illustrates how vulnerable our systems are to this rapidly evolving threat. David Smith might have intended, and believed, that his Melissa virus was little more than a prank, but in a world that is increasingly networked, malware can have devastating consequences. As already noted, malware writers have, for the most part, become professionals who are motivated by financial gain. According to one study, "professional, targeted attacks" have replaced the malware "hobbyism" of the 1990s.[172] Unfortunately, this is part of a larger trend.

Cyberspace + Crime = Cybercrime

As the first decade of the twenty-first century ended, cybercrime was becoming big business on a global scale.[173] Experts estimated cybercriminals raked in more than $100 billion a year.[174] And the influence of the Willie Sutton effect was not limited to hacking and malware. Computer technology was being used to commit traditional crimes—fraud, theft, extortion, and copyright violations—in new ways that were at once more profitable and less likely to lead to the perpetrator being apprehended.

Other cybercriminals exploited the technology for different purposes. They used computers to inflict nonfinancial "harms"—some old, some new —in new ways. The twenty-first century saw a dramatic rise in online stalking, harassment, defamation, and invasion of privacy. The Christian Hunold case was an early indicator of what was to come.

By 2000, it was apparent that computer technology could be used to facilitate the commission of most—if not all—of the crimes that had so far been recognized. It was also apparent that, as with the Love Bug, criminal law was going to have to expand to encompass new types of criminal activity. It was no longer possible to equate cybercrime with hacking or phreaking, malware, and a few related activities. Cybercrime was beginning to permeate all areas of criminal activity.

In 1999, I began working with law enforcement officers on cybercrime. For the next several years, I would hear officers say, "Some day every crime is going to be a cybercrime." For the last several years, I have heard officers say we are almost to that point—that almost every crime is a cybercrime. When I say that, I do not mean that the commission of EVERY crime involves the use of a computer and cyberspace as an integral criminal tool. I mean that computers increasingly, if not inevitably, play some role in the commission of crimes of all types. That reality is simply a function of the fact that computers are increasingly pervading every aspect of our lives.

When lawyers and law enforcement officers analyze cybercrime, they usually divide it into three categories, as we will see in Chapter 3. In that chapter, the categories are not defined with scientific precision. Instead, they are a way of sorting cybercrimes according to the type of "harm" inflicted and the role the computer played in the commission of the offense. After we review the categories in the next chapter, we will examine the crimes that fall into each of the categories in Chapters 4, 5, and 6.

Three Categories of Cybercrime

As noted in Chapter 2, law enforcement officers divide cybercrime into three categories: crimes in which a computer is the target of the offense, crimes in which a computer is used as a tool in committing the offense, and crimes in which a computer plays an incidental role in the commission of the offense.[1] The classification dates back to the mid-1990s.[2]

It emerged as a way to help officers draft applications for computer search warrants: If a computer was the target of the crime being investigated, it essentially becomes the crime scene on which investigators need to focus. Therefore, target crime search warrants generally need to be more comprehensive in scope and execution than, say, warrants for a computer that played an incidental role in the commission of a crime.

Here, we will simply define the three categories of cybercrime. In the next three chapters, we will examine the laws that apply to each of the categories in more detail.

TARGET CYBERCRIMES

When a computer is the target of criminal activity, the perpetrator attacks the computer by breaking into it or bombarding it from outside. In Chapter 2, we examined what so far are the two main types of target crimes: hacking and malware.

As we saw in Chapter 2, hacking is a kind of trespass. Trespass has been a crime for centuries, probably for millennia. Definitions of the crime are straightforward, as this Colorado criminal trespass statute illustrates: "A person commits . . . criminal trespass if such person unlawfully enters or remains in or upon premises of another."[3] Real-world criminal trespass statutes are designed to protect the privacy and sanctity of real property (i.e., land and structures built on land) by discouraging people from going where they have no legal right to be.

As we saw in Chapter 2, hacking is analogous to trespassing, in that hackers gain access to computers without being authorized to do so. Because computers are a kind of property (personal property, instead of real property),[4] hacking is similar to trespassing on someone's land. Therefore, we could have expanded criminal trespassing statutes so they outlawed hacking as well as trespasses on real property,[5] instead of creating a new "hacking" crime. The problem with trying to adapt traditional, criminal trespassing laws to encompass hacking is that one type deals with conduct in the physical world while the other deals with conduct "in" the virtual world. As we will see in Chapter 4, that difference undermines the viability of analogizing hacking and trespass. Trespassers physically "go into" a place or "go onto" land; hackers neither "go into" nor "go onto" the computers they attack. The evil to be outlawed in hacking laws is not unauthorized physical presence in a "place"; it is, as we will see in Chapter 4, something far more complex and elusive.

Disseminating malware can also be analogized to a traditional real-world crime: vandalism. Vandalism laws make it a crime to intentionally damage or destroy "real or personal property of another" without the owner's consent.[6] As we saw in Chapter 2, viruses and worms can damage computer systems and/or destroy data, both of which qualify as personal property. So we could expand our definition of vandalism, which currently focuses on inflicting physical damage to property, to also encompass the damage and destruction caused by viruses, worms, and other types of malware. No U.S. jurisdiction seems to have taken that approach, presumably because of the conceptual and practical differences between physical damage and intangible damage to property.

If someone takes a sledgehammer to my laptop, that would clearly be vandalism; my laptop, my personal property, has been damaged (or, more likely, destroyed). If that same someone creates and spreads a virus that infects my computer and deletes data, that could reasonably be characterized as vandalism; the virus has destroyed personal property (the data). If that virus infects my laptop, but instead of deleting data, it interferes with the operating system on which my computer relies to function,[7] it is not at all clear that this would constitute vandalism. The laptop itself has neither been destroyed nor damaged; it is still capable of functioning. The software constituting the operating system has not been deleted (destroyed) nor has it been damaged, at least not in the traditional sense; it is presumably still capable of functioning once the virus has been neutralized. In this and similar malware scenarios, the "harm" inflicted is at once more subtle and more complex than the "harm" encompassed by vandalism statutes.

Unlike the physical damage inflicted on tangible personal property in vandalism cases, the "harm" inflicted on the laptop in this scenario can be remediated, and the laptop can be restored to its original condition with comparatively little effort. Compare this scenario to one in which someone throws paint or acid on Rembrandt's *The Night Watch*.[8] If the vandal threw paint, it *might* be possible to restore the painting to a state only somewhat degraded from its original condition. If the vandal threw acid, it will be impossible to restore the painting to any semblance of its original condition. As I hope this hypothetical case demonstrates, the ultimate difference between real-world vandalism and the dissemination of malware lies in the elasticity and malleability of digital property. The "harm" I sustain in my original scenario is more akin to interference—or nuisance—than it is to the "harm" inflicted by vandalism.[9] For that and other reasons, the law has not sought to bring malware within the definition of vandalism. Instead, as we will see in Chapter 4, it created new and distinct malware crimes.

There is one other target crime we need to consider before we take up the tool cybercrimes: Distributed Denial of Service (DDoS) attacks. In a DDoS attack, attackers overwhelm Web sites and servers by bombarding them with data, or "traffic." The effect of a DDoS attack is similar to what would happen if someone used an automated dialing system to repeatedly call a small pizza delivery business; the automated calls would tie up the phone lines of the business and prevent legitimate customers from placing orders. The consequence would be that the business would lose business at least for as long as the attack continued. It might also lose some residual business if customers decided not to try calling again, either on that occasion or in the future.

In a DDoS attack, the perpetrators use a network of compromised computers—known as "zombies"—to send massive bursts of data at the target (s) of the attack. The zombies are computers that have been taken over by "bots"—software that subtly and usually invisibly infiltrates a computer. Bot software turns innocent computers—those used by individuals, businesses, and governmental, educational, or other agencies—into zombie computers.[10] The owners of these compromised computers usually have no idea their equipment is now moonlighting as a minion of some more-or-less sinister force.[11] The computer will operate more or less normally. The user may notice that it is running a little slower than usual, but that may be the only indication it has become a zombie.

Zombie computers will be integrated into a network—a "botnet"—controlled by a cybercriminal known as the "botherder." Botnets are becoming huge; law enforcement officers report botnets consisting of two million zombies, and the size only increases. A botnet is, in effect, a digital zombie army. Botherders usually rent their digital armies to cybercriminals, who use them to make money by shutting down Web sites and extorting money from their owners, sending spam e-mails, enticing users into online fraud scams, or installing adware on users' machines.

A botnet-based DDoS attack does not fit into the definition of any of the crimes countries have traditionally recognized. A pure DDoS attack is not theft, fraud, extortion, vandalism, trespass, or any other heretofore known type of criminal activity. DDoS attacks require the adoption of new laws, which we will examine in Chapter 4.

TOOL CYBERCRIMES

Instead of being the target of a cybercrime, a computer can be the implement—the tool—that is used to commit it. For the cybercrimes in this category, the role of the computer is analogous to the role telephones play in telephone fraud.[12]

Fraud is a type of theft. As a court noted, one commits theft when he or she takes personal property owned by someone else and carries it away "with intent to steal the property."[13] Theft consists of taking someone's property without his or her permission and with the intent to permanently deprive the victim of the possession and use of that property. Fraud is a relatively new variation of theft. The crime of fraud was created to encompass the situation in which the victim willingly gives the property to the criminal—the fraudster. If the owner of property consensually gives that property to someone, intending that the person will keep it, this is not theft; it must be something else. Centuries ago, English common law developed the crime of fraud, which consists of persuading someone to give you their property under false pretenses, such as falsely telling a person that in exchange for the property, you will give that person title to the Brooklyn Bridge. Fraud is also known as theft by trick.

Until the twentieth century, fraud could be committed only by mail or in person. In the twentieth century, fraudsters began using the telephone to commit fraud because it allowed the fraudster to remain anonymous and speed up the process. A perpetrator could contact people more quickly by using the telephone than he could in person. The telephone became a tool that is used to commit fraud; in the same way, and for many of the same reasons, computers have become a tool that is used to commit fraud and a variety of other crimes.

Perhaps the best example of a tool cybercrime is the Citibank theft case. In August 1994, Carlos Arario, head trader at the Argentinian firm Invest Capital, came to work one morning and discovered that more than $200,000 had disappeared overnight from his firm's account with Citibank.[14] Four anonymous wire transfers were made from the Invest Capital account to four unknown accounts. Arario called Citibank executives in New York to tell them what had happened; unfortunately, it continued to happen, and over the next months, someone siphoned almost $10 million from 20 Citibank accounts.

Citibank executives assembled a "war room" of experts to try to stop what was happening, but they could only watch as funds were transferred from client accounts into accounts in California, Tel Aviv, Rotterdam, Athens, Latin America, Finland, and Israel. The experts launched a global investigation as they sought to track the transfers and prevent more from occurring. They got a break when the unknown cyberthief transferred $218,000 from an Indonesian businessman's account to a BankAmerica account in San Francisco. Citibank experts and federal agents traced the account to Evgeni and Erina Korolkov, Russian nationals who had come to the United States from St. Petersburg. Erina was arrested when she tried to make a withdrawal from the San Francisco account. (She and Evgeni had allegedly opened this and other accounts to launder the funds being stolen from Citibank.) Federal agents flew to St. Petersburg and were given access to records that showed the Citibank accounts were being accessed from a computer at AO Saturn, a software company in St. Petersburg.

By December, Erina was cooperating with federal authorities and encouraged her husband to help them identify the Citibank thief. After the FBI promised Evgeni they would treat him leniently if he cooperated, he identified Vladimir Levin, who worked at AO Saturn, as the cyberthief. Levin was then a 29-year-old computer programmer who allegedly used a laptop computer at the AO Saturn offices to carry out the Citibank fund transfers. As these agents were identifying Levin, other federal agents were arresting Russian mules in the Netherlands and other countries The mules' role was to collect the funds that had been transferred from Citibank accounts to foreign accounts. Citibank ultimately claimed it had recovered all but $400,000 of the stolen funds.

Because the United States and Russia did not have an extradition treaty, Levin was safe as long as he remained in Russia. For some reason, he flew to London in 1995, where British authorities arrested him. He spent 18 months in a British jail, fighting extradition. Levin was finally sent to the United States and indicted on federal charges of theft and hacking. In 1998, he pled guilty and was sentenced to three years in prison.

Many do not believe Levin was the sole architect of the Citibank thefts (or almost thefts). Many found it difficult to believe Levin, even working with associates, could have developed and implemented the complex international network of bank accounts and mules that was to have been used to launder the proceeds. Many also did not believe Levin had the computer skills necessary to hack the Citibank accounts. Various theories emerged to explain what "really" happened. According to one theory, a Russian hacker group known as Megazoid figured out how to access the Citibank computers. One of them sold that information to Levin—or to someone working with Levin—for $100 and two bottles of vodka.[15] As to how Levin implemented the network of international bank accounts and mules, some, including then-U.S. Attorney General Janet Reno, suggested Levin was directly or indirectly working for the Russian mafia, which was, and still is, involved with cybercriminals.[16]

We will probably never know exactly what happened with the Citibank crimes: whether Citibank did, indeed, recover most of the money; whether Levin acted alone in hacking the Citibank system and transferring the funds from the Citibank accounts; and whether the Russian mafia was involved, either at the outset or as a broker for the stolen funds. At the time, Citibank confessed that its experts had never quite figured out how the crimes—or frustrated crimes—were executed. All of that, though, is irrelevant to the point at hand. Whoever he or she was, the architect of the Citibank thefts was a post-twentieth-century bank robber. Instead of using a mask and a gun to steal from a bank, the thief used computers. He or she used a new tool to commit a very old crime.

As we will see in Chapter 5, theft is only one of a host of traditional crimes that can be committed by substituting computer technology for more conventional means. Tool cybercrimes also include fraud, embezzlement, stalking, forgery, threats, extortion, defamation, gambling, terrorism, homicide, and the dissemination of child pornography. None of the tool crimes is a "new" crime, but it may be difficult to prosecute tool crimes under existing law, an issue we will take up in Chapter 5.

COMPUTER INCIDENTAL

The third and final category consists of cybercrimes in which the use of a computer is incidental to the commission of the crime; the computer plays a minor role in the offense. This category encompasses cases in which a computer is used to commit a crime; however, its use is so trivial that the computer does not rise to the level of being a tool, the use of which is integral to the commission of the crime. To understand the difference, it is helpful to consider an example.

Armed robbery is a type of theft. As we have already seen, theft is taking someone's personal property without his or her permission and with the intent to permanently deprive him or her of its possession and use. Theft requires only that the thief take the property without the owner's consent. It is theft if I take your laptop while you are not looking. I took it without your consent, but I did not use force to take it. Robbery consists of using force to commit theft. A Colorado statute, for example, defines robbery as taking "anything of value from . . . another by the use of force."[17] The force can consist of inflicting "bodily injury" on the victim or threatening to inflict such injury. The most serious theft crime is armed robbery, which, as its name implies, consists of using a deadly weapon (usually a gun) to commit robbery. Armed robbery is considered the most serious theft offense because the use of such a weapon increases the risk that someone will be killed in the commission of the offense. Armed robbery cannot be committed without using a deadly weapon; such a weapon is the tool the robber uses to commit this particular crime and, as such, is an integral element of the offense.

Computers were essential to the commission of the thefts in the Citibank case; Vladimir Levin, or whoever committed these crimes, could not have siphoned funds from the Citibank accounts without using computers (and the Internet). Computers played an integral role in the commission of these crimes; they were the tool the use of which was essential for the crimes to have been committed as they were. Now, that does not mean we need to define a new crime—computer theft—to encompass what Levin and others have done. We define armed robbery as a distinct type of robbery because the use of a deadly weapon—another tool for committing theft—raises distinct concerns about the "harm" inflicted in these crimes. As we will see in Chapter 5, while the use of computers to commit theft enables the crime be committed in new ways, it does not increase the actual or potential "harm" inflicted in a way that requires us to define a new crime. We can simply treat the computer as one of many tools that can be used to commit theft.

Now consider a different scenario: In 2007, Melanie McGuire was convicted of killing her husband William. According to prosecutors, Ms. McGuire used chloral hydrate to sedate William and then shot him "three or four times" before dismembering his body and dumping the remains in the Chesapeake Bay.[18] After the remains were discovered, police began investigating the crime. They learned Ms. McGuire had purchased a gun of the type used to kill her husband shortly before the murder; the murder weapon was never found. Police computer forensic investigators examined the couple's home computer and found that in the weeks before the murder, someone—presumably Melanie McGuire—used the computer to research topics such as "how to commit murder," "how to illegally purchase guns," and "undetectable poisons." They also found "romantic e-mails" between Melanie and her boss, a married physician. At trial, prosecutors used the computer evidence to establish that Melanie had a motive for killing her husband (i.e., to be with her lover) and had researched methods of committing homicide, including methods that were used in her husband's murder. On April 23, 2007, Melanie was convicted of murder; on July 19, she was sentenced to life in prison for the crime.

The McGuire computer played an important, although peripheral, role in William's murder. Melanie used it to research how to commit the crime but not to commit it. As we will see in Chapter 5, computer technology can—and no doubt will—be used to kill human beings. Here, however, the McGuires's home computer played an incidental role in the commission of the offense; it facilitated the commission only in the most indirect sense. Its actual role—as is true whenever a computer plays an incidental role in the commission of a crime—was as a source of evidence. The police clearly suspected Melanie of killing her husband, but the evidence preserved on the computer made their case much stronger than it would have been otherwise.

The McGuire case illustrates the role the computer plays in this final category of cybercrime. As people increasingly use computers, computers are increasingly used in criminal activity. It is, for example, common for drug dealers—especially those who deal on a large scale—to use computers to track their drug purchases, inventory, and sales.[19] As in the McGuire case, these computers become a valuable source of evidence when a drug dealer has been apprehended and will go on trial. The same is true for a variety of crimes: white-collar crimes such as embezzlement and economic espionage; other murders; blackmail; extortion; and essentially any crime we can imagine. We will examine this aspect of cybercrime in detail in Chapter 5.

Because the computer is merely a source of evidence in these types of cases, they do not require us to adopt new legislation to be able to prosecute the crimes at issue. But as we will see in Chapter 6, the intricacies of digital evidence can make it necessary to revise laws that govern the acquisition of evidence and its introduction at trial.

Target Cybercrimes: Hacking, Malware, and Distributed Denial of Service Attacks

As we have seen, there are (so far, anyway) three types of target cybercrime: hacking, malware, and Distributed Denial of Service (DDoS) attacks. In this chapter, we will examine how the law deals with each of these target crimes.

More precisely, we will examine how U.S. law deals with these target crimes. We will focus primarily on U.S. law for several reasons, the most important of which is that the United States has the most extensively developed set of cybercrime laws in the world. This is attributable to the facts that the United States has had a great deal of experience with cybercrime and is composed of 52 distinct jurisdictions. Each U.S. state plus the District of Columbia has its own cybercrime law, as does the U.S. federal system. Because each jurisdiction is, to a great extent, free to fashion its law as it likes, this can give rise to a fair amount of statutory diversity and complexity. As a result, U.S. law has been influential in shaping the cybercrime laws of other countries.

We will not ignore the cybercrime law of other countries. I will, as appropriate, compare how U.S. law and the law of certain countries approach similar issues. In Chapter 10, we will examine the effort to create a coordinated global effort against cybercrime.

HACKING

As noted in Chapter 3, from a legal perspective, hacking is functionally analogous to the crime of trespass; in both, the perpetrator violates use restrictions on property. In trespass, the restrictions govern who can legitimately enter onto, or into, real property—land, buildings, and so forth. In hacking, the restrictions govern who can legitimately make use of computer technology.

This notion of hacking as a violation of use restrictions on computer technology shaped how U.S. law and the law of other countries dealt with this type of activity. Although there is a great deal of consistency in the approach these laws take, there are variations in how they define hacking. We will examine those variations in the first section, which deals with the laws that criminalize "outsider" hacking.

In the next section, we will examine the laws that criminalize "insider" hacking, a not-entirely-new phenomenon that has become a matter of growing concern over the last decade. "Insider" hacking occurs when someone who is legitimately entitled to access a *portion* of a computer system—a business system, for example—exceeds the scope of his or her authorized access to the system. People do this for various reasons—some innocent, some not so innocent. However, in every instance, this ostensibly more innocuous variety of hacking raises concerns analogous to those that led us to outlaw trespassing in the real world.

Before we examine hacking law, I need to note a caveat: We are dealing only with "simple" hacking. That is, we are dealing only with criminal conduct that consists of gaining access to a computer without being authorized to do so. This is the cyber-analogue of a hunter going onto someone's land to pursue a deer. "Simple" hacking is a target crime and, as such, properly falls within the scope of this chapter. In the next chapter, we will examine "aggravated hacking": accessing a computer without being authorized to do so for the purpose of committing a crime. Aggravated hacking is not trespass; it is, in effect, burglary. Burglary is defined as entering a "dwelling" or other building without being authorized to do so and "with the intent to commit an offense therein."[1] Burglary is essentially aggravated trespass; burglars break into a building to commit a crime—theft, arson, rape, murder—once inside. As we will see in Chapter 5, many cybercriminals are burglars; they break into computers to commit a crime—such as stealing or destroying data—once inside.

"Outsider" Hacking

"Outsider" hacking is conceptually very similar to trespass in the physical world. Similar to trespass, it involves a violation of a use restriction on property that is committed by someone who has *no* right to access the property. As courts have noted, the rationale for criminalizing trespass is "the protection of one's property from unauthorized intrusion by others."[2] The rationale assumes an intrusion onto someone's land; courts and legal dictionaries consistently define "trespass" as "wrongful entry on another's real property."[3]

Because criminal trespass is synonymous with an intrusion into real, physical space, legislatures have not tried to define hacking as trespass by bringing it within the scope of their criminal trespass statutes or by adopting new "computer trespass" statutes. Instead, they have created a new crime: unauthorized access to computers. In the United States, the federal hacking statute makes it a crime to intentionally access a computer without being authorized to do so and thereby "cause damage."[4] Arkansas's statute is representative of the laws adopted by other U.S. states: "A person commits unlawful . . . access to computers if the person knowingly and without authorization, . . . accesses . . . or causes access to be gained to a computer, system [or] network."[5]

Other countries have taken the same approach in outlawing hacking. The United Kingdom's Computer Misuse Act makes it a crime to cause "a computer to perform any function with intent to secure access to any program or data held in any computer" if the access is unauthorized and if the person knows it is unauthorized.[6] The hacking laws of other countries in Europe and elsewhere are similar to this provision and to the U.S. laws previously noted here.[7]

In this type of hacking, therefore, an "outsider" intentionally accesses a computer or computer system without being authorized to do so. The hacker must know that he or she is not authorized to access the system, but this is generally not a problem. It is, if not impossible, extraordinarily difficult to hack by accident. Most of the time, hacking a system requires a fair degree of effort.

The hackers we are dealing with here are not motivated by a desire to access a computer to commit theft, sabotage, or any other traditional crime. Similar to the original hackers we examined in Chapter 2, they tend to be motivated by curiosity about the intricacies of a particular computer network or about what is inside that network.

Gary McKinnon is a good example of this kind of hacker. Born in Glasgow in 1966, he got his first computer when he was 14 and has been using computers since then.[8] Although McKinnon enjoyed working with computers, he became a hairdresser when he was 17. In the early 1990s, McKinnon changed careers; he took courses and qualified as a computer technician. He worked uneventfully in that field until 1999, when he began using "a cheap PC" in his London flat to break into the "most secure computer systems in the world."[9]

Between 1999 and 2002, McKinnon broke into 97 computer networks used by NASA, the U.S. Army, the U.S. Navy, the U.S. Department of Defense, and the U.S. Air Force.[10] The United States later claimed it spent approximately $700,000 tracking McKinnon's intrusions and correcting problems caused by them. McKinnon has denied causing any damage but admits hacking the systems.[11]

According to McKinnon, his hacking was "humanitarian"—a research project meant to benefit mankind.[12] He was researching unidentified flying objects (UFOs). His interest in UFOs was sparked by what he read on The Disclosure Project, an Internet site maintained by UFO enthusiasts. The site features "testimonies" from people who confirm the existence of UFOs. Some of these testimonies are allegedly from former military personnel who say the U.S. military reverse-engineered UFO technology.[13] McKinnon began hacking U.S. military systems in an effort to confirm this; he was particularly interested in whether the United States had developed "free energy." McKinnon believed "free energy" was an antigravity propulsion system extracted from recovered alien spacecraft.[14] "I felt if it existed it should be publicly available," he later said.[15]

McKinnon admits "posting anti-war diatribes on" some computers but insists he never damaged systems he invaded.[16] The U.S. government sees him very differently. In November 2002, the U.S. Attorney for New Jersey pointed out that one of his hacks shut down the computer system at the Earle Naval Weapons Station in Colts Neck for a week after the 9/11 attacks. Because the station supplies munitions for the Atlantic fleet, this "grave intrusion" impaired the ability of the United States to respond at a "perilous" time.[17]

The U.S. Attorney for the District of New Jersey made his comments while announcing that a New Jersey grand jury had indicted McKinnon for hacking in violation of the federal statute previously quoted. At almost the same time, a Virginia grand jury indicted McKinnon for violating the same statute by hacking 92 U.S. military systems and shutting down the computer network for the Military District of Washington.[18] McKinnon was indicted on one count of violating that statute—18 U.S. Code § 1030(a)—in each of the two indictments and faced two counts of violating the federal anti-hacking statute.

At NASA's behest, officers from the United Kingdom National Hi-Tech Crime Unit (NHTCU) arrested McKinnon in March 2002. The NHTCU officers seized McKinnon and his computer equipment but let him go without filing charges. Britain *could* have prosecuted McKinnon under the Computer Misuse Act, which is previously quoted here. Instead, the British government's view was that because the crimes targeted computers in the United States, "[n]inety-nine per cent of the witnesses are in the US and the technical evidence is also in the US. The most practical approach is to prosecute in the US."[19]

Because McKinnon was not in the United States, U.S. officials had to extradite him to put him on trial for the charges in the New Jersey and Virginia indictments.[20] McKinnon fought extradition for years and consistently lost. He argued that he should be prosecuted in the United Kingdom (if at all) and that he needed to remain in the United Kingdom to obtain treatment for his recently diagnosed Asperger's syndrome (a type of autism).[21] McKinnon's claims attracted a fair amount of support in the United Kingdom. There were sympathetic press stories and a "Free Gary McKinnon" movement, complete with a Web site and demonstrations.[22]

Much of the support for McKinnon may be attributable to the fact that the British press consistently misstated the penalties he faced if convicted in the United States. As a *Wired* reporter noted, under U.S. law, McKinnon would serve between "six months to six-and-a-half years in prison," depending on the amount of damage he is found to have caused and whether he takes responsibility for his actions.[23] As the reporter also noted, through a "quirk of the metric system, this becomes 60 years, 70 years, 80 years and a life sentence in the British press."[24] McKinnon's supporters also ignored the fact that in 2003, he turned down a plea offer that would have let him serve between six months and a year in a minimum security U.S. prison and then be returned to the United Kingdom, where he would spend six months on parole.[25]

Much of the sympathy for McKinnon seemed to be based on the premise that he, similar to David Lightman in *War Games*,[26] did nothing "wrong." Some of the stories in the British press contrasted McKinnon—an "innocent," traditional hacker—with the modern, professional cybercriminals who hack for profit instead of in an (alleged) effort to benefit mankind.[27] A few claimed the United States was using him as a scapegoat to conceal lax security on military computers. Some characterized McKinnon as an inept hacker who stumbled into barely secured networks.[28] The implicit refrain was that while McKinnon accessed the U.S. military computers without being authorized to do so, he never meant to cause harm and so should not be held responsible for any damage he inadvertently inflicted. There was also another implicit assumption in many of the British press stories about McKinnon: the notion that the U.S. military was, in effect, to blame for what he did because it did not adequately secure its computer systems.

Some of the sentiment in the refrains derived from the resentment British citizens felt at seeing one of their own facing (what were inaccurately characterized as) horrific penalties in the United States. Much of it, though, was the product of attitudes about hackers and hacking that date back to the 1960s and 1970s, when hacking was, in fact, an innocent intellectual endeavor.

As we saw in Chapter 2, hacking evolved in a mainframe culture that encouraged users to elide restrictions as they explored what computers were capable of doing. As we also saw, the perception of hacking as a constructive endeavor carried over from mainframe culture to the early years of Internet culture. In the *War Games* era, hacking was seen as part prank and part scientific exploration. It was to be encouraged, not prosecuted. The premise on which this attitude was based was, however, inextricably linked to the use of mainframes. As noted earlier, mainframes are closed systems. In a mainframe culture, hacking is an activity that is necessarily carried out by those who have some legitimate affiliation with the mainframe computer that is the object of their efforts. It is, in other words, an "inside job"; only those with some level of authorized access to a mainframe can hack it (i.e., go beyond the scope of what they were specifically authorized to do). That, plus another characteristic of mainframe hacking, distinguish it from the kinds of hacking we see today.

The other characteristic is the nature of the mainframes to which early hackers had access. As we saw in Chapter 2, hacking emerged in an academic environment. The computers used by the early hackers were university computers, and the hackers were university students. The mainframes were used for academic research and instruction. As students, the early hackers' access to the computers was, more or less explicitly, for educational purposes. The conception of hacking as an intellectual endeavor akin to scientific research is a logical product of this confluence of this context (education) and the bounded technology (mainframe computers) then available. Hacking was implicitly accepted in the universities from which it emerged because it was, in fact, an intellectual and educational endeavor. Most hackers were enrolled in computer science or electrical engineering programs. Testing the capacities and limits of their school's mainframes was part of their course of study. That, in turn, tended to mitigate the impropriety associated with their bending mainframe user rules established by the institution. Given the context, going beyond one's authorized access to a mainframe could not harm anyone outside the institution, could not *really* harm the institution, and had the benefit of enhancing the skills of certain students. In this context, hacking could legitimately be seen as something that was not "wrong."

That changed once hacking moved into cyberspace. It was no longer a bounded, educational endeavor—an "inside job." Cyberspace hacking may have been prompted by simple curiosity, analogous to what motivated the original mainframe hackers. But curiosity has become a purely idiosyncratic phenomenon. Anyone who is curious about a person or issue and has certain computer skills can hack computer(s) that might contain the answer. The motivation now is purely selfish. And because the computers probably belong to someone else, the hacks—unlike the mainframe hacks—violate property rights. They violate the various computer owners' rights to exclude others from their systems.

Hackers such as McKinnon, who claim their hacks were intellectual endeavors, are attempting to resuscitate what I submit is an outmoded premise. The premise that simple hacking—simply gaining access to a computer system without being authorized to do so—is not "wrong." I agree that the original mainframe hacking was not "wrong" as criminal law construes "wrong." Those hackers were motivated by intellectual curiosity, and that motivation was relevant, given the bounded context in which they hacked. They were, in effect, violating internal use restrictions imposed by and binding upon the members of a single community: their university. The impact of their transgressions was felt only within that community; it was therefore up to that community to decide how to deal with them. My impression is that universities tended to wink at hacking during the mainframe era and to regard it as a sometimes annoying but essentially innocuous prank.

The transgressions of contemporary hackers such as McKinnon are not so limited; they impact strangers who may be in another city or in another country. They also inflict "harm," even when "harm" is not intended and is relatively minor. McKinnon is probably telling the truth when he says he did not cause damage to the U.S. military systems. He never *intended* to delete or alter data in the systems, and there seems no evidence that he did either. However, he did, interrupt legitimate users' ability to access the systems he explored and, in so doing, deprived the owner of those systems (the U.S. government) of a portion of the value and use of that property.[29] This deprivation of the right to control access to a system constitutes "damage" under the federal computer crime statute—18 U.S. Code § 1030.

Section 1030(e)(8) defines "damage" as "any impairment to the integrity or availability of data, a program, a system, or information."

"Outsider" hacking may once have been an innocuous and constructive pursuit, but that is no longer the case. Similar to those who explore property that does not belong to them in the physical world, these virtual trespassers at a minimum violate a property owner's exclusive right to determine who has access to his or her property. They can also inflict additional "harm" on the property owner by inadvertently altering or deleting data in the systems they hack. For these reasons, countries criminalize "outsider" hacking.

"Insider" Hacking

"Insider" hacking occurs when someone who is authorized to access *part* of a computer system exceeds the scope of that authorization and, in effect, trespasses on other parts of the system. Although "outsider" hacking is defined as gaining "unauthorized access" to a computer system, "insider" hacking is defined as "exceeding authorized access" to such a system.

Colorado's computer crime statute, for example, defines "insider" hacking as a person "knowingly" exceeding authorized access "to a computer, computer network, or computer system or any part thereof."[30] A related statute defines to "exceed authorized access" as "to access a computer with authorization and to use such access to obtain or alter information, data, computer program, or computer software that the person is not entitled to so obtain or alter."[31] The federal statute—18 U.S. Code § 1030—defines it in almost identical terms[32] and makes it a crime to exceed one's authorized access to obtain information from a "computer."[33] Other countries—including the United Kingdom, Singapore, and Japan—also criminalize the act of exceeding one's authorized access to a computer.[34]

"Insider" hacking cases range from the trivial to the unnerving, in terms of both the motivations of the hacker and the "harm" he or she caused. Among the trivial, and more common, "insider" hacking cases are cases in which a law enforcement officer exceeds his or her access to a police computer, usually for some personal reason.

In *State v. Moning,*[35] for instance, Cincinnati Police Officer Matthew Moning was charged with, and convicted of, exceeding his authorized access to police databases. According to the Ohio Court of Appeals, Moning was assigned to the Cincinnati Police impound lot, where vehicles seized by the police were being held. The office at the lot had a computer that police officers could use for legitimate law enforcement purposes, such as looking up the owner of a vehicle. Although Moning knew he was authorized to use the computer only for law enforcement purposes,[36] on September 3, 2000, he used it to access the Regional Crime Information Center (RCIC) database and run a search on James Heileman. As the court's opinion notes, the RCIC database is "one of three databases available to law enforcement personnel to investigate the criminal history of a subject."

Moning accessed the database to check Heileman's crimnal history, apparently out of curiosity and a desire to embarrass Heileman. The court's opinion says Moning and Heileman "had grown up in the same area and both frequented a neighborhood bar, but the men did not get along." Moning discovered Heileman had a drug conviction. After he got off work, Moning obtained a copy of the printout showing the conviction, took it to the bar the two frequented, and gave it to Heileman. Heileman called the Cincinnati Police to ask why Moning had run a check on him. When police investigated, they found there was no legitimate reason to run such a search; Heileman was not suspected of criminal activity. Because the investigation of Heileman's complaint showed Moning had used the RCIC system for an unauthorized purpose, Moning was indicted for exceeding authorized access to a computer in violation of Ohio law. A jury convicted him of the offense, and the Court of Appeals upheld the conviction. Similar to all "insider" hackers, Moning simply went too far. He abused his privilege of accessing the police computer system.

Also similar to many "insider" hackers, Moning seems to have been motivated by simple curiosity (plus, perhaps, a desire to intimidate someone toward whom he felt some antagonism). In 2008, Lawrence Yontz, an intelligence analyst for the U.S. Department of State, pled guilty to exceeding his authorized access to State Department computers, including the Passport Information Electronic Records System (PIERS).[37] The PIERS database includes images of all passport applications files since 1994, including the applicant's photography and personal information. In pleading guilty, Yontz admitted that between 2005 and 2008, he used PIERS to view applications filed by approximately 200 athletes, celebrities, and presidential candidates. As a State Department analyst, Yontz had authorized access to its databases, including the PIERS database. However, because he had no legitimate purpose for viewing the applications of these people, he exceeded his authorized access to the system. In his plea agreement, Yontz said he was motivated by "idle curiosity." While his transgression may seem trivial, it caused great concern to those who discovered their information had been accessed improperly. Yontz proved harmless, but someone else might have used the information to "harm" the individuals involved by, say, using it to stalk them or publicizing the information and perhaps embarrassing those who might not want their dates of birth or other personal information in public circulation.

Perhaps the strangest "insider" hacking case I recall is *Commonwealth v. McFadden*.[38] According to the opinion in the case, in 2001 Gina McFadden and her partner Dawn Norman were Philadelphia Police officers. On October 18—a little more than a month after the 9/11 attacks—they were on patrol in a Philadelphia Police vehicle. Similar to other police cars, theirs was equipped with a mobile data terminal (MDT), a computer terminal that officers can use to communicate with the police dispatch system and to look up information, such as license plates.[39] All that day, MDT terminals in Philadelphia Police cars had been repeatedly broadcasting a message about a missing truck containing hazardous materials. At approximately 1:00 p.m. that day, McFadden used the MDT terminal in her patrol car to send a message over the system that read, in part, "We have anthrax in the back of our car." The rest of the message consisted of profane comments expressing hatred of the United States.

Naturally, the message generated concern among other officers, including those who supervised McFadden and Norman. The two officers were called back to their police station and asked about the message. Both said they knew nothing about it. McFadden said they left their patrol car unattended while they ate lunch and again when they made a bathroom stop. The implication was that someone else had sent the message. After being questioned about the episode over several days, McFadden finally admitted she had sent the message. She would later claim she typed the message as a joke to be seen only by her partner but somehow transmitted it by mistake.

McFadden, who soon became a former police officer, was charged with and convicted of exceeding her authorized access to the MDT computer in her patrol car. She appealed, arguing that the evidence presented to the jury was insufficient to prove she committed the crime. The court that heard her appeal did not agree. It held that the evidence "established that, while [McFadden] was authorized to access the MDT for purposes of official police business, she was not authorized to access the computer for any other purposes. . . . She certainly was not authorized to access the computer for the purpose of distributing a message that implied that a Philadelphia police car had been contaminated with anthrax by terrorists."

In these three cases, the evidence unambiguously established the "exceeding authorized access" crime. In each case, it was clear that the defendant exceeded the scope of his or her access to the computer system and did so knowingly and intentionally. In the Moning and McFadden cases, the police departments had policies specifying that officers were authorized to use police computers only for law enforcement purposes, and in each case, the officer was aware of these policies. Yontz, too, was clearly aware that his passport snooping exceeded the bounds of his legitimate access to Department of State computers.

The issues of whether someone actually exceeded the scope of his authorized access to a computer system and, if so, whether he did so intentionally are not always so straightforward. The "exceeding authorized access" crime is by definition committed by an insider, and it can sometimes be difficult to prove beyond a reasonable doubt that the accused not only exceeded his or her legitimate access, but knew that what he or she was doing was outside the bounds of what was permissible. The case that perhaps best illustrates this difficulty is *Fugarino v. State*.[40]

Fugarino was a programmer for a Georgia company that designed software for land surveyors. All we know about what led to his being charged with exceeding his authorized access to his employer's computer comes from a Georgia Court of Appeals decision. Fugarino was apparently a "difficult employee" before the events described here took place; the opinion says his employer had been "concerned about his unusual behavior." According to the decision, Fugarino "became very angry" when he learned someone had been hired "in an unrelated technical support position." He told another employee that the code he had been working on "was his product" and that he "was 'going to take his code with him.'"[41] The employee saw Fugarino "deleting massive amounts of files" before the owner of the company finally made him leave. An investigator later found that "large amounts of data had been deleted from the system."[42]

Fugarino was charged with and convicted of "exceeding authorized access" to his employer's computer system.[43] He appealed, claiming the evidence presented at trial did not prove beyond a reasonable doubt that he *knew* he was exceeding his authorized access to his employer's computer when he deleted substantial amounts of code. Before I explain how the appellate court dealt with this argument, we need to consider its merits. Fugarino's argument may seem specious because we all know, as a matter of common sense, that he went too far—that what he did clearly did not fall within the scope of what he was *supposed* to do with his access to the company's computer. The problem here is that we cannot base the imposition of criminal liability on what we presume someone knew.

The Georgia statute requires that a defendant must have *known* that what he did was outside the bounds of his legitimate access to a computer system.[44] This is consistent with all hacking statutes; both "insider" and "outsider" hacking statutes require either that the defendant (1) *knew* he was doing something he was not authorized to do or (2) not only knew he was doing something he was not authorized to but *intended* to do precisely that. In criminal law, these mental states (knowingly and intentionally) constitute what is called *mens rea*, or "guilty mind." American criminal law uses four mental states—four levels of *mens rea*—to calibrate the liability we impose for particular crimes: negligence, recklessness, knowledge, and intention.[45] Most serious crimes require either knowledge or intention; we tend to reserve recklessness and negligence for lesser offenses.

Under the Georgia statute, the prosecutor had to prove Fugarino *knew* he was exceeding his authorized access to the system in order to convict him. To have acted knowingly, Fugarino had to have been consciously aware—at the time he was deleting the code—that he was doing something he was not authorized to do. When knowledge is the applicable level of *mens rea*, the evidence must show that this specific person—this defendant—actually *knew* he was doing something "wrong." If the prosecution can show only that a reasonable person in the defendant's situation would have known this, its evidence merely proves the defendant was negligent, which is not enough to support a conviction under a statute such as the one under which Fugarino was charged.[46]

That brings us back to the Fugarino case. The prosecution could not sustain its burden of proving beyond a reasonable doubt that Fugarino knew what he was doing by arguing that a reasonable person would have known that deleting the code exceeded his authorized access to the system. Instead, it had to somehow prove that *he* knew. The prosecutor did this in two ways: He had the owner of the company testify "he did not give Fugarino authority . . . to delete portions of the company's program." Also, he used Fugarino's words against him: The prosecutor apparently had the employee who saw Fugarino deleting code and the owner of the company describe his comments about ensuring that "no one would be able to sell" the code and about "taking it with him."

The owner's testimony that he did not authorize Fugarino to delete the code is what the law calls direct evidence. Direct evidence is evidence that directly proves a fact at issue; an eyewitness testifying about what he saw is the classic example of direct evidence. If the jury believes the witness, his or her testimony becomes proof of that fact. The employee's and owner's testimony about Fugarino's comments is what the law calls circumstantial evidence. Circumstantial evidence is indirect evidence, consisting of evidence (testimony or physical evidence) from which the jury can infer the existence of a fact at issue in the case.

Law professors often use this example to illustrate circumstantial evidence: You work in an interior office in a large high-rise building. Your office has no windows and is effectively soundproof. You see a co-worker walk by your open office door carrying an umbrella that is dripping water. What you have seen is circumstantial evidence from which you can infer that it is raining outside. The fact her umbrella is wet because she has been outside where it is raining is not the only conceivable inference you could draw from what you have seen. Perhaps the sprinkler system went off in another part of the office and soaked her umbrella. The inference that her umbrella is soaked because it is raining outside is, though, more likely to be correct. Inferences are based on common sense, and our common sense tells us umbrellas are more likely to be wet because of rain than because of defective sprinkler systems.

So the Fugarino prosecutor had eyewitnesses describe what Fugarino said as he deleted large amounts of program code. Then the prosecutor asked the jury to infer from those comments that Fugarino knew he was doing something he was not authorized to do. The jury did so, and the Georgia Court of Appeals held it was reasonable for them to infer from "the vindictive and retaliatory manner in which Fugarino deleted large amounts of . . . code . . . that he knew he lacked authority to do so."[47]

Had Fugarino not made those comments and had he not acted in the "vindictive" manner he did, the prosecutor might not have been able to prove his *mens rea* beyond a reasonable doubt. Fugarino was a programmer; his job was to develop software. To do that, he had to write and delete code; in software development, as in writing and other endeavors, the job description and authorization necessarily entail both creating and editing what one has created. Editing encompasses deleting parts of what one has created. Literally, then, Fugarino *was* authorized to delete code; the problem was that he went too far by deleting *too much* code. Had he done so calmly and surreptitiously —without letting anyone know why he was deleting so much code—it might have been impossible for the prosecution to prove he did, in fact, know he was exceeding his legitimate authority over the company's code and its computer system.

There are two approaches organizations can take to minimizing ambiguity as to the scope of employees' authorized access to their computers: contract and code.[48] The Moning case illustrates the contract approach; the police department had a set of written policies specifying the purposes for which officers could use law enforcement databases. Officers were required to acknowledge their understanding of and willingness to comply with these policies by signing a consent form. The contract approach is predicated on the premise that employees will not exceed authorized access to a system if they know what they are *supposed* to do. The other alternative relies on software, not policies. In the code approach, the employer uses software to circumscribe what each employee is *able* to do in using the employer's computer system. This approach is predicated on the premise that the best way to prevent employees from exceeding authorized access is to deny them the ability to do so.

The code approach is no doubt effective in many instances, but it simply will not work in others. It *might* be possible to configure police databases to limit the types of searches individual officers can conduct, but that seems impracticable as a general rule. It might have been possible to limit the access by a special assignment officer such as Moning to police databases by restricting his ability to search for information other than that which related to the duties of an impound officer. It would probably not have been possible to limit McFadden's access to the MDT terminal in her patrol car to prevent her from sending the prank message. And it certainly would not have been possible to limit Fugarino's access to the company's computer system in such a way as to prevent him from doing what he did because, as already noted, deleting code was a necessary and inevitable part of his job as a programmer.

That brings us back to the contract approach, which I believe is the best option. The contract approach is consistent with the approach we use in a variety of other areas. Organizations have policies that put employees on notice as to what types of conduct are expressly forbidden and what the consequences are if an employee engages in such conduct. This is a well-established, familiar dynamic in many aspects of our lives in the real world. When we see a speed limit sign, for example, we know that if we drive faster than what is allowed, we run the risk of incurring certain consequences (a ticket). Speed limit signs are, in effect, a kind of contract; it tells drivers that within this particular area, they are authorized to operate their vehicles at speeds below, say, 45 miles per hour. Rules and policies such as speed limits are not perfect; some people speed anyway. But they serve two essential purposes: They discourage most of us from speeding; and they provide a clear standard that can be enforced when someone speeds—when they exceed their authorized access to that stretch of highway.

The contract approach is, I submit, the more likely of the two to remain viable as technologies increase in complexity. When workers perform simple, mundane tasks (such as data entry), it is not particularly difficult to define their access to the computer system in a way that effectively deprives them of the ability to exceed that access. As computers and tasks become more complex, it becomes increasingly difficult to do so. The utility of the code approach consequently erodes. The contract approach has the virtue of targeting people, not technology. Policies that specifically restrict the scope of an employee's legitimate use of a computer system essentially have the same effect as speed limit signs. That is, they discourage most people from violating the rules, and they provide an objective benchmark that can be used to discipline those who do so.

That leaves us with one final issue we need to address before we move to our next topic—laws criminalizing the creation and dissemination of malware. The issue is *whether* it is possible to craft policies that specifically define the scope of the access an employee such as Fugarino legitimately has to his employer's computer system. It would be very difficult, I think, to structure such policies in terms of the discrete actions such an employee is authorized to carry out on the system. It would not, as already noted, have been feasible to develop a policy that allowed Fugarino to delete *some* code but not *too much* code. Such a policy would leave the issue of access ambiguous and, in so doing, would give the employee a fair degree of latitude to argue that blatantly unreasonable acts (such as deleting substantial parts of a program) were not unauthorized. The solution, I think, lies in focusing not on technical processes but on the purpose with which the processes are initiated and carried out. If Fugarino's company had required employees to sign a policy that, say, committed them to using the company's computers only in a manner that was constructive and beneficial for the company, it would not only have put employees on notice as to what was forbidden, it would also have provided a clear benchmark from which to infer that a particular employee's actions were intentionally outside the bounds of what was permitted.

MALWARE

As noted in Chapter 2, malware has, for the most part, ceased to be an activity carried out by amateurs and instead has become a business dominated by professionals. As one article noted, malware is now a "big business"[49] and an international one. Research conducted in 2008 showed that while Russia, China, and Brazil have been "hotspots of malware creation" since 2003, the focus is likely to shift over the next five years to Mexico, India, Africa, and China.[50]

The malware business—the "online shadow economy of malware," as one analyst described it—is estimated to produce more than $100 billion in revenue each year.[51] According to those who study this "shadow economy," it is based on a sophisticated division of labor among specialists, each of whom is responsible for discrete tasks.[52] The first set of specialists is the malware writers, who create viruses, Trojan horse programs, and spyware. They create generic and customized malware. For prices that can run less than $300, someone can hire a malware writer to create a special-order virus or other type of malware. For as little as $25 a month, he or she can subscribe to a software update service that helps the malware evade detection by antimalware software.

Malware writers sell their product either directly to someone who wants it for a particular purpose or to middlemen who use botnets to disseminate malware as a step toward the commission of various types of financial crimes. In Chapter 3, we saw how botnets were used to launch DDoS attacks. They can also be used to spread malware that sends out millions of spam e-mails or attacks Web sites and steals credit card and other data. The middlemen who use botnets to distribute malware usually rent a botnet from its owner, who is known as the "botherder." The middlemen profit in any of several ways: from sending out millions of spam e-mail; from installing spyware and adware on unsuspecting computers; or from selling the credit card and other data they harvest, courtesy of malware. They may sell the data to another category of specialists who use them to purchase items online. The items are then sent to a "drop site," a person or location where they can be delivered and held until they are sold. Studies show that organized crime is often involved in this activity, as well as in using banks to launder the proceeds of credit card thefts.

The increasing specialization of the malware writing and distribution processes makes attacks more common and more effective. A 2008 study found that the number of malware attacks had more than doubled in the last year and that antivirus software was less effective in identifying and frustrating attacks.[53] The effectiveness of antivirus software erodes because new varieties of malware are being written faster than the antivirus companies can come up with countermeasures for them.[54]

What about prosecutions? Is law enforcement mounting an effective campaign against those who write, disseminate, and use malware? The answer, for the most part, is no.

It is illegal to *use* malware but not to *create* it.[55] The federal computer crime statute makes it illegal to "knowingly" cause "the transmission of a program, information, code, or command" and thereby intentionally cause "damage" to a computer.[56] While Congress took this rather indirect approach to criminalizing malware,[57] U.S. states have been more direct. A number make it a crime to "knowingly" introduce a "computer contaminant into any computer, computer system or computer network."[58] They define "computer contaminant" as a virus, worm, or other software that is designed to disrupt the functioning of a computer system and/or alter data.[59] Other states simply make it a crime to spread a computer virus,[60] and they define "computer virus" in a fashion similar to the definition of "computer contaminant."[61]

Although the federal government and most, if not all, states criminalize the use of malware, I can find *no* reported state cases in which someone was prosecuted violating these laws, and only a few federal prosecutions.[62] The lack of state prosecutions is not surprising given what we have already seen (i.e., malware has become a tool of professional, organized criminals, the majority of whom operate outside the United States). The U.S. states are not equipped to pursue malware writers who operate from Brazil, China, or Russia. State and local prosecutors lack the resources and expertise for such an endeavor.[63]

That leaves the federal government, which, at least since the 9/11 attacks, has had other priorities. Federal prosecutors have brought a few prosecutions against those who created and disseminated malware, but malware charges tend to be unusual, and the defendants tend, as one observer noted, to be "low-hanging fruit."[64] That is, the prosecutions tend to be brought against people who committed their crimes while they and the targets of their attacks were in the United States. This makes it much easier to identify and apprehend them.

In August 2003, for example, FBI agents arrested Jeffrey Lee Parson and charged him with creating and disseminating a version of the "Blaster worm."[65] The Blaster worm initially surfaced on August 11; the original version appeared after a Chinese group known as XFocus reverse engineered a patch Microsoft had developed for a vulnerability in its software. XFocus released code for software that could be used to exploit the vulnerability. The exploit code could be used to gain remote access to and take over compromised computers.

Parson used the exploit code to create and launch his version of the worm later in August. It was not difficult for FBI agents to find Parson because he included a link to his Web site—http://www.t33kid.com—in the code he used for his version of the worm. FBI agents tracked the site to a Web hosting company and then to two other contacts, one of which finally gave them the information they needed to find Parson, also known as t33kid.

On August 29, FBI agents arrested Parson—an 18-year-old, 6-foot 4-inch 320-pound high-school student—at his home in a Minneapolis suburb. The FBI claimed his version of the Blaster worm had infected at least 7,000 computers. It is estimated that the combined versions of the worm had infected more than 500,000 computers around the world. Parson was charged with knowingly causing the transmission of a program, information, code, or command and thereby intentionally causing damage to a computer.[66] He was charged with multiple counts of committing this offense, but on August 11, he pled guilty to only one count as part of a plea bargain. He was sentenced to 18 months in a federal prison, followed by three years of probation. Parson was also ordered to perform 225 hours of community service upon his release from prison.

Parson was the poster boy for how *not* to be a successful cybercriminal. He made it incredibly easy for law enforcement officers to identify him (putting his Web site address in his malware) and apprehend him (living in the United States under his own name). He also released his version of the Blaster worm approximately two weeks after he turned 18 and became an adult in the eyes of federal law enforcement. That is important because the federal system is not set up to deal with juvenile offenders. The Federal Bureau of Prisons does not have its own juvenile detention centers; instead, it places juveniles through agreements with state and local governments or "contracts with privately-operated . . . juvenile facilities."[67]

As a result, perhaps, juveniles are rarely charged with violating federal cybercrime law, and when they are, they usually receive probation. The "other" Blaster worm case illustrates this. In September 2003, an unnamed 14-year-old juvenile was arrested for releasing his version of the Blaster worm. Similar to Parson, he was charged with knowingly causing the transmission of a program, information, code, or command and thereby intentionally causing damage to a computer.[68] His version of the worm, like Parson's, was designed to infect computers and then use them to launch a DDoS attack on a Microsoft Web site. The juvenile, like Parson's, launched such an attack. However, unlike Parson's attack, his August 14 DDoS attack shut down a Microsoft site for approximately four hours. (Parson's August 16 attack failed to shut down the site; by then, Microsoft knew it was the target of the Blaster attacks and had taken it offline.) But because he was 14 years old when he committed the crime, the juvenile was given only three years of probation and was required to perform 300 hours of community service.

Parson and the juvenile were the only ones convicted of disseminating a version of the Blaster worm; the Chinese hackers who created the exploit code that was the launching pad for all the versions of the Blaster worm were never identified and were never prosecuted for what they had done. In Parson's case, Microsoft claimed his version of the Blaster worm caused $497,546.55 in damage to the company. Because his worm did not actually shut down Microsoft's Web site, this figure was based on costs the company incurred in defending itself against the Blaster worm.[69] If Microsoft's damage estimate is accurate, then the company must have incurred millions of dollars in damage from the combined effects of the other variants of the Blaster worm. Some suggested that federal agents investigated Parson and the juvenile only because "Microsoft pursued the issue so aggressively."[70]

If that is true, it is neither particularly surprising nor particularly objectionable. The victim of a crime—and Microsoft was the primary victim of the Blaster worm—usually has a legitimate stake in seeing that the perpetrators of the crime are brought to justice. It is true that the involvement of corporate victims in the process of investigating cybercrimes has, at least on occasion, been somewhat controversial. Some see this kind of involvement as inviting bias by at least implicitly guaranteeing a higher level of justice for those who can support law enforcement's investigatory efforts. This, however, is not a legal issue, as such. Instead, it goes to issues we will deal with in Chapters 8 and 9 regarding the resource and other problems that cybercrime creates for law enforcement.

The real issue, as I see it, in prosecutions such as the two Blaster worm cases is whether they actually accomplish anything. As we will see in Chapters 8 and 9, the purpose of criminal law and the criminal justice system is to keep crime under control by capturing, prosecuting, and punishing enough criminals to deter others from following their lead. The purpose is, in other words, to create disincentives that are sufficient to deter most of a country's population from engaging in criminal activity. To that end, law and law enforcement sometimes make an example of a particular offender, someone who has been caught when others escaped. We see this all the time when it comes to enforcing traffic laws: We all know that police officers simply cannot catch everyone who speeds, doesn't signal when changing lanes, or violates any of the other myriad laws that govern our activity when we drive our vehicles. Police officers understand that as well, so they try to stop and ticket people in a way that creates an example that will deter others from engaging in similar conduct (at least for a while). That same dynamic operates in many other areas of the law, although some crimes (such as homicide) are so serious they require especially rigorous enforcement efforts.

Where do prosecutions such as the Blaster worm prosecutions fall in that dynamic? On the one hand, I could argue that they serve the same purpose as a traffic officer stopping someone and giving that person a ticket for speeding. They make an example of someone who has violated a law and, as a result, will presumably deter others from following their lead. Although that argument is no doubt literally true, I think it misses the point. Studies show that the deterrent effects of someone being caught and punished for committing a crime are directly related to others' perception of how likely they are to be caught and punished if they commit the same crime.[71] If someone believes there is little chance of being caught if they commit a particular crime, they are not likely to be deterred by prosecutions of those who have committed that crime. The deterrent effect of nominal prosecutions is even less likely to deter other would-be offenders if the commission of the crime is likely to be financially or otherwise rewarding.

That brings us to the problem the United States and other law enforcement agencies confront in dealing with malware. The two adolescents prosecuted for disseminating the Blaster worm were obvious, easy targets. They were in the United States, and they targeted a U.S. victim. The former makes them relatively easy to find, and the latter gives U.S. law enforcement officers a greater incentive to do just that. Neither made any serious effort to conceal their identities, so it was easy for federal agents to find both of them. None of this is true for the professional malware criminals who emerged during roughly the last decade and have become the dominant players in this area during the last several years. They tend to operate from outside the United States, are adept at concealing their locations and identities, and may exploit gaps in national cybercrime laws to further shield themselves from prosecution. Because of all that, they know there is little, if any, likelihood of being caught and prosecuted for what they do. They can also make money, more than they can make by any other means, by writing and dealing in malware. The combination of a strong financial incentive and the lack of a real disincentive inevitably encourages the rise of an underground malware industry.

That all adds up to a discouraging, perhaps even dangerous, scenario for the potential victims of malware. We will return to these issues in later chapters. For now, we need to consider how law and law enforcement deal with DDoS attacks.

DDOS

For at least the last five years, DDoS attacks have been used primarily as a tool—a device used to commit a traditional crime. The crime that DDoS attacks generally are used to commit is extortion, and the best example of DDoS extortion is the attacks that target online casinos.

Obviously, online casinos make money when they are online and available to gamblers, and they lose money when they are not. That dichotomy creates an irresistible opportunity for cybercriminals. They launch a DDoS attack that effectively takes a casino offline. Then they send the casino's management an e-mail, explaining that the site is under attack or there is a "problem" with the casino's network that will go away if the casino pays a given sum. In a case from several years ago, the extortionists demanded $40,000, telling the casino it would "lose more than $40,000 in the next couple of hours if you do not resolve this problem."[72]

Casinos pay off because they really have no choice. As one observer noted, when a casino is offline for several hours, it can lose "$500,000 to $1 million of action" in lost wagers.[73] If a casino pays, the attack stops but only for a while, probably a few months. Then the DDoS extortionists, similar to their Mafia counterparts in the 1950s, come back, launch another attack, and demand more money. If a casino refuses to pay, the attacks continue until the company finally gives in. Because casinos do not publicize the extent to which they are the victims of DDoS extortion, we do not know precisely how much it has cost them over the years. However, experts estimate that DDoS extortion has cost casinos millions of dollars since it began to become a serious problem in the early 2000s. According to one estimate, online extortion cost British bookmakers more than $70 million in 2004;[74] by 2008, casinos were reportedly receiving "blackmail demands for sums in excess of $100,000 from DDoS extortionists."[75]

The attacks were also becoming more sophisticated. In early 2008, Gala Coral, a British gambling company, reported that its gambling sites were taken down by a "next generation" DDoS attack.[76] Unlike early DDoS extortion attacks, which were effective but sometimes haphazardly organized, the Gala Coral attackers spent four months setting up this attack. They used stolen credit-card numbers to open thousands of accounts on Gala Coral sites and concealed the "build up of traffic" leading to the attack by "analyzing and reproducing the browsing habits of the sites' typical users."[77] This let them fly under the radar of Gala Coral's security staff, who, as a result, did not spot the evolving attacks and take steps to frustrate them . . . not, it seems, that this would have mattered. After the initial attack, Gala Coral's security team used a port firewall to try to prevent another attack, but the botnet assembled by the extortionists bypassed the firewall and continued with the second attack.

Online casinos were the original targets of DDoS extortion, but the cybercrime expanded to target other types of online businesses as well. Some believe the Russian Business Network (RBN), "a multi-faceted cybercrime organization" based in Russia, is responsible for many of these attacks.[78] According to researchers who study the RBN, its extortion schemes are based on an updated version of an old Mafia racket: Using its army of botnets, the RBN launches a DDoS attack on a Web site and shuts it down for a period of time. Then RBN representatives, posing as parties unaffiliated with those who launched the attack, contact the company that owns the Web site and "encourage" it to buy DDoS "protection" service from them, usually for $2,000 a month.[79] Companies usually agree because $2,000 a month is much less expensive than sustained DDoS attacks. This tactic is an updated and refined version of the "protection racket" that real-world Mafiosi have used for decades.[80]

Experts say DDoS extortion, similar to other types of cybercrime, is increasing as the result of economic problems and ineffective law enforcement.[81] Some experts also cite the "inadequacy of cybercrime laws" as contributing to the increase, but that is less of a problem in the United States than it may be elsewhere.

The federal statute used to prosecute malware can also be used to prosecute DDoS attacks. As noted earlier, 18 U.S. Code § 1030(a)(5)(A) makes it a crime to "knowingly" cause "the transmission of a program, information, code, or command" and intentionally cause "damage" to a computer. The statute has been used to prosecute those who launched DDoS attacks. In December 2005, for example, Anthony Scott Clark pled guilty to one count of violating 18 U.S. Code § 1030(a)(5)(A), based on his participation "with several others" in launching DDoS attacks on eBay and other targets.[82] Some U.S. states have criminal statutes that address DDoS attacks, and many, if not most, of the others may be able to prosecute such attacks under their general computer crime statutes.[83] Other countries—including the United Kingdom—also criminalize DDoS attacks.[84]

The real problem here—as with all cybercrimes—is enforcement. Everything I said about the elusiveness of malware writers applies with equal force to the architects of DDoS attacks. Similar to malware writers, most maintain their anonymity and operate from outside the United States and other target countries, such as the United Kingdom. We will, as already noted, take up in Chapters 9 and 10 the difficult issue of transnational enforcement of cybercrime law. Before we leave this topic and this chapter, however, I want to describe the investigation and prosecution of a domestic DDoS attack, a prosecution that went sadly awry.

In 2004, Massachusetts businessman Jay Echouafni was charged in a federal indictment with aiding and abetting DDoS attacks on the Web sites of companies he regarded as competitors.[85] Echouafni allegedly used an Ohio man—Paul Ashley—to arrange the attacks, while Lee Walker of England and Axel Gembe of Germany carried them out. The attacks targeted two online businesses—Miami-based Rapid Satellite and Los Angeles-based WeaKnees—that competed for sales with Echouafni's Orbit Communication Corporation. All three companies sold satellite dishes.[86] The DDoS attacks crippled the Rapid Satellite and WeaKnees sites, costing the companies hundreds of thousands of dollars in lost sales.

FBI agents investigating the attacks traced activity involved in the WeaKnees attack to Walker, whom the FBI knew from an earlier investigation into a DDoS attack on someone else. FBI agents interviewed Walker, who admitted his role in the attacks and identified Ashley as the person who arranged them. The FBI raided Ashley's home in Ohio, and he confessed to his role in the attacks. He identified Gembe and Walker as the attackers and Echouafni as the person who contracted for them. Echouafni was arrested in Massachusetts and released on $750,000 bail secured by his house.

That was a mistake. While Echouafni was out on bail, his attorney persuaded the court to allow Echouafni, his wife, and children to "travel freely" outside the United States.[87] Their passports, which had been seized, were returned, and the family disappeared. Echouafni is a citizen of Morocco, which is where he is believed to be. If he stays in Morocco, he can probably avoid U.S. law enforcement for the rest of his life. Although both Echouafni and Ashley were indicted in 2004, Gembe and Walker were not indicted for their role in the DDoS-for-hire scheme until late 2008.

If nothing else, the Echouafni case illustrates how slowly, and sometimes ineptly, law enforcement deals with cybercriminals. We will return to this issue in Chapters 8 and 9.

Tool Cybercrimes: Fraud, Harassment . . . Murder?

As we saw in the Chapter 4, target cybercrimes require the adoption of new, cybercrime-specific laws because the conduct involved in the commission of and/or the "harms" inflicted by target cybercrimes do not fit into traditional criminal law.[1] Because tool cybercrimes consist of using computer technology to commit what is already a crime,[2] it may seem that they should not require any new laws.

The extent to which a tool cybercrime requires modifying existing law or adopting new law is a function of the specific activity at issue. But before we get into specific tool cybercrimes, I want to describe a case that illustrates how the use of computers to inflict harms of varying types challenges existing law.

HACKING CASINOS

In 2001, someone accessed the computers used by two online casinos and manipulated their software to alter the poker and video slot games.[3] The games were set so that "every roll of the dice in craps turned up doubles, and every spin on the slots generated a perfect match." During the "few hours" the manipulation was in effect, 140 gamblers won $1.9 million, which the casinos dutifully paid out.[4]

I like to use that case in cybercrime presentations because although the facts are straightforward, the law is not. I begin by asking the audience what, if any, crime the hacker (who was never caught) committed. Some people immediately say "theft," and I ask why. They say the casinos were unlawfully deprived of property that belonged to them, which may or may not be true and does not constitute theft even if it is true.

The problem with characterizing what the unknown hacker did as theft is that theft is defined as taking "possession . . . of the property of another . . . with the intent to deprive the other thereof."[5] In other words, I take your property so I can use it, give it to someone I care about, or sell it. The unknown hacker did not do any of those things; he (or she) never took possession of the money the casino paid out and therefore never personally benefited from the payouts.

(The fact that those who manipulated the software to guarantee payouts in these two games did not personally benefit from the manipulation is the primary *legal* obstacle a prosecutor would face in convicting that person[s] of theft. But I can also see another problem, an evidentiary one: How could the prosecutor prove beyond a reasonable doubt that those who won when the manipulation was in effect would not—either individually or collectively—have won if it had not been in effect? We all know the odds in casinos favor the casinos, but people do win, notwithstanding the skewed odds in honest games. I wonder how a prosecutor could have convinced a jury, beyond a reasonable doubt, that what happened could not have happened but for the manipulation of the software.)

People then say the hacker committed fraud. Similar to theft, fraud is a property crime; both involve the unlawful acquisition of property belonging to another. The difference between them lies in how the perpetrator obtains the property. In theft, he takes it from the victim without his or her consent. In fraud, the perpetrator tricks the victim into handing over the property willingly (e.g., convinces him or her to buy the Brooklyn Bridge).

Fraud seems a viable charge for what the unknown casino hacker did because the casinos voluntarily paid the money the poker and slot players won but did so under a misapprehension. The misapprehension was that the games were operating correctly. Had the casinos known the games had been altered to guarantee payouts, they would certainly have halted play—and payouts—in the poker and video slots sections of their Web sites. The casinos paid because they assumed the games were legitimate; therefore, we have the trick required for fraud. The question is whether we have the traditional fraud dynamic, in which the trick is used to convince the victim to give his or her property to the fraudster (i.e., to the person who perpetrated the fraud).

Fraud crimes implicitly assume that the one who plays the trick and the one who obtains the victim's property are the same.[6] Why else would someone commit fraud? Because fraud crimes implicitly incorporate this assumption, we have the same problem we had with theft. The hacker who manipulated the casino software to make every poker and video slot player a winner did not do so to benefit himself. As far as we know, he in no way profited from the trick he pulled on the casinos. If that is true, then it would be impossible to charge him with fraud.

If the casino hacker cannot be charged with theft or fraud, does that mean he would face no criminal liability if he were apprehended? It does not, because there is one crime that clearly applies to what he did: gaining unauthorized access to a computer. The casino hacker could be prosecuted under the federal computer crime statute. As we saw in Chapter 4, 18 U.S. Code § 1030(a)(5) makes it a crime to access a computer without being authorized to do so and to cause "damage." As we also saw in Chapter 4, the federal statute defines "damage" as "any impairment to the integrity . . . of data, a program, a system, or information."[7]

The hacker "accessed" the casino computers because he was able to make changes in the software each used. Because he was an "outsider" with no authority to access either computer system, prosecutors would have no difficulty proving his access was unauthorized. Finally, his manipulation of the software impaired the "integrity" of the casino computer systems and/or programs, thereby causing "damage."

The question is whether convicting the casino hacker of violating 18 U.S. Code § 1030(a)(5) would be enough to qualify as justice. There is no doubt he or she committed this crime, but the reaction I get when we reach this point in a presentation is "But that's not enough. He did a lot more than just hack computers. He cost these companies a lot of money." That, of course, is true, and it brings us to tool cybercrimes. The incremental damage unauthorized intrusions and other criminal uses of computers can cause is one reason why tool cybercrimes are so important.

In the remainder of this chapter, we will examine the more commonly committed tool cybercrimes. I am dividing this discussion into two parts: crimes against property and crimes against persons.

CRIMES AGAINST PROPERTY

In this section, we will see how computers can be used to commit traditional crimes against property, such as theft, fraud, extortion, and vandalism.

Theft

In Chapter 3 we reviewed what is probably the classic instance of computer theft: the Vladimir Levin case. Levin used computers to siphon millions of dollars from Citibank accounts. His crime was simply a high-tech version of the cases in which thieves break into a bank vault and make away with the funds. In either instance, we have what we did not have with the casino hacker: The perpetrator takes property (cash) from its rightful owner without the owner's consent.

That type of computer theft is straightforward, as far as the law is concerned. It is the only type of theft known in the real, physical world because real-world assets are necessarily tangible (e.g., cash, jewels, cars, electronics). The theft of tangible items is therefore a simple, zero-sum transaction, in which the possession and use of the item(s) moves from the rightful owner to the thief. One is wholly deprived of the items; the other is wholly enriched by them. Because this is the only type of theft that can occur in the real world, our laws assume zero-sum theft.

This is not the only type of theft that can occur when property becomes intangible. Certain types of computer data have great value, but data are intangible. Unlike property in the real world, digital property is not an either-or commodity. It does not exist in only one place at a time. Digital property can be duplicated, which means it can exist in two (or more) places at the same time.

That aspect of digital property became an issue in the Oregon case of *State v. Schwartz*.[8] According to the Oregon Court of Appeals, Schwartz was an independent contractor who worked in Intel's Supercomputer Systems Division (SSD), which created systems that were "used for applications such as nuclear weapons safety."[9] Everyone at SSD had to use a password to gain access to its computers and the information stored on them. The information was stored "in an encrypted or coded fashion."[10]

After he worked at SSD for awhile, Schwartz had a disagreement with a systems administrator that led to his ending his contract with SSD. Intel disabled his passwords for all but one of the SSD computers. It inadvertently failed to disable his password for the computer known as Brillig. Schwartz continued to work as a contractor for a different Intel division and accessed the Brillig computer without being authorized to do so. About a year and a half after he quit working for Intel's SSD division, Schwartz downloaded a password-guessing program called Crack. When he ran Crack on Brillig, he discovered the password for Ron B., one of Brillig's authorized users. Although he knew he was not authorized to do so, Schwartz used "Ron B.'s password to log onto Brillig" and copy the "entire SSD password file onto another Intel computer, Wyeth. Once the SSD password file was on Wyeth, [he] ran the Crack program on that file and learned the passwords of more than 35 SSD users. . . . [Schwartz then] stored the information while he went to teach a class in California."[11]

Intel systems administrators discovered what Schwartz had been doing and called the police. Schwartz was charged with using a computer for the purpose of committing "theft of proprietary information."[12] He was convicted and appealed, arguing that at his trial, the prosecutor had not proved he "had taken property," which, as we saw earlier, is an essential element of a theft charge.

An Oregon statute defines theft as follows: "A person commits theft when, with intent to deprive another of property" he "[t]akes, appropriates, obtains or withholds such property from" its owner.[13] Schwartz said he did not commit theft because although he moved a copy of the password file to Wyeth, the file and passwords were still on Intel's computers. "[U]sers . . . could still use their passwords just as they had before. Intel continued to 'have' everything it did before . . . and consequently, . . . [he] cannot be said to have 'taken' anything away from Intel."[14] The prosecutor said that by copying the passwords, Schwartz "stripped them of their value. . . . [L]ike proprietary manufacturing formulas, passwords have value only so long as no one else knows what they are." The prosecutor argued that after Schwartz copied the passwords, they became "useless for their only purpose, protecting access to information in the SSD computers. The loss of exclusive possession of the passwords . . . is sufficient to constitute theft."

The prosecutor won. Schwartz lost because instead of being charged under a regular theft statute, he was charged with violating a statute that made the theft of *information* a crime. The Court of Appeals was able to use the fact that this statute was designed to protect information to rationalize what was problematic: non-zero-sum theft of property.[15] If the charge had been brought under a regular theft statute, it would have been difficult, if not impossible, for the Court of Appeals to uphold Schwartz's conviction.

This notion of theft as a zero-sum transfer of property has its roots in English common law, which is the basis of U.S. criminal law. At English common law, theft was defined as "the felonious taking and carrying away of the personal goods of another."[16] The "taking and carrying away" element required that the possession of the goods be wholly transferred from the rightful owner to the thief. The Oregon court would therefore have had more trouble upholding the conviction if it had been a simple theft charge.

The *State v. Schwartz* case illustrates why governments need to revise their laws to encompass new variations of old crimes. One approach is to expand the definition of "deprive." In Delaware theft statutes, "deprive" means "to withhold property of another person permanently or for so extended a period or under such circumstances as to withhold a major portion of its economic value or benefit."[17] The last option captures the kind of non-zero-sum data theft that was at issue in the *State v. Schwartz* case.

Data theft is not the only tool cybercrime involving theft, at least not according to some. In a number of instances, people have been charged with theft for using wireless Internet networks provided by coffee shops, libraries, and other institutions. In June 2006, for example, 20-year-old Alexander Eric Smith of Battle Ground, Washington, was charged with theft after he made a habit of parking his truck in the parking lot of Brewed Awakenings, a coffee shop, and using its wireless network.[18] Smith was charged after Brewed Awakenings employees called the police to report that he had been using the shop's wireless network—without buying anything from the shop —for three months.[19]

The charge against Smith and other wireless freeloaders[20] is not a traditional theft charge. They are charged with "theft of services," a crime that until recently encompassed only obtaining telephone, electricity, cable, and professional services without paying for them. Theft of services is a relatively new crime. At common law, "time or services" were not "recognized as a subject" of theft because there can be no "taking and carrying away" of either.[21] In the United States, the criminalization of the theft of services began in the 1960s as a result of the American Law Institute's Model Penal Code.[22] The Model Penal Code—which, as its name implies, is a template for drafting criminal statutes—appeared in 1962 and introduced a new theft-of-services crime.[23]

Under the Model Penal Code, someone commits theft of services if he or she obtains services "he [or she] knows are available only for compensation" without paying for them.[24] "Services" include "labor, professional service, transportation, telephone or other public service."[25] The Model Penal Code's theft-of-services crime—which has been adopted by most, if not all, states[26]—differs from traditional theft crimes. In traditional theft, the possession and use of property is transferred completely from the owner to the thief. In theft of services crimes, the victim's property is the ability to offer services in exchange for pay. When a theft of services occurs, the victim is completely deprived of a quantum of the services he or she offers or, more accurately, of the remuneration he or she should have been paid for the services, without being deprived of the ability to offer such services. The drafters of the Model Penal Code recognized that this is still theft because the victim is being deprived of a commodity that lawfully belongs to him or her.[27]

When the Model Penal Code was written, there was neither an Internet nor wireless Internet access. But there is no reason why its theft-of-services crime cannot apply to freeloading on a wireless network. If nothing else, the theft of wireless services comes within the Model Penal Code's definition of "services" as including "telephone or other public service."[28] The difficulty comes with another aspect of the crime:the requirement that the person being charged must have known the services "are available only for compensation." When someone taps an electric line to get free electricity, he or she *must* know that the service is legally available only to those who pay for it. We can infer his or her knowledge from the fact that she surreptitiously tapped into the company lines and from the fact it is common knowledge that one must purchase electricity in the same way that one purchases other commodities. The same logic applies when someone obtains other services, such as telephone or television cable service, because he or she cannot obtain those services without doing something to bypass conduits or other devices that are intended to make the service available only to those who pay for it.

The problem in applying theft of services to wireless freeloading is that wireless Internet service, unlike other services, is sometimes given away for free. In the Smith case described earlier, the coffee shop—Brewed Awakenings—was intentionally giving free wireless access to its customers. The same has been true in most, if not all, of the cases in which people have been prosecuted for wireless freeloading. As a result, many say it is not theft of services to use an open wireless network to check e-mail or to surf the Web. As one person put it, "Complaining to the police about someone 'stealing' your unsecured Internet access is like complaining that your neighbours are 'stealing' from you when the smell of your rose bushes wafts into their windows.'"[29]

Many say the theft of wireless services cannot occur unless the network is secured. Some point out that in many cases, the owner of the network left it unsecured for the express purpose of providing free wireless service and claim it is impossible to steal what is being given away. Others disagree, saying that when an establishment gives away free wireless, it intends to provide the service to its customers alone. The problem is that wireless service bleeds outside the immediate area of the establishment that provides it, making it possible for both patrons and nonpatrons to use it.

Most lawyers and computer security experts think the solution to wireless freeloading lies not in law but in technology. If the owners of wireless networks would secure their networks, wireless freeloading would no longer be a problem (or, at least, no longer be a widespread problem). Securing wireless networks would be a somewhat more complicated process for institutions and establishments that offer free wireless access to a particular constituency, but even that is possible.[30]

The debate over whether legal or technical solutions are the appropriate approach for a particular cybercrime is not limited to the wireless freeloading context. This is an issue we will take up again in later chapters. For now, we need to turn our attention to some other tool cybercrimes against property.

Extortion and Blackmail

At common law, extortion consisted of a public official using the power of his office to coerce someone into paying him money.[31] The term "blackmail" originated in England, where it referred to a similar practice, in which "freebooting chiefs" extorted money from villages in exchange for not attacking them.[32]

In U.S. law, extortion consists of using a threat to obtain "the property of another, with intent to deprive him of the property."[33] As that definition suggests, extortion is a type of theft. The extortionist forces the rightful owner of property to surrender it to avoid certain consequences that the extortionist threatens to inflict.

Blackmail has become a subset of extortion. It consists of using a threat to coerce someone to give the blackmailer money or property. Some statutes also include making a threat "to compel action or inaction by any person against his will."[34] The distinctive characteristic of blackmail lies in the nature of the threat. Blackmail usually involves threatening to expose a secret that can damage the victim's reputation.[35]

Blackmail and extortion have both migrated into cyberspace, but extortion is far more common than blackmail. It is more common because it is easier to commit. To blackmail someone, the perpetrator must have access to secret information about the person's private life. To commit extortion online, all the extortionist needs is the ability to attack Web sites with DDoS attacks.

Ironically, although generic definitions of extortion such as the one quoted here are usually broad enough to encompass online extortion, specialized "computer extortion" statutes sometimes are not. The case that best illustrates this is Myron Tereshchuk's improbable attempt to extort $17 million from MicroPatent, an intellectual property company.[36] Because Tereshchuk believed MicroPatent had wronged him, he hacked into its network and obtained confidential proprietary information. He then used alias e-mail accounts to send MicroPatent a series of e-mails in which he threatened to release the information publicly unless he was paid $17 million. Federal agents spent weeks investigating the threats. Their task became much easier when Tereshchuk demanded that the $17 million be paid via a check made "payable to Myron Tereshchuk" and delivered to an address he provided (which, if I recall correctly, was his parents' home).

Prosecutors wanted to charge Tereshchuk with computer extortion under 18 U.S. Code § 1030(a)(7), but they had a problem: The method Tereshchuk used did not fit within the language of 18 U.S. Code § 1030(a)(7) as it existed when he made his threats to MicroPatent. At the time, 18 U.S. Code § 1030(a)(7) made it a crime to threaten to damage a computer to extort "any money or other thing of value." Tereshchuk did not threaten to damage a computer; he threatened to release confidential information. Because 18 U.S. Code § 1030(a)(7) did not apply to what Tereshchuk had done, he was prosecuted under a generic extortion statute: the Hobbs Act, 18 U.S. Code § 1951. Section 1951(a) makes it a federal crime to obstruct, delay, or affect commerce by engaging in extortion. 18 U.S. Code Section 1951(b)(2) defines "extortion" as obtaining property "from another . . . by wrongful use of . . . threatened force, violence, or fear." Because Tereshchuk sought to induce MicroPatent to surrender property—money—by inducing fear that he would release confidential proprietary information, his conduct fell under this provision.

In 2008, Congress revised 18 U.S. Code § 1030(a)(7),[37] now making it a crime to send a threat to damage a computer or impair the confidentiality of information obtained from a computer without authorization. Tereshchuk could be prosecuted under this version of the statute, even though he never received his $17 million. Because extortion criminalizes the act of making the threat, the crime is complete when the threat has been sent to the victim.[38]

Tereshchuk's unsuccessful effort is not typical of cyber-extortion. Financially motivated extortion predicated on DDoS attacks and directed at online casinos and other businesses is the most common, and most successful, type of cyber-extortion.[39] Similar to its real-world counterpart, extortion is almost always a property crime. It generally involves forcing the victim to pay money or to do something that ultimately benefits the extortionist.

In the real world, blackmail is usually a property crime because it is really a version of extortion. Online blackmail also tends to be a property crime,[40] but sometimes cyber-blackmail takes on a different aspect, something akin to a crime against persons.

Perhaps no case better illustrates this than one student's bizarre attempt to blackmail a fellow student at the University of the Cumberlands in

Kentucky.[41] On October 1, a female student at the university went to police and told them someone was trying to force her to make a video of herself masturbating and send it to him. She said she got an e-mail from an unknown male who said he had Web cam clips of her having sex with a young man. He said unless she made the video he wanted, he would send the clips to her friends and professors. The woman said she made the videos with her boyfriend several years earlier. Police and federal agents investigated and identified Sungkook Kim, a South Korean student, as the blackmailer. Kim told a federal agent he found the clips after he noticed a student fail to log off a computer in the university computer lab. He found the Web cam clips on that computer and saved them to a portable flash drive, which he took with him.

Kim's blackmail scheme shows how a crime can morph online. The tactic he used clearly qualifies as blackmail because he threatened to reveal information that would expose his victim to contempt or ridicule, but it is not clear that he used the threat in an attempt to obtain "property" from her. Because they derive from extortion statutes, blackmail statutes often require that the blackmail must have been designed to obtain property from the victim.[42] Kim did not demand money. The video he wanted would constitute "property" after it came into existence, but Kim was not demanding a video (property) that already existed. He demanded that his victim create a video to his specifications. That could present a problem if blackmail statutes, such as extortion statutes, criminalized *only* threats designed to obtain property.

Under traditional blackmail statutes, the threat must be to obtain money or property, but modern blackmail statutes tend to be phrased much more broadly.[43] Kansas, for example, defines blackmail as "gaining or attempting to gain anything of value or *compelling another to act against such person's will*" by threatening to reveal information that would subject the person to "public ridicule, contempt or *degradation*."[44] Kim's conduct clearly constitutes blackmail under a statute such as this. He sought to use his threats to compel his victim to do things she did not want to do, things that would certainly subject her to public degradation if she had made his video and it had come to public light.[45]

Kim's actions may seem extraordinary, but they are not. Financially motivated blackmail still tends to be the most common, even when cyberspace is involved, but there are other cases in which males use threats in an attempt to force females to create sex videos for them. In 2006, Michigan police brought charges against Babir Majid Chaudhry for using threats to coerce a 15-year-old girl into taking nude photos of herself and sending them to him. According to the girl, Chaudhry e-mailed financial information about her parents to her and threatened to destroy their credit rating if she did not send him the photos.[46] Chaudhry e-mailed the girl from Dubai, which is where he lived. He was arrested when he came to Fort Wayne to visit his brother.

In one of the most peculiar of these types of cases, a St. Charles, Illinois, mother was accused of using nude photos in an attempt to force her daughter's ex-boyfriend to start seeing her again.[47] According to news reports, before the 13-year-olds broke up, they exchanged nude photos via their cell phones. After they broke up, the girl's 42-year-old mother threatened to post the 13-year-old boy's nude photos online unless he started dating her daughter again. She apparently sent him "hundreds" of e-mails and text messages to coerce him into doing what she wanted. The district attorney referred the matter to the unit of his office that handled online crimes, calling it "an odd situation." I suspect no criminal charges were filed in this case because, although it could constitute blackmail under modern statutes, prosecution would only have compounded the humiliation, ridicule, and other pain this incident must have caused the two children.

Fraud

As we saw in Chapter 3, fraud consists of tricking someone into giving you his or her property. Fraud has exploded in cyberspace. One Web site lists 12 different kinds of online fraud.[48] Although the list may be accurate for the moment, new varieties are inevitable because the Willie Sutton effect[49] is particularly influential in this context.

We will not review all 12 varieties of online fraud because each is simply a variation of the basic fraud dynamic. We will review two of the most common types of online fraud: 419 fraud and identity theft.

419 Fraud

This type of fraud is known as 419 fraud because many of the scams originate in Nigeria and § 419 of the Nigerian Criminal Code criminalizes fraud.[50] A 419 scam begins with an e-mail, the subject line of which will be something such as "From the Desk of Mr. [X]" or "Your assistance is needed." The e-mail will say that its author knows of

a large amount of unclaimed money or gold which he cannot access directly, usually because he has no right to it. . . . The money could be . . . bullion [or] . . . a bank account. . . . The sums involved are usually in the millions of dollars, and the investor is promised a large share, typically ten to forty percent, if they will assist . . . in retrieving the money.[51]

The e-mail will say the money belongs to a wealthy foreigner who has died in the author's country, leaving no heirs, or belongs to a deposed African leader or general who cannot return for it. If the recipient of the e-mail agrees to assist and sends money to the author, that will begin a process in which "difficulties" continually arise in retrieving the money, difficulties that require the victim to continue to contribute funds to the retrieval effort. As with many scams, the process will continue until the victim is out of funds or realizes he has been had.

People fall for this scam, as they have fallen for versions of it since the sixteenth century.[52] No one knows how many respond, but a probably conservative estimate is that a fraudster receives one or two interested replies for every thousand e-mails he sends.[53] Because 419 scammers send millions of e-mails, that is a very satisfactory return rate. It means a fraudster receives up to 2,000 interested responses for every million e-mails. If even five percent of those who respond go on to participate in the scam, it will, at the very least, have been worth the fraudster's time. 419 scammers have essentially no overhead; they often operate from Internet cafes, so their primary expenditure is the effort they put into composing the initial e-mails and responding to those who become victims.

The victims are encouraged to wire funds to the fraudster, and many do. Estimates of how much they send vary; a 2006 report from Britain estimated that the average UK victim lost £31,000.[54] A few victims go completely overboard. In 2007, Thomas Katona, former treasurer of Alcona County, Michigan, was charged with embezzlement after he siphoned more than $1.2 million dollars of the county's money and wired it (plus $72,000 of his own money) to "overseas bank accounts . . . closely linked to the Nigerian Advance Fee Fraud Scheme."[55]

In 2008, Janelia Spears, a registered nurse from a small town in Oregon, wound up sending $400,000 to a Nigerian con man.[56] It began with an e-mail promising her $20 million left by her grandfather, with whom her family had lost touch years earlier. Spears said the fact the e-mailer knew her lost grandfather's name piqued her interest and convinced her there must be something to the story. She started by sending $100 but kept responding to the scam e-mailer's escalating demands for money. By the time she was done, she had mortgaged the house in which she and her husband lived, put a lien on their car, and spent her husband's retirement money.[57]

The Katona and Spears cases are extreme examples of the personal harm the Nigerian fraud scam can inflict, but personal harm is not the only reason governments are concerned about 419 scams. The scams also inflict an aggregate harm. In 2006, a British report estimated that this type of fraud cost the

UK economy £150 billion a year,[58] and estimates put the losses to U.S. citizens in the hundreds of millions of dollars.[59] Any estimate of the amount lost to 419 fraud is likely to be understated because most victims do not report the crime to the police, usually out of embarrassment at having been taken. The one point on which everyone agrees is that online fraud is a booming industry . . . a criminal enterprise that has so far had very little to fear from law enforcement, for reasons we will examine in Chapters 9 and 10.

Identity Fraud (Identity Theft)

Cori Godin was prosecuted for identity theft in violation of federal law.[60] She defrauded eight banks and eight credit unions of $40,000 by opening accounts using seven Social Security numbers she fabricated by altering the

fourth and fifth digits of her own social security number. Godin's social security number is 004-82-XXXX. Of the seven fabricated numbers, only one, number 004-44-XXXX, belonged to another person. Godin opened an account at Bank of America with the fabricated 004-44-XXXX number but provided the bank with her . . . name, address, date of birth, driver's license number, and telephone number.[61]

Godin used all seven fabricated numbers to open accounts, some of which she closed and then deposited checks drawn on those accounts into the still open accounts. She withdrew money from the falsely inflated accounts, leaving the banks and credit unions with losses of $40,000.

Godin was charged with identity fraud under 18 U.S. Code § 2018(A)(a) (1), which makes it a crime to "knowingly" and unlawfully use "a means of identification of another person" in perpetrating a felony under state or federal law. The prosecution said she used "a means of identification of another" in committing bank fraud because she used fake Social Security numbers to trick the banks and credit unions into giving her money to which she was not entitled. Godin was convicted of identity fraud and appealed.

Godin claimed the government did not prove beyond a reasonable doubt that she "knowingly" used another person's identity. Godin said that as far as she knew, none of the cloned numbers belonged to a real person. At trial, the government called two witnesses to prove Godin had knowingly used a means of identification of another person. One was a Bank of America employee, who testified that Godin used her name and other identifying information in opening the account. The other witness was a special agent from the Social Security Administration, who said that "by searching a secure and password-protected Social Security Administration database, he determined that social security number 004-44-XXXX was assigned to a man who resided in Maine. The Agent also testified that he could not tell by looking at the number that it belonged to another person because there are millions of unassigned numbers."[62]

The issue the Court of Appeals had to decide was whether "knowingly" applied to the fact that this "means of identification" belonged to another person. At trial, the district court instructed the jury that the government "is not required to prove that she knew the means of identification actually belonged to another person."

In ruling on the issue, the Court of Appeals noted that the language of the statute is ambiguous as to whether "knowingly" applies to the fact that the means of identification belongs to someone else. It explained that if "a statute contains a 'grievous ambiguity,' " it must be resolved in the defendant's favor.[63] So the court held that "knowingly" applies to the fact that the means of identification belongs to another person, which meant the district court instructed the jury incorrectly. After reviewing the evidence presented at trial, the Court of Appeals held that a rational jury could not "find beyond a reasonable doubt that Godin knew the false social security number was assigned to another person."[64] So it reversed her conviction and remanded the case to the district court, instructing it to dismiss the 18 U.S. Code § 2018(A)(a)(1) charge against her.

The Godin case points out the ambiguity in the crime of "identity theft." What we call identity theft is not "theft" in the traditional sense because the victim is not deprived of his or her identity. As we saw earlier, theft used to be a zero-sum phenomenon, but law has expanded its conception of theft to encompass copying data. The question is whether that is appropriate in this context.

I think it is. In analyzing the legislative history of 18 U.S. Code § 2018 (A), the Godin court found that Congress meant the statute to be a theft statute—that it was intended "to punish 'thieves,' or those who knowingly use another's identification." I think the government implicitly recognized that in the Godin prosecution because it charged her with only one count of identity theft, which was based on the fact that, coincidentally, one of the Social Security numbers she cloned happened to belong to a real person.

I think the best argument for construing the unauthorized use of another's means of identification as a "theft" crime is that it gives us the ability to address a harm that will otherwise be neglected. In identity theft cases, we have two types of victims: the banks and businesses that were defrauded by the identity thief, and the person whose identity was misused. The crime against the banks and businesses is fraud because they were tricked out of their money or property. We could stop at this point because charging the perpetrator with fraud addresses the financial harm he or she inflicted. But that ignores the other victim—the person whose identity was misused. That person was not defrauded of money or property and may not have suffered any direct financial loss, but he or she has "lost" something. Identity theft laws are intended to address that loss by allowing the government to seek justice for the indirect victims, for the people whose identities were misappropriated and used to commit fraud. Because that is the purpose of these laws, it follows that the perpetrator (1) must misuse the identifying information of a real person and (2) must know he or she is doing so.[65]

The Godin case is a good example of a traditional identity theft crime. I want to end our examination of fraud by describing a very unusual identity theft case.

Christopher Baron was an emergency medical technician (EMT) for the city of Jefferson, Wisconsin.[66] Mark Fisher was the director of the Jefferson Emergency Medical Service (EMS) program and Baron's boss. One day, Baron "hacked into" Fisher's work computer and forwarded e-mails he found in Fisher's e-mail account to "about ten people."

Because he used Fisher's account, the e-mails seemed to come from Fisher. They were e-mails Fisher had sent to a female EMT, and they suggested the two were having an affair. They basically consisted of sexual innuendo and attempts to set up meetings to engage in the affair. The e-mails indicated Fisher was using an apartment owned by the EMS Department to conduct the affair. Baron sent the e-mails to local and county EMS workers, as well as to Fisher's wife. The day after he sent them, Fisher committed suicide.[67]

Baron told the officers investigating the case that he sent the e-mails to get Fisher in trouble. He knew Fisher's password because he had helped Fisher with his computer. Baron used his home computer to hack Fisher's work computer and forward the e-mails. He originally intended to send them only to Fisher's wife but decided to send them to others so they could see that Fisher was not "golden."

Baron was charged with identity theft under a Wisconsin statute that makes it a crime to use another's "personal identifying information" without authorization and "by representing" he is that person, obtain any "thing of value," or "harm the reputation . . . of the individual." This is an unusual identity theft law because most jurisdictions define the crime solely in terms of using another's identity for profit. For some reason, Wisconsin's legislature added the "harm the reputation" provision to what is otherwise a standard identity theft statute. Had it not done so, there probably would not have been any crime with which Baron could have been charged that captured the most serious harm he inflicted: using Fisher's identity to destroy his reputation and, in so doing, cause him to destroy himself.

The Baron case illustrates how cyberspace can be used to harm people as well as property. In the next section, we will examine some of the other ways this is being done.

CRIMES AGAINST PERSONS

There arc so many ways people can use cyberspace to harm each other, it is impossible to cover them in one chapter. I am going to use some of the more common online crimes against persons to illustrate the issues that arise in this context. The discussion is divided into two categories: psychological harm and physical harm.

Psychological Harm

Criminal law historically did not concern itself with psychological harms; they were consigned to the civil arena. So someone who thought his or her reputation or feelings had been damaged by someone either sued the perpetrator for damages or got over it.

Criminal law historically focused on "hard" harms, which are physical damage to persons or property.[68] It focused on these harms because they are the first priority for a society. Societies must keep the infliction of such harms under control or they will disintegrate, as we have seen recently in some failed states.[69]

In the latter part of the twentieth century, U.S. criminal law began to target some "soft" harms. Unlike hard harms, which involve tangible injury to persons or property, soft harms are difficult to categorize. Essentially, they involve inflicting some type of injury to any of several interests, which include affectivity (or human emotion). In the next sections, we will examine two types of soft harm crimes, one old and one new.

Threats

Threats became a crime under English law in 1754, when a statute made it a crime to send a letter threatening to "kill or murder any of his Majesty's . . . subjects, or to burn their houses or other property."[70] The English threat crime migrated to the United States and has been incorporated into federal law and the laws of every state.[71]

There is some dispute as to whether threat crimes target soft harms. Some say threat crimes are what the law calls an inchoate, or incomplete, crime. Attempt is an inchoate crime because it criminalizes incomplete efforts toward committing a crime. Assume the FBI learns John Doe intends to rob the First National Bank. The FBI observes Doe as he "cases" the bank and tracks him as he heads to it on the day he intends to commit the crime. FBI agents arrest him outside the bank before he is able to begin the process of robbing it. Doe will be charged with attempting to rob the bank; he cannot be charged with robbing it because he never got the chance to do that.

Modern criminal law criminalizes attempts on the theory that it protects public safety. If we did not criminalize attempts, the FBI would have to wait for Doe to rob the bank and try to arrest him afterward. Aside from letting him take money that is not his, this could also expose people in the bank to the risk of death or injury if something went wrong or Doe simply became trigger-happy. Criminal law developed inchoate crimes such as attempt to give law enforcement the ability to stop crime before it can occur.

Some say threats are inchoate offenses, on the premise that a threat is the first step in an attempt to commit the target crime, such as robbing a bank.[72] Others say threats are not inchoate crimes but crimes that target the infliction of a soft harm; they protect the victim "from fear and disruption."[73] The U.S. Court of Appeals for the Sixth Circuit had to decide which view was correct in an early—and disturbing—cybercrime case: *United States v. Abraham Jacob Alkhabaz a.k.a. Jake Baker.*[74]

In 1994, Alkhabaz, who apparently used his mother's name (Baker), was an undergraduate at the University of Michigan. In October, Baker began submitting stories depicting the rape, torture, and murder of young women to the alt.sex.stories usenet group. One of the stories graphically described the rape, torture, and murder of one of his classmates, a woman I will call Jane Doe. This story, similar to the others Baker posted, are notable both for the extreme violence they depict (such as raping the victim with a hot curling iron or hanging her upside down, cutting her with a knife, pouring gasoline over her and setting her on fire) and for the sadistic enjoyment the writer seems to take from the victim's pain.

A Michigan graduate who read the Doe story and recognized the victim's name contacted university authorities, who called the police. When police searched Baker's computer, they found more stories and an e-mail correspondence he maintained with a Canadian known as Arthur Gonda. The e-mails outlined a plan by which the men would meet in real life, abduct a young woman, and carry out the fantasies in Baker's stories and e-mails to Gonda. The police believed Baker and Gonda represented a threat to Jane Doe and other potential victims, so they brought in the FBI. (I also suspect they brought in the FBI in because they were not sure that what Baker had done could be prosecuted under Michigan law as it existed at the time.) The FBI arrested Baker, and a grand jury charged him with sending threats via interstate commerce.

The charges were brought under 18 U.S. Code § 875(c), which makes it a federal crime to transmit "in interstate . . . commerce any communication containing any threat to kidnap . . . or to injure the person of another." Baker moved to dismiss the charges against him, arguing that while he had sent communications via interstate commerce,[75] neither his alt.sex.stories postings nor his e-mails to Gonda constituted "threats" to kidnap and/or injure anyone. Baker said they were fantasies he was sharing with Gonda. The district court agreed and dismissed the charges. The government appealed the dismissal to the Sixth Circuit Court of Appeals.

The Sixth Circuit upheld the dismissal. The judges found that although Baker's stories were disturbing, they were not "threats." They noted that to constitute a "threat," a communication must "be such that a reasonable person . . . would take the statement as a serious expression of an intention to inflict bodily harm." The Sixth Circuit held that Baker's stories and e-mails did not constitute a threat under this standard.

Essentially, the court found that the notion of "threat" implicitly assumes that the communication is directed *at the victim* for the purpose of effecting change or achieving a goal through intimidation. That is how threats worked in the past, and it is how they usually work, even in an era of electronic communication. In *Irizarry v. United States*,[76] for example, Irizarry was convicted of violating 18 U.S. Code § 875(c) after he sent his ex-wife hundreds of e-mails in which he threatened to kill her, her new husband, and her mother.

I believe the Sixth Circuit reached the right conclusion in the Alkhabaz case. As that court noted, any other result would mean I could be convicted of violating 18 U.S. Code § 875(c) if I took notes at a trial in which a defendant admitted sending death threats to his former spouse, and then I e-mailed my notes to someone else. If my notes quoted the threats he made, I would literally be sending threats to injure another via interstate commerce. However, common sense tells us I would not actually be threatening someone.

The problem with the decision in the Alkhabaz case is that it opens possibilities for doing something new: using online communications passively, in a way that makes someone uncomfortable or even fearful but does not rise to the level of a "threat." In 2001, William Sheehan, a computer network engineer who lived in Washington, put a Web site called JusticeFiles.org online.[77] It listed the home addresses, telephone numbers, Social Security numbers, and other personal information of local police officers. Some entries included a map to the officer's home. All the information on the site came from public sources, so Sheehan committed no crime in collecting and compiling it.

Police saw the JusticeFiles.org as providing information someone could use to retaliate against an officer or his family. Sheehan denied any improper motive even though he had two criminal convictions: one for harassing a police officer and the other for growing marijuana and for theft.[78] In an interview, Sheehan said, "police have too much power. . . . In putting the information up in the fashion that I have, it makes it much easier . . . for a citizen to hold police accountable for any wrongful act that may happen."[79] He explained that when he said police should be held "accountable," he meant they should be able to be sued or subpoenaed to testify in court. Sheehan said that because many officers have unlisted addresses and phone numbers, citizens who want to sue them or call them as witnesses "often can't find them."[80] And Sheehan pointed out that his site included this disclaimer: "THIS SITE DOES NOT ENCOURAGE VIOLENCE."[81]

Neither Sheehan's disclaimer nor his disavowing a desire for revenge convinced officers his site was not a threat to their safety and that of their families. The Washington legislature adopted, and the governor signed, a law that prohibited publishing personal information of police or other law enforcement personnel with "the intent to harm or intimidate" them.[82] Sheehan sued, claiming the statute violated the First Amendment.

The First Amendment protects speech but does not protect *all* speech. Some speech, such as "true threats" can be criminalized because the harm it inflicts outweighs the value of the speech. According to the Supreme Court, "true threats" are "statements where the speaker means to communicate a serious expression of an intent to commit an act of unlawful violence to a particular individual or group."[83] In the Sheehan case, police said releasing their personal information was a "true threat," but the federal judge disagreed. He found no law that defined publishing "truthful lawfully-obtained, publicly-available personal identifying information" as a threat.[84] He also found that "disclosing and publishing information obtained elsewhere is precisely the kind of speech the First Amendment protects" and therefore held that the statue was unconstitutional.[85]

As Sheehan argued, he was in effect publishing a phone book. Similar to his Web site, telephone directories provide information that can be used to find someone, which is why many police officers have unlisted numbers. It is also why some countries have laws that prevent the publication of such information.[86]

Stalking and Harassment

Stalking and harassment are the only offenses in U.S. law that directly target soft harms. They are relatively new crimes. We will begin by reviewing the evolution of these crimes and then examine some stalking and harassment cases.

The Crimes

The criminalization of harassment began a century ago, when people realized telephones could be used for less than legitimate reasons. The initial problem came from callers who used "vulgar, profane, obscene or indecent language."[87] Concerned about the harm being done to the women and children who received such calls, states responded by making "telephone harassment" a crime.[88] Initially, the crime focused on obscene or threatening calls, but some states broadened their statutes to encompass more general conduct, such as "anonymous or repeated telephone calls that are intended to harass or annoy."[89] As a 1984 article noted, the harassment statutes then in effect failed to encompass more problematic conduct, such as touching someone, insulting them, or following them.[90]

That began to change in 1989, when actress Rebecca Schaeffer was stalked and killed by an obsessive fan.[91] Shocked by her murder and five similar murders, California legislators passed the nation's first criminal stalking law in 1990.[92] By 1995, all the states and the District of Columbia had outlawed stalking;[93] most of their statutes followed the California model.[94] The California statute had two elements. The first element was willful and repeated harassment; harassment was defined as "a course of conduct . . . over a period of time that shows a continuity of purpose." The second element was a credible threat "intended to cause the victim to reasonably fear death or great bodily injury."[95]

California's approach led some to describe stalking as an inchoate crime, on the theory that the harm it addresses is the "murder, rape or battery" the stalking "could ultimately produce."[96] Others said stalking is not an inchoate crime because it is concerned with the infliction of a distinct, soft harm. As a law review article noted, stalking "is wrongful because the threat of future violence causes emotional injury to the victim."[97]

As society became more familiar with stalking, states revised their statutes. Modern stalking statutes not only encompass threatening conduct, they also address conduct that would cause a reasonable person to "suffer severe emotional distress."[98] Missouri's stalking statute, for example, says anyone "who purposely and repeatedly harasses . . . another person commits the crime of stalking" and defines "harasses" as engaging "in a course of conduct directed at a specific person that serves no legitimate purpose, that would cause a reasonable person to suffer substantial emotional distress, and that actually causes substantial emotional distress to that person."[99] The Missouri statute does not define "emotional distress," but other statutes do. Michigan's stalking statute defines it as "significant mental suffering or distress that may . . . require medical or other professional treatment or counseling."[100] Other states have similar provisions,[101] and some courts have specifically noted that stalking statutes are intended to prevent "emotional harm to victims."[102]

Some states have broadened their harassment statutes so they, to, encompass emotional distress. Delaware's harassment statute, for example, makes it a crime to harass someone by engaging in a course of conduct "which serves no legitimate purpose and . . . which the person knows is likely to . . . cause a reasonable person to suffer substantial emotional distress."[103]

Cases

Online stalking is often a form of revenge. An Ohio case began when James Cline met three women in an Internet chat room. After Cline had been on several dates with each of them, they all refused to have any further contact with him. In what seems an attempt at revenge, Cline used his computer expertise and access to the women's personal information to create havoc in their lives. "Cline locked the women out of their internet accounts, and he scheduled dates for the women, unbeknownst to them. He used their names to send vulgar messages to others, and he sent vulgar messages about the women to others."[104]

What Cline did is not a threat; nothing he did would make a reasonable person believe he was going to harm any of the women physically. Instead, he disrupted the women's lives. Maneuvers such as the ones Cline used cause emotional distress by making each victim feel she has lost control of her life. Can you imagine how unnerving it would be to have a strange man (or woman) show up at your home for a date about which you knew nothing?

Cline targeted his victims directly, but other stalkers act indirectly. Can someone be convicted if he uses innocent people to cause his victim to suffer emotional distress? A few cases have dealt with this issue, one of which is State v. Parmelee.[105]

When Renee Turner married Allan Parmelee, she found out he corresponded with "incarcerated people" and had been an inmate in an Illinois federal prison. After three years and a child, Renee filed for divorce. Allan reacted by creating a Web site and posting material on it that was "highly offensive" to Renee. Renee obtained a protective order that barred Allan from doing certain things. When Allan sent her printouts of material on the site, which violated the order, Renee called the police. He was charged with violating the protective order and incarcerated until the case was resolved.

Renee began receiving letters from prisoners at the institution where Allan was being held. She said one "was a letter like you want to be a pen pal," but others were "very graphic and described the sexual acts the prisoner wanted to perform with" her. She gave the letters to the police. They discovered Allan had not only encouraged inmates to contact his wife (who, he said, liked "nasty" sex), he had posted notices that described her, gave her home address, and said she sought sex partners.

Allan was charged with stalking, but his conduct is distinguishable from Cline's conduct and that usually involved in stalking cases. Allan used intermediaries to inflict emotional distress on Renee. Allan therefore *might* have argued that because he did not engage in activity that directly affected Renee, he could not be charged with stalking her.

He did not, and for good reason. Criminal law long ago recognized that a clever perpetrator can use innocent dupes as a way to avoid being held liable for the crimes he or she instigates. It therefore treats a guilty person who convinces innocents to engage in conduct that constitutes a crime as the real perpetrator of the crime.[106] The prisoners did not commit stalking; the letters they sent caused Renee emotional distress, but that was not their purpose. They had no idea that was what they were doing; they believed what Allan told them. they lacked the intent for stalking, they committed no crime. To ensure the truly guilty person is held accountable, criminal law imputes the prisoner's conduct to Allan, who intended to commit the crime of stalking.

The case of *State v. Parmelee* is not an online stalking case. Although Allan posted offensive material on a Web site at one point, his stalking primarily involved the use of the mail. I use it because it illustrates how stalkers manipulate others to achieve their ends. In one case, a security guard whose interest in a woman was not reciprocated retaliated by posting ads online that said she "was seeking to fulfill fantasies of being raped. On six occasions, men showed up at her door in response to the ads."[107] The victim became so desperate she put a note on her apartment door, which said the ads were fakes. The stalker then updated the ads so they said the note was part of her fantasy and anyone showing up to carry out the fantasy should simply ignore it. He was finally identified and prosecuted for stalking.

That brings me to another case in which the perpetrator pretended to be the victim. It was reported in the media as a cyberstalking case, but I do not think it is. I am not sure precisely what kind of crime this perpetrator actually committed.

We will call the perpetrator Mr. X.[108] He was a 23-year-old man who worked at a church in Wabash, Indiana. (I do not know in what capacity he worked there.) He decided to assume the identities of two sisters—one 28 and the other 16—whose family attended the church.[109] Mr. X created Facebook pages in each of the sisters' names and pretended to be them online. On the Facebook pages, he created the posted photos of each sister, listed their addresses and phone numbers, and described their after-school activities and work places in detail. This went on for two years.

Why did he do this? If this were stalking, he would have done it to torment the sisters. He would have posted false information to damage their reputations in the community or used the Facebook pages to do other things that would unnerve or even terrify the sisters. As one observer noted, true stalking is "a form of mental assault, in which the perpetrator repeatedly, unwontedly and disruptively breaks into the life-world of the victim."[110] Stalkers focus their efforts *on their victims*, whether they carry out the activity in the real world or in the virtual world of cyberspace.

Mr. X did not do that. The sisters did not learn about the Facebook pages for two years. Instead of targeting the women whose identities he used, Mr. X acted for his own benefit. He used the Facebook pages to "have virtual sex with men around the world."[111] According to a news story, the language used in these encounters was so graphic, the reporter could not describe it in print.[112] However, that is a routine aspect of online sex; people use graphic language and their imaginations to simulate physical encounters.

Mr. X simply used these women's identities to have a good time, in his own way. He must have had no desire for them to learn about what he was doing in their names because that would bring his online frolic to an end. Unlike a stalker, he did not *want* them to know what he was doing online. How did the sisters find out about their secret lives? The pastor of their church found the Facebook sites when he was "compiling an Internet list of his congregation" he could take with him when he left for a new post.[113]

We have to assume that the pastor initially believed the sisters created the presumably raunchy Facebook pages. The process of sorting out everything must have been frightening and painful for them. I assume it took awhile to figure out that it was Mr. X, and not the sisters, who was responsible for the pages. Because I received a message from one of the victims after I did a blog post on the case,[114] I know she and her sister were terrified when they found out what Mr. X had been doing. Because he created the pages in their names and posted their addresses, photos, and other identifying information on them, one of the men with whom Mr. X fraternized online could have decided to show up in Wabash at one of the sister's homes, prepared to continue the online affair in the real world.

I also received an e-mail from Mr. X's sister. She said his mother has an "addiction to sex and using the Internet to meet people and his father is a convicted child molester and molested" Mr. X when he was a child.[115] So we can perhaps understand what drove Mr. X to do what he did, but the real question is whether he committed a crime.

Mr. X was charged with felony harassment.[116] Indiana Code § 35-45-2-2 (a) defines harassment as doing any of the following with the intent to harass someone: calling the victim, sending him or her a letter, or using a computer to communicate with him or her. Mr. X did not call the sisters, send them letters, or use a computer to communicate with them. Because Mr. X did not direct any of his activity toward either victim, he did not commit the crime of harassment.

What happened to Mr. X? According to the e-mail from his sister, his defense lawyer and the prosecutor knew the "jury would convict if he went to trial on the original charges and he would be in prison until it was overturned (and they both agreed it would be overturned) on appeal."[117] The problem the defense saw was that Mr. X would be in prison while his case went through the appeal process, which could take a year or even longer. The defense attorney and the prosecutor negotiated a deal, under which Mr. X pled guilty to a lesser charge of some sort. He was sentenced to serve 30 days in the local jail, spend a year on probation while attending counseling sessions, and surrender his computer.[118] The impetus for the deal seems to have been a concern for Mr. X's safety. According to his sister, the judge commented that the plea deal probably saved his life because he would not have survived in prison.[119] The victim who contacted me seemed to find the outcome satisfactory. In what I think was a remarkable display of charity and maturity, she said she and her sister "were not out for vengeance, we only wanted him to get help to stop it from happening again."[120]

Concluding Thoughts

The Mr. X case is an atypical soft harm case in one respect—he did not intend to cause harm to the women whose identities he appropriated—but typical in another. As we saw with the security guard who pretended to be a woman who wanted to be raped, stalkers and harassers can use their victims' own identities against them. This is a new phenomenon, at least as far as criminal law is concerned.

Several years ago, I remember reading about a woman who was a distin-guished commentator on online culture and who had a peculiar experience: When she went to work one day, her co-workers and others repeatedly com-plimented her on the insightful comments she posted in an online chat room the previous night. The problem was that she was not in that chat room and had no idea what everyone was talking about. She investigated and discov-ered that someone pretending to be her had been in the chat room and posted comments that, fortunately, were not harmful. Her theory was that someone simply wanted to be her—to be an acknowledged online expert—for a night.

Although that may seem a trivial use of another's identity, I do not think it is. I, for one, would be unnerved and aggravated if someone did that to me. The harm here is the loss of control over our "self." The soft harm and iden-tity theft laws we have in place are all about using someone's identity to *do* something. The crime consists of using the identity to inflict a hard or soft harm on a victim. In the preceding incident, the imposter did not use the identity to inflict any type of harm on anyone . . . at least, not any type of harm the criminal law currently addresses. It seems we should have the right to control how our identity is used in any regard.

I think we need a new crime: imposture. Imposture has not historically been a crime, probably because it is a difficult feat to pull off in the real world. In the real world, I cannot pretend to be a male (a judge, say), and am likely to have difficulty pretending to be an identifiable female (a senator, say). In the real world, there has been no need for criminal imposture stat-utes. Most states make it a crime to pretend to be a police officer or a "public servant," but few have statutes that could be used to prosecute someone who assumes a regular person's identity. Yet that is precisely what happened in the Mr. X case, and it is what happened—in a different way and for a very differ-ent reason—in *State v. Baron*, the Wisconsin case we examined earlier.

Baron pretended to be Fisher in forwarding the e-mails that Fisher sent to a lover. Baron may have intended to cause Fisher emotional distress, but he cannot be prosecuted for stalking or harassment. Both require that he must have targeted the victim. Baron did not send messages to Fisher or engage in other activity directed at Fisher. Most stalking and harassment statutes also require that the perpetrator has engaged in a continuing course of conduct. That requirement is meant to ensure that I cannot be prosecuted for stalking or harassment if I send a nasty e-mail to a boyfriend. The premise is that although my e-mail may cause him emotional distress, and although that may have been my intention, it is neither just nor practical to criminalize every instance in which we cause emotional harm to each other. Baron did not engage in a persistent course of conduct. Forwarding the e-mails was a single event, one that probably took less than a minute.

As we saw, Wisconsin law offered another alternative: using someone's personal identifying information to harm that person's reputation. This is essentially a criminal impersonation statute. I think other states should criminalize criminal impersonation. Such an offense is a useful alternative in cases that cannot be prosecuted as stalking, harassment, threats, or any of the other crimes that currently exist.

Physical Harm

There are few cases in which computer technology has been used to inflict physical injury or death. As I argue elsewhere, I think it is impossible to use cyberspace to commit rape.[121] Rape is defined as having sexual intercourse with someone without his or her consent. It often involves the use of force to compel the victim to have sex with the perpetrator. As long as we define rape as a physical sexual assault, I do not see how it can be committed in cyberspace.[122]

That leaves two types of physical harm: nonsexual physical injury and death. Because nonsexual physical injury is a lesser-included offense—a subset—of homicide, we will analyze only the use of cyberspace to cause someone's death. My assumption is that if cyberspace can be used to kill someone, it can also be used to inflict injuries that do not cause death.[123]

There are two ways cyberspace can be used to kill someone. One is to cause them to take their own life, and the other is to use cyberspace as a murder weapon.

Suicide

There are instances in which what someone did in cyberspace seems to have prompted another person to kill himself. We saw this with the Baron case we examined earlier. As far as criminal law is concerned, it is difficult to hold one person criminally liable for another's suicide.

For one thing, suicide itself is not a crime. It was a felony at common law, which meant someone could be prosecuted for the crime of attempting suicide if he failed to kill himself.[124] By the twentieth century, lawmakers realized that making suicide a crime was not only futile, it was cruel. Today, no U.S. state makes suicide a crime.

There is a profound difference between committing suicide and *causing* someone else to commit suicide. Because the drafters of the Model Penal

Code realized that causing someone to kill himself or herself is a "clever way" to commit murder,[125] they included this provision in the Model Penal Code: "A person may be convicted of criminal homicide for causing another to commit suicide only if he purposely causes such suicide by force, duress or deception."[126] This provision does not define a new crime; it merely makes it clear that if I (1) purposely cause Jane Doe to kill herself (2) by using force, duress, or deception, I can be prosecuted for murder.

The provision was adopted in the early 1960s. As far as I can tell, no one in the United States has ever been prosecuted for causing someone to commit suicide. One problem in bringing such a prosecution is intent. Baron's act of forwarding Fisher's e-mails clearly prompted Fisher to take his life. But nothing suggests this was Baron's intent; he said he forwarded the e-mails to discredit his boss. It is unlikely Baron ever imagined Fisher would kill himself because of the e-mails. Suicide is an extraordinary step and one we do not expect. We may know we are doing something that will upset someone—we may even know we are being cruel—but we do not expect the person to kill himself or herself as a result.

I am sure there are cases in which a jilted lover committed suicide after being rejected. Because the person's death is at least to some extent the result of being spurned, we may have what the law calls "but for" causation: but for the person breaking up with the victim, he presumably would not have committed suicide when and as he did. But we cannot hold the other partner criminally liable for what happened after she broke up with him unless we can prove beyond a reasonable doubt that she acted intentionally—that she wanted to cause him to kill himself. We basically use intent to weed out the cases in which someone's suicide was a horrible surprise from cases in which it was a carefully calculated result.

That is difficult to do. To illustrate why it is difficult, I am going to use the Meier case.[127] Thirteen-year-old Megan Meier lived with her parents in a Missouri suburb. She had attention deficit disorder, battled depression, and had "talked about suicide" when she was in the third grade. She had been heavy but was losing weight and was about to get her braces off. She had just started a new school and was on their volleyball team. She had recently ended a friendship with a girl who lived down the street.

Megan had a MySpace page. A "cute" 16-year-old boy named Josh contacted Megan via MySpace and said he wanted to add her as a friend. Megan's mother let her add him, and they corresponded for six weeks. Josh told her she was pretty and gave her the impression he liked her . . . until he sent her an e-mail saying he did not know if he wanted to be her friend because he had heard she was not "very nice" to her friends. Josh followed up with other not-very-nice e-mails, such as one that said "Megan Meier is a slut." After this had gone on for awhile, Megan hung herself and died the next day. Her father went on her MySpace account and saw a final message from Josh, one that ended with Josh telling Megan the "world would be a better place without her."

Megan's parents tried to e-mail Josh after she died, but his MySpace account had been deleted. Six weeks later, a neighbor told them that the mother of Megan's former friend created Josh and his MySpace page. According to the police report, the girl's mother—Lori Drew—and a "temporary employee" of hers created the MySpace page so Lori Drew could "find out" what Megan was saying about her daughter.

When this became public, many wanted Lori Drew to be prosecuted for causing Megan Meier to commit suicide. The first problem is intent: What Lori Drew did was amazingly juvenile and irresponsible but, similar to Baron, we have no evidence showing she wanted Megan to commit suicide. Why would she? Unless a prosecutor can prove that her purpose in creating the Web site and sending the "Josh" e-mails was to drive Megan to kill herself, she cannot be charged with homicide in the form of causing suicide.

Even if a prosecutor could show this *was* Lori Drew's motive, the prosecutor would still have to overcome the biggest problem, which would be the probably insurmountable problem in prosecuting someone for causing suicide. How can you say Lori Drew "caused" Megan Meier to kill herself? The decision to take one's life is always ultimately up to that person. The cruel trick Drew played on Megan may have contributed to her decision to commit suicide; it might even have been the tipping point that pushed her over the edge. But people play cruel pranks on others all the time without the victim committing suicide.

It may be impossible to convict someone of causing a suicide. Even if it is, that does not mean someone like Lori Drew is immune from prosecution. Depending on the circumstances, it may be possible to prosecute them for stalking or harassment.

Murder

Murder is intentionally causing the death of another human being.[128] Murder is not method-specific; it encompasses the use of any technique (e.g., stabbing, poisoning, shooting) that can kill someone.[129] The focus in a murder case is on the defendant's intent to kill someone and whether the defendant did, in fact, kill that person.

As far as I can tell, no one has been charged with using cyberspace to commit murder. Here, of course, the killer uses cyberspace as a murder weapon, not as a way to persuade the victim to kill himself or herself. In a cyber-murder case, the perpetrator uses cyberspace instead of a gun or poison.

There is a UK case that *might* have involved an attempt to use computers to kill someone. In 1994, Dominic Rymer, a 21-year-old male nurse, hacked the IBM mainframe at Arrowe Park Hospital and modified two patients' prescriptions.[130] According to a news story, Rymer added "heart disease and high blood pressure" drugs to a nine-year-old boy's prescription. The boy was "saved from serious harm" when a nurse "spotted" the alteration. Rymer also gave antibiotics to a geriatric patient. Fortunately, she "suffered no adverse reaction."

The alterations were traced to Rymer, and he was prosecuted for unauthorized access to a computer. At trial, the prosecutor said Rymer had memorized a doctor's password and used it to access the hospital computer system. Rymer could not explain why he altered the prescriptions but "denied having any malicious intent." The judge found him guilty and sentenced him to a year in jail.

The Rymer case illustrates how someone might use networked computers to commit murder. A book published several years ago described another way to commit cyber-murder.[131] "Knuth" wants to eliminate a man who helped him orchestrate a large financial cybercrime. Knuth knows the man will be going into a hospital for surgery, so he tricks a computer science student into hacking the hospital's computer and changing the blood type in the victim's file. Knuth tells the student he is the CEO of the hospital and wants the student to test the security of its wireless network. He says that if the student changes the record, he can use that to require better security on the network. Knuth also tells the student that the test does not involve a real patient. The student makes the change, the victim goes in for surgery a month later, and he dies on the operating table because he is given blood of the wrong type.

That, I think, is a very clever cyber-murder scenario. Personally, I hope it is also a very unlikely cyber-murder scenario. With at least one exception, I suspect cyber-murder is a generally unlikely prospect now and for at least the immediate future.

In 2008, medical researchers came up with a way to commit what might be the perfect murder: using wireless signals to shut off someone's pacemaker.[132] Computers use wireless signals to program a pacemaker so it can deal with the patient's particular defibrillation requirements. Unfortunately, pacemakers are not protected by encryption or any other security. They are unsecured because they were introduced long before we had wireless networking and the destructive opportunities it creates. It is therefore *possible* to use wireless signals to shut off a pacemaker and presumably kill the person to which it belongs.

It is also highly unlikely at this point in time. The technology the researchers used is complex and expensive, which puts this technique outside the reach of most people. For now, the attacker must be within three to five feet of the victim to shut off the pacemaker; according to some reports, although researchers are working on a more sophisticated device that could shut down a pacemaker from 30 feet.[133]

Cyber-murder will no doubt become a reality, perhaps in the near future. Because, as noted earlier, the method used to kill the victim is irrelevant to the crime of homicide, cyber-murder should not be legally problematic. As long as the prosecution can prove the defendant acted with the necessary intent and can show a causal nexus between what the defendant did and the victim's demise, it should be able to win a conviction.

Cyber-*CSI*: Computer Crime Scene

INTRODUCTION

As we saw in Chapter 3, law enforcement officers divide cybercrime into three categories: target crimes; tool crimes; and crimes in which computer technology plays an incidental role in committing an offense. We examined target crimes in Chapter 4 and tool crimes in Chapter 5.

In this chapter, we will examine the final category: crimes in which the role of the computer is incidental. Because the computer is a source of evidence in these crimes, we will focus on the challenges cybercrime investigations create for cybercrime investigators. The challenges fall into two categories: evidentiary and privacy. Because we will examine digital privacy in Chapter 11, this chapter focuses on evidentiary challenges. Here, we will briefly review how privacy concerns impact cybercrime investigations, returning to that issue in Chapter 11.

Instead of examining the evidentiary and privacy issues in the abstract, we will use a famous hacking prosecution as a case study. The next section outlines the crime, the investigation, and the trial. The next two sections use these facts to demonstrate the challenges cybercrime cases pose for prosecutors and investigators.

THE PORT OF HOUSTON ATTACK

On September 20, 2001, the computer system at the Port of Houston in Texas was shut down by a DDoS attack.[1] It crashed the system, denying pilots and mooring and support companies access to databases they needed to help ships navigate into and out of the eighth busiest harbor in the world. As one observer noted, the attack "could have had catastrophic repercussions to life and limb"[2] but fortunately did not. It was still unnerving for a country reeling from the 9/11 attacks.

The U.S. authorities "followed an electronic trail" to a home in the United Kingdom, where an 18-year-old hacker named Aaron Caffrey lived. More precisely, digital investigators examined the system log files for the Port of Houston computer system and identified the Internet Protocol (IP) address of the computer that launched the attack and the IP address of the system he targeted.[3] An IP address is a numerical formula identifying a computer or other device that is connected to a computer network; each IP address is unique.[4] Every IP address includes data that identify the network to which a computer belongs and the computer itself. Once the Houston investigators found the IP address that launched the attack and the IP address of the system that was the real target of the attack, they could begin to track down the person responsible.

The investigation showed that the attacker's target was not the Port of Houston computers but a computer in a different country. The Houston computer system was shut down when the software the attacker used seized that system—and others—to use as tools in an attack on the real target. The investigators identified the software used in the attack as custom-written software ("coded by Aaron") intended to exploit a known vulnerability in the software the servers were using.[5] As already noted, they traced the attack to the home in Fairland, Shaftesbury, Dorset, where Aaron Caffrey lived with his parents.

British officers confiscated Caffrey's computer system and arrested him on "suspicion of unauthorized modification of computer material," a crime under UK law.[6] After officers from the Computer Crime Squad conducted a forensic examination of the computer, Caffrey was charged with hacking the Port of Houston system. In this case, unlike the McKinnon case, the United States was content to leave the matter to British authorities.[7]

The case went to trial in October 2003. The prosecution did not claim Caffrey meant to shut down the Port of Houston system. Its theory was that the Houston attack was an inadvertent but foreseeable consequence of a "revenge" attack against someone Caffrey thought insulted his American girlfriend. Prosecutors said Caffrey was "deeply in love"[8] with Jessica, an American with whom he had an online relationship, and launched the attack after a South African Internet Relay Chat (IRC)[9] user called Bokkie made anti-American comments in an IRC chat room. Crown investigators not only tracked down Bokkie's comments, they also found a comment from "Aaron" that said he wanted to see Bokkie " 'time-out' " because " '[i]f she hates America, she hates Jessica.' "[10]

The evidence not only showed a link between Caffrey's computer and the Port of Houston system, it also showed that after Bokkie made the anti-American comments, Caffrey ran a search to find her IP address.[11] When he had Bokkie's IP address, he fed it into the custom-coded DDoS attack software on his computer and launched the attack that, incidentally, shut down the Port of Houston system.

That was the Crown's theory, and it was well supported by the digital evidence the Crown's forensic examiners had found and analyzed. Because the evidence against Caffrey was so strong, his attorney did not challenge most of the prosecution's case. The defense conceded Caffrey's computer launched a DDoS attack that shut down the Port of Houston computers. However, instead of arguing that he should not be held liable because his real intention (at least according to the prosecution) was to attack Bokkie, the defense took a very different approach.

The defense's theory was that while Caffrey's *computer* launched the attack, *Caffrey* did not. According to his attorney, "someone" installed a Trojan horse program on Caffrey's computer without his knowledge and used it to launch the attack that shut down the Port of Houston system.[12] A Trojan horse is malicious software that installs itself surreptitiously on a computer and enables the owner of the Trojan take control of the computer.[13]

Caffrey blamed "Turkish hackers" for trying to frame him, claiming they regularly seized control of chat rooms and other Internet sites.[14] He said his computer operating system allowed remote access and control and therefore was vulnerable to Trojan horse programs. Caffrey claimed the log files on which the investigators relied in holding him responsible for the attack had been altered to frame him. According to Caffrey, someone " 'edited' those log files. Just because something says something, it doesn't mean it happened."[15] Finally, when asked about the "coded by Aaron" attack software investigators found on his computer, Caffrey said, "Aaron is a very, very common name."[16]

It was up to the Crown to rebut Caffrey's claim that a Trojan horse manipulated by "someone" shut down the Port of Houston system. The prosecution responded with the only argument it had: Crown experts testified that they examined Caffrey's computer very carefully and found no trace of a Trojan horse program on it.[17] Caffrey, who was the defense's only expert witness, told the jury it would have been impossible for the Crown experts to test every file on his computer. He also said the Trojan might have been self-erasing, so after it launched the attack, it deleted itself from his computer.[18]

The Crown tried to rebut Caffrey's claim of a self-erasing Trojan horse program by pointing out that when prosecution experts examined his computer, they not only found no trace of a Trojan, they found no evidence of log files having been altered and no evidence a "deletion tool" had been used to eliminate a Trojan horse.[19] Prosecution experts contended that even if the Trojan horse program Caffrey blamed for the attack had erased itself, the process of erasure would have left traces on his computer, Crown experts found no such traces.[20]

The case went to the jury after two weeks of trial. The five men and six women deliberated for three hours before acquitting Caffrey on all charges.[21] The verdict left prosecutors and police stunned. As an expert who testified for the prosecution noted, "It's very difficult to counter the argument that someone else did it and then ran away. We had hoped to show that if someone else did it they would have left footprints and . . . there weren't any."[22]

EVIDENTIARY CHALLENGES

The Caffrey case illustrates several of the evidentiary challenges prosecutors can face in cybercrime prosecutions. One challenge is proving the defendant's guilt beyond a reasonable doubt.[23] Other challenges concern the prosecutor's ability to have certain types of evidence admitted.

Trojan Horse Defense

The Trojan horse defense Caffrey used so successfully is an updated version of an old defense: the SODDI ("Some Other Dude Did It") defense.[24] As a law review article explains, when a defense attorney is trying to persuade a jury that her client is not guilty either because that client did not commit the acts with which he is charged (actual innocence) or because the prosecution has not proven his guilt beyond a reasonable doubt (failure of proof), the lawyer will have to give the jurors an alternative theory— another suspect.[25] The assumption is that it is easier for a jury to acquit if they can find reason to believe someone else committed the crime than it is if they have to weigh the prosecution's evidence and find it lacking.

The SODDI defense has long been the device defense attorneys use to make it easier for a jury to acquit. It is usually not successful in prosecutions for real-world crimes, although there have been exceptions (e.g., the O.J. Simpson murder case).

The major obstacle to successfully presenting a SODDI defense in a prosecution for a real-world crime is credibility. Assume Caffrey was charged with breaking into the Port of Houston's offices. Assume further that the officers investigating the crime found Caffrey's muddy footprints leading up to and into the offices and found his fingerprints on furniture in an office and on the office safe he is accused of robbing. At trial, the officers testify as to what they found, and a fingerprint expert explains why the fingerprints in the office are definitely Caffrey's. We could make the case against Caffrey even stronger by assuming that the officers find his DNA in the office with the safe.

Caffrey tells his attorney he did not commit the crime but has no alibi; the only option the defense has is a SODDI defense. His attorney makes the same arguments to the jury Caffrey's attorney made in the real case: He says the footprints were made by someone trying to frame Caffrey. He says the same thing about the fingerprints and the DNA. He also says the fingerprint and DNA evidence were altered to frame Caffrey. The prosecutor notes the difficulty of leaving footprints indistinguishable from Caffrey's and reminds the jury that neither fingerprint nor DNA evidence can be altered. Altering any of the evidence would be extraordinarily difficult because it is tangible, physical evidence. In this version of the Caffrey case, the jury will, without any doubt, reject his SODDI defense and convict him. His defense is simply not credible as a matter of common sense. The jury understands and has confidence in footprints, fingerprints, DNA, and the experts who explain how and why they point to Caffrey.

Caffrey's case, though, arose in the virtual world of cyberspace, hard drives, and software. Anyone who uses a computer understands that digital data are not as solid, not as immutable, as the physical evidence in the hypothetical case in which Caffrey is charged with burglary. Anyone who follows the news knows there are hackers and knows those hackers can penetrate computer systems. So that part of Caffrey's defense is credible because it gives the jury what the defense arguments in the burglary hypothetical did not—an identifiable "Other Dude."

In this instance, the Other Dude is not a specific person. Instead, he or she is a group of persons: the Turkish hackers who hijack Web sites and computers. This gives the jury an identifiable human predicate for Caffrey's SODDI defense. Their relative or total ignorance of digital evidence and the intricacies of computer forensics adds the missing element by making it possible for them to believe Caffrey and ignore the more credible testimony of the Crown experts. In the burglary hypothetical case, the jury has a common-sense understanding of footprints and faith in the validity of DNA and fingerprint evidence, which makes it easy for them to reject the SODDI defense. Here, the jurors' common sense tells them digital data is malleable and insubstantial. In their experience, data can be altered or erased without leaving any trace; therefore, Caffrey's SODDI defense seems a " 'reasonable' alternative theory" to them. He wins.

So have others.[26] Caffrey was charged with a target cybercrime, but the defense he pioneered has been used successfully in cases in which the use of a computer was incidental to the crime. Defendants have used it to avoid being convicted of possessing digital child pornography, and an Alabama accountant used a variation of the defense to convince a jury to acquit him of tax fraud. He blamed a computer virus for underreporting income on his tax return.[27] Some have used the Trojan horse defense to avoid going to trial by persuading prosecutors to let them plead to lesser charges.[28]

If the Trojan horse defense is routinely used to win acquittals in U.S. cybercrime cases, that is not being reported by the media. Because the media tends to report the outcome of cases that go to trial, the lack of media reports of Caffrey-style victories suggests his success may be something of an aberration. Therefore, if the defense is being used successfully in the United States, it must be used to persuade a prosecutor either to accept a plea to reduced charges or to forego prosecution entirely. It is difficult to determine the extent to which this may be occurring because plea bargains and failures to prosecute are not widely reported by the media and do not appear at all in the official case reports for federal and state courts.[29]

From the cases that are reported, it appears prosecutors are deflecting the use of the Trojan horse defense by having their computer forensic examiners tell the jury they found no trace of a Trojan horse program on the defendant's computer.[30] No one in the United States, anyway, has had the temerity to raise the improbable "self-erasing Trojan horse program" theory Caffrey used.

The dearth of U.S. cases involving the Trojan horse defense may be due to the fact that defense attorneys are not—or are not yet—particularly familiar with it. In some of the reported cases, for example, the defense claimed a virus was responsible for the child pornography found on the defendant's computer.[31] The prosecutors in these cases were able to rebut the "virus defense" by showing that only a Trojan horse program or a worm program would be able to download child pornography onto someone's computer without that person knowing it.[32] In other cases, the prosecutor rebutted the defendant's attempt to blame a Trojan horse by showing that the defendant not only had child pornography on the hard drive of his computer (which is where a Trojan horse *could* have deposited it), he also had child pornography on DVDs, flash drives, and other media.[33]

After the Caffrey verdict, there was occasional speculation that someone might exploit the Trojan horse defense either by installing Trojan horse programs on his or her hard drive or by simply leaving it unsecured and vulnerable to malware.[34] We have no way of knowing whether this has happened because, as noted earlier, we really have no way of knowing if the defense has been, or is being used, to persuade a prosecutor to accept a plea to a lesser crime or to forego charging someone with a cybercrime. This might be happening, but it seems unlikely. If defendants were exploiting the Trojan horse defense to avoid prosecution or bargain for lesser charges, there should be some mention of this in the media . . . but there is not.

Before we move on to other evidentiary challenges, it is important to note one thing: The Trojan horse defense can be perfectly valid. It is possible to frame someone by using a Trojan horse or similar program to put child pornography or other evidence of a crime on someone's computer.[35] It is also possible to install the material in an area of the hard drive where the person will never notice it. Think about it: Do you know what every file on your computer is? As a former federal prosecutor commented, the "scary thing" about the Trojan horse defense is that it "might be right."[36]

Admissibility of Evidence

Every court system has rules that govern the admissibility of evidence. The rules are intended to ensure that the finder of fact in the case—the jurors in a jury trial and the judge in a bench trial[37]—considers only evidence that is authentic and reliable.[38] In the United States, the Federal Rules of Evidence govern the admissibility of evidence in federal trials; each state has similar rules that govern the admissibility of evidence in state trials.

The rules of evidence in any jurisdiction tend to be complex, so we will not attempt to review all the evidentiary issues that can arise in a cybercrime case. Instead, we will focus on the two issues that are most likely to be problematic: whether evidence is authentic and whether it is inadmissible hearsay.

Authenticity

One of the things the prosecution (or defense) must do to introduce items into evidence at trial is to "authenticate" them, that is, to show they are what they purport to be. An Ohio Court of Common Pleas case—*State v. Bell*[39]—illustrates the approach one court took to authenticating e-mail.

Jaysen Bell was charged with "one count of rape, three counts each of sexual battery and sexual imposition, and one count of gross sexual imposition stemming from alleged improper sexual conduct involving two foster children, T. T. and T. W., between July 2003 and June 2006."[40] He filed a number of motions seeking to prevent certain evidence from being used at trial, one of which was directed at e-mail and online chats that allegedly occurred between Bell and one of the alleged victims.

The police officers who investigated the case got a "search warrant for computer equipment located in defendant's home. A search of the seized hard drives uncovered stored pornographic images, e-mail messages, and MySpace chat messages. . . . The state seeks to introduce the images and . . . e-mail and chat messages . . . [at] trial."[41] Bell moved to bar the state from introducing the e-mails and MySpace chats, arguing that the prosecution could not authenticate them. He claimed, "MySpace chats can be readily edited after the fact from a user's homepage. Furthermore, he points out that while his name may appear on e-mails to T. W., the possibility that someone else used his account to send the messages cannot be foreclosed."[42]

Because Bell was challenging the state's ability to authenticate the e-mails and chats, the court had to decide what the prosecution would have to do to show that they were, in fact, what the prosecution claimed they were. It began by explaining the Ohio standard for authenticating evidence, which is relatively undemanding:

"The requirement of authentication . . . as a condition precedent to admissibility is satisfied by evidence sufficient to support a finding that the matter in question is what its proponent claims." . . . [T]he evidence necessary to support this finding is quite low. . . . Other jurisdictions characterize documentary evidence as properly authenticated if "a reasonable juror could find in favor of authenticity."[43]

The Court of Common Pleas found that, under this standard, T. W. could authenticate the electronic communications through testimony that (1) he has knowledge of the defendant's email address and MySpace user name, (2) the printouts appear to be accurate records of his electronic conversations with defendant, and (3) the communications contain code words known only to defendant and his alleged victims. In the court's view, this would permit a reasonable juror to conclude that the offered printouts are authentic.[44]

A Nebraska federal court reached a very different conclusion in *United States v. Jackson*.[45] Jackson moved to prevent the government from using a "cut-and-paste" document that allegedly recorded online conversations between himself and Postal Agent David Margitz, who had posed online as a 14-year-old girl. Based on online chats allegedly conducted between Jackson and the person he believed to be a 14-year-old girl, Jackson was charged using a computer to induce a minor to engage in sexual activity in violation of 18 U.S. Code § 2422(b).[46]

The problem was that the prosecution did not have printed transcripts of the alleged communications between Margitz and Jackson or access to the hard drive on which they were stored. Margitz had wiped the hard drive at some point without making a backup copy of its contents, and he apparently never printed the conversations he allegedly had with Jackson.[47] Instead, Margitz had created a "cut-and-paste" synopsis, or set of excerpts, of the conversations, and it was this synopsis that the prosecution wanted to introduce into evidence at trial.

The prosecution lost in the *United States v. Jackson* case. The federal district court held that the synopsis was not admissible because it was not authentic:

[T]here are numerous examples of missing data, timing sequences that do not make sense, and editorial information. . . . [T]his document does not accurately represent the entire conversations that took place between the defendant and Margitz. The defendant argues that his intent when agreeing to the meeting was to introduce his grandniece to the fourteen-year-old girl. Defendant is entitled to defend on this basis. . . . Defendant alleges such information was excluded from the cut-and-paste document. . . . The court agrees and finds the missing data creates doubt as to the trustworthiness of the document. . . . Changes, additions, and deletions have clearly been made to this document, and accordingly, the court finds [it] is not authentic as a matter of law.[48]

Because the prosecution lost its primary evidence against Jackson, it could not prove its case beyond a reasonable doubt. That, aside from anything else, illustrates how important the requirement of authentication can be.

Before we move on to hearsay, we need to review a related principle that also ensures the authenticity of evidence offered in court: chain of custody. As Wikipedia explains, "chain of custody" refers to the need to document the

seizure, custody, control, transfer, analysis, and disposition of evidence . . . to avoid later allegations of tampering . . . which can compromise the case. . . . The idea behind recording the chain of custody is to establish that the alleged evidence is fact related to the alleged crime—rather than . . . having been planted fraudulently to make someone appear guilty.[49]

A federal case illustrates the importance of the chain-of-custody require-ment. John Wyss was charged with possessing child pornography in violation of federal law.[50] The charge was based on child pornography investigators found in a computer they claimed belonged to Wyss; Wyss raised the chain-of-custody issue. He said the government had not documented the seizure, custody, and analysis of the computer in a manner sufficient to satisfy the chain-of-custody requirement. Because the computer was the only evi-dence on which the government relied at trial, Wyss argued that the lack of authentication of the computer meant he was entitled to be acquitted. In other words, he said the government's failure to establish chain of custody for its only piece of evidence meant it could not prove the case against him beyond a reasonable doubt.[51]

The federal judge began his ruling on Wyss' motion for an acquittal by pointing out that the only evidence the government had offered to prove the computer belonged to Wyss was "a bill of sale covering a computer."[52] Although the government did not offer "testimony as to serial numbers or any other definite identification of the computer," the judge assumed for the purpose of ruling on Wyss' motion that the bill of sale was for the com-puter the government had seized and on which it found child pornography.[53] In other words, the government assumed—without deciding—that Wyss had bought this specific computer.

The judge made this assumption because the chain-of-custody problems were not in the government's ability to demonstrate that Wyss had owned the computer but in its ability to show that Wyss, and only Wyss, was the person who put the child pornography on the computer.

Wyss had been renting a house from Stanley Felter's father. When Wyss fell behind in his rent, Stanley Felter entered the house. Felter "made an inspection" and "removed items," including a computer, from the house Wyss was renting.[54] Ten days later, Felter contacted a police officer, Deputy Manley, and got him to remove property—"including a computer"—from "a storage unit on Highway 61."[55] Felter apparently persuaded Manley to seize the computer by telling him it had child pornography on it.[56] When the computer was examined, it did have child pornography on it, which led to the charge against Wyss.

The problem was that there was a complete gap in the chain of custody of the computer. As the federal judge pointed out, assuming "the computer found in the storage unit is the same computer which was found at the home, there is no evidence regarding what happened to the computer after it was removed from the home and before it came into the custody of Officer Man-ley, a period of . . . ten days."[57] The judge held that the "failure to prove the chain of custody raises a reasonable doubt as to whether this defendant is responsible for the images on the hard drive, since the images could have been placed there by someone else after the computer was removed from his household and before it came into official custody."[58] He therefore granted Wyss' motion for an acquittal, which meant Wyss was in the same position as a defendant who has been acquitted by a jury.

The Wyss case is an exception. State and federal law enforcement officers are usually meticulous about maintaining and documenting the chain of custody for digital evidence because they know that it is uniquely susceptible to claims of tampering or alteration. The Wyss case is an unusual instance in which there was a total failure to comply with the chain-of-custody requirement, presumably because Mr. Felter, a civilian, played such an active role in the investigation.

Hearsay

The authentication and chain-of-custody requirements are really concerned with the pedigree of evidence that is to be offered in court. That is, they are concerned with ensuring that evidence is what it purports to be (Wyss' computer) and is in the state in which it was obtained from the defendant (chain of custody). Essentially, these rules are designed to prevent the use of corrupted evidence. In the Wyss case, the computer that the prosecution wanted to use *might* have belonged to Wyss, but even if it did, there was no way to know if someone else put the child pornography on it. If the court had relied on that evidence in convicting Wyss of the charge against him, the conviction would have been based on evidence that might have been corrupted (i.e., might not have been what it was claimed to be).

The rules governing the admissibility of hearsay are also concerned with ensuring the integrity of the trial process, but they focus on a different issue. To understand what that issue is and why it is important, we need to review the rules governing hearsay.

Hearsay is not admissible unless it falls within certain exceptions to the blanket rule deeming it inadmissible. Rule 801(c) of the Federal Rules of Evidence defines hearsay as "a statement, other than one made by the declarant while testifying at the trial or hearing, offered in evidence to prove the truth of the matter asserted." Every state has a similar provision. Rule 802 of the Federal Rules of Evidence (and comparable state provisions) states that hearsay "is not admissible unless provided by these rules."

Why is hearsay excluded unless it comes within certain exceptions to rules such as Rule 802? It is a matter of common sense and fairness. If hearsay were not excluded, then John Doe could take the stand and say that Jane Smith told him the defendant—Richard Roe—confessed to the murder for which he is on trial. That puts Roe in a very difficult situation. If the jury believes what John says (i.e., that Jane heard Roe confess to the murder), they are almost certainly going to convict him, unless he claims he was insane or acted in self-defense. Roe can try to show that *John* is a liar, is mistaken, is insane, or otherwise cannot be believed. However, neither Roe nor his lawyers can do much in terms of challenging the person whose credibility really matters: Jane Smith. Jane is a declarant who is not testifying at trial and whose statement is being offered to prove the truth of the matter asserted (i.e., that Richard killed the victim). If Jane were present and testifying, we would not have a hearsay issue.

Allowing secondhand evidence—John repeats what Jane allegedly told him—opens all kinds of possibilities for unfairness and error. We have all probably played the rumor game in which something is whispered to one person and passed along by others, only to come out garbled. The hearsay rules are in part intended to prevent that kind of inadvertent error from infecting a trial.; They are also intended to guard against intentional error (i.e., fabricated evidence).

Hearsay is increasingly an issue in cases involving digital evidence. To illustrate why it often becomes an issue, we will examine two cases that involved digital evidence. We will begin with the Iowa case in which Aaron Cowell appealed his conviction on two counts of making a false report under this statute:[59] "A person who, knowing the information to be false, conveys . . . false information concerning the placement of any incendiary or explosive device or material or other destructive substance or device in any place where persons or property would be endangered commits a" felony.[60]

According to the Iowa court, the charges against Cowell arose from these facts:

On March 11, 2004, the Bloomfield Foundry received two telephone calls warning foundry management of an alleged bomb on the premises. The employees were evacuated and authorities conducted a search of the foundry, which confirmed that the calls were false. Telephone records secured by the police showed that two calls originating from the same phone number were made to the foundry at the time of the bomb-threat calls. During the investigation, it was determined that the originating number was the home number of a foundry employee, Aaron Colwell. Colwell consistently denied making the calls, claiming that he was at a gas station about ten miles from his home around the time the calls were made. Colwell was charged with two counts of making a false report and found guilty following a jury trial in December 2004.[61]

On appeal, Colwell argued that the trial court erred by admitting "two telephone records documenting calls between Colwell's residence and the foundry" into evidence.[62] He claimed the records were inadmissible hearsay. Similar to Rule 801(c) of the Federal Rules of Criminal Procedure, Iowa Rule of Evidence 801(c) defined hearsay as an out-of-court statement that is offered into evidence to prove the truth of the matter asserted. The prosecution responded to Colwell's argument by claiming the records were not hearsay because they were not a "statement" made by a "declarant":

The evidence . . . shows that the computers which generated Exhibits 1 and 2 are programmed to automatically log and compile a record of calls made to or from a certain number. . . . The State does not dispute that it offered the telephone records to prove the truth of the matter asserted in them—that calls to the foundry at the time the bomb threats were made originated from Colwell's home phone. However, the State [claims] the records are not hearsay because they were produced by a computer that automatically records the trace between numbers when calls are placed.[63]

The Iowa Court of Appeals agreed with the prosecution: "We conclude that the computer-generated records tracing calls . . . in this case are not hearsay, as they lack a human declarant required by our rules of evidence."[64] As a Louisiana court explained a quarter of a century ago, the printout of the results of a computer's internal operations is

not hearsay. . . . It does not represent the output of statements placed into the computer by out of court declarants. Nor can we say that this printout itself is a "statement" constituting hearsay. . . . The underlying rationale of the hearsay rule is that such statements are made without an oath and their truth cannot be tested by cross-examination. Of concern is the possibility that a witness may . . . misrepresent what the declarant told him or that the declarant may . . . misrepresent a fact or occurrence. With a machine, . . . there is no possibility of . . . misrepresentation, and the possibility of inaccurate or misleading data only materializes if the machine is not functioning properly.[65]

Similar to these courts, other courts have held that because the rule excluding hearsay is concerned with the fallibilities and falsehoods of humans, it does not apply to records generated by computers. So far, anyway, computers cannot lie; and although they can be fallible, the party offering computer-generated records can, as in the Colwell case, offer testimony or other evidence to show that the computers from which the records were generated were functioning properly.

Computer-generated records may not be hearsay, but computer documents that are generated by a human being usually are considered hearsay.

Therefore, when the prosecution or defense wants to introduce such a document, they have to show that it can come in under one of the exceptions to the general rule barring the use of hearsay.

The applicability of such an exception was the issue in the Florida murder case of *Thomas v. State*.[66] Here is how the Florida Court of Appeals summarized the facts and what happened at trial:

Chaka Baldwin, [Steven] Thomas's girlfriend of four years, was stabbed to death. No physical evidence tied him to the crime, but the State presented circumstantial evidence in support of its contention that [he] was the murderer. One piece of . . . evidence was an email written by Natalie Zepp to Michelle McCord, both employees of the apartment complex where Ms. Baldwin and Mr. Thomas shared an apartment. Defense counsel made hearsay objections, not only to the introduction of the email as a whole, but also to the introduction of statements within the email that Ms. Zepp, the employee who wrote the email, reported Ms. Baldwin made to her.[67]

Here is what the Zepp e-mail said: "This resident called and says that *she's had someone (Steven Thomas) living in her ap[artmen]t for the past year that is not on the lease* and . . . wants him out but *he refuses to leave*. What can we do? [H]er number is (754)2241958, but I asked that she call you back tomorrow morning as well.' "[68] The italic portions of the e-mail are the parts to which the defense particularly objected, as being inadmissible hearsay.

The rest of the e-mail consists of statements describing matters of which Ms. Zepp had firsthand knowledge and could, had the prosecution so desired, have testified about them at trial. These portions of the e-mail did, and could, come under the business records exception to the hearsay rule. The exception is codified in Rule 803(6) of the Federal Rules of Evidence and in similar state rules. The rationale is that employees are under a duty to be accurate in observing, reporting, and recording business facts. The belief is that special reliability is provided by the regularity with which the records are made and kept, as well as the incentive of employees to keep accurate records (under threat of termination or other penalty). The exception functions to allow the record to substitute for the in-court testimony of the employees, but it can substitute only for matters about which the employee could testify.[69]

In the *Thomas v. State* case, Michelle McCord, who was the recipient of the Zepp e-mail, testified that one of her duties as the property manager of Campus Walk Apartments was to keep track of records pertaining to the individual apartments. She inspected the e-mail written by Ms. Zepp, and testified that it was a record kept in the ordinary course of business at Campus Walk Apartments. She further testified that the record was made at or near the time the information it contained was provided by a person with knowledge. Finally, she testified it was a regular practice of Campus Walk Apartments to keep records such as the e-mail . After the trial judge determined that "clearly this email is within the firsthand knowledge of Ms. Zepp" and "it's clearly within her duty to try to assist tenants," the trial judge ruled that "assuming the other requirements for the business record are met, I will admit that part of the record."[70]

The defense objected to the admission of the italic statements in the e-mail. The defense attorney argued that "Ms. Baldwin's statement [to Zepp] constituted a separate layer of hearsay—hearsay within hearsay—which could not come in without qualifying under an exception of its own."[71] In making that argument, he relied on a Florida statute that says "[h]earsay within hearsay is not excluded . . . provided each part of the combined statements conforms with an exception to the hearsay rule."[72]

According to the defense, although the remainder of the e-mail could come in under the business records exception, the italic statements could not. The only way they could come in was if another exception to the hearsay rule applied to these statements, and it did not, at least according to the defense attorney. The prosecution argued that all of the information in the e-mail was "within the personal knowledge of Ms. Zepp," so it did not constitute hearsay within hearsay.[73]

The Court of Appeals agreed with the defense. It held that the trial court erred in admitting the italic portions of the e-mail because while "the employee who wrote [it] had firsthand knowledge of Ms. Baldwin's desire to evict—and could . . . have so testified—there was no evidence she had personal knowledge of any of the surrounding circumstances."[74] As the court explained, the e-mail contained two levels of hearsay:

The email is itself hearsay because it is an out-of-court statement being offered for the truth of the matters asserted. . . . It is Ms. Zepp's account of what Ms. Baldwin told her. Its accuracy depends both on Ms. Zepp's veracity and on Ms. Baldwin's veracity. Within the email—the first tier of hearsay—lies another layer of hearsay: the statement made by Ms. Baldwin to Ms. Zepp, viz., "that she's had someone (Steven Thomas) living in her ap[artmen]t for the past year that is not on the lease and . . . refuses to leave." There was no evidence Ms. Zepp had firsthand knowledge of these matters. Rather, her "knowledge" that Ms. Baldwin "had someone (Steven Thomas) living in her ap[artmen]t for the past year . . . and . . . refuses to leave" was hearsay. She was recounting statements she said she heard Ms. Baldwin make. Ms. Baldwin's statements were not . . . business records themselves. As recounted by Ms. Zepp, they were not admissible, because they did not qualify for an exception to the hearsay rule in their own right.[75]

The Court of Appeals not only found the admission of the e-mail was error, it found that it constituted reversible error (i.e., required the reversal of Thomas' murder conviction):

The hearsay was used . . . to prove motive, a critical component of the State's case. . . . The State used hearsay to show a possible reason for Mr. Thomas's wanting to kill his live-in girlfriend of four years. No other evidence tended to show that Ms. Baldwin had asked him to move out and that he had refused to leave.

Not even Ms. Baldwin's best friend . . . testified . . . to any problems in the couple's relationship. . . . Because there is a reasonable possibility that admission of Ms. Baldwin's hearsay statement that "[Mr. Thomas] refuses to leave" contributed to Mr. Thomas's conviction, we are constrained to reverse for a new trial.[76]

Thomas v. State illustrates the complexity and the importance of the rules governing the use of hearsay, not only in cybercrime cases but in any case in which one side relies on digital evidence.

PRIVACY

The U.S. Constitution, as such, does not establish privacy rights that are enforceable against the government. The text of the Constitution is, for the most part, concerned with constructing a government. It defines the three branches of the federal government (executive, judicial, and legislative), articulates the powers assigned to and limitations imposed upon each, and deals with related structural issues.

The federal Constitution is not the only constitution in force in the United States. The U.S. system of government is a federal system in which power is allocated between a central federal government and the states. Each state has its own constitution, some of which establish privacy rights that are enforceable against the government of that state.[77] Because we cannot examine the constitutional guarantees of privacy in the federal system and each of the 50 states, the discussions in this chapter and in Chapter 11 focus exclusively on the privacy guarantees that derive from federal law.

Although the Constitution does not create a general right to privacy,[78] the Supreme Court has interpreted three amendments to the Constitution as creating specific rights to privacy. It derived these rights from the First Amendment's protection of free speech and freedom of assembly, the Fourth Amendment's prohibition on unreasonable searches and seizures, and the Fifth Amendment's privilege against self-incrimination. According to the Supreme Court, these amendments protect privacy in different ways.

The First Amendment protects the privacy of certain acts. More precisely, the Supreme Court has held that as a function of protecting free speech and freedom of assembly, the First Amendment guarantees the rights to speak anonymously and to preserve the confidentiality of one's associations.[79]

The Fourth Amendment historically protected certain physical areas—those constitutionally deemed "private"—from unauthorized governmental intrusions. As we will see in Chapter 11, the twentieth-century Supreme Court extended this notion of privacy to encompass at least certain uses of technology.[80]

Finally, the Fifth Amendment's contribution is more limited. While the Supreme Court has said that the Fifth Amendment privilege against compelled self-incrimination protects "personal privacy,"[81] it has never applied the privilege when the government's acquisition of evidence "did not involve compelled testimonial self-incrimination of some sort."[82] The only role the Fifth Amendment currently plays in the U.S. skein of privacy, therefore, is to prevent the state from forcing citizens to divulge their guilty testimonial secrets. We will return to this issue in Chapter 11.

Beyond *War Games*: Who Are the Cybercriminals?

This chapter deals with an issue we have been covering throughout this book: the people who commit cybercrimes. In many of the previous chapters, we focused on the cybercriminals of years past, the teenaged hacker of *War Games* being the prime example.

In this chapter, we will examine what are, in effect, cybercriminal archetypes. That is, we will examine the kinds of people who commit three types of cybercrime: two target crimes (hacking and insider attacks) and two tool crimes (fraud and stalking). We focus on these crimes because they tend to be the most frequently committed types of cybercrime. The frequency with which these crimes are committed makes it possible to generalize with some accuracy about the people who are most likely to commit them.

HACKERS

For many people, hacking is the archetypal cybercrime, and the *War Games*-style hacker is the archetypal cybercriminal. That is not an unreasonable conception of cybercrime and cybercriminals. As we saw in Chapter 2, cybercrime really began with hacking, and the first hackers were sport hackers—students who saw hacking as an intellectual exercise. The original hackers hacked for fun, not for profit.

As we saw in Chapter 2 and succeeding chapters, that model of hacking is in decline, if it has not disappeared entirely. We still have occasional sport hackers, but today, even adolescents tend to hack for instrumental reasons (i.e., because they are seeking some benefit or advantage). In 2008, for example, Omar Khan, a high-school student in Orange County, California, was charged with 69 felonies under state law, based on his allegedly having hacked the computer system in his high school.[1] Among other things, Khan was accused of hacking into the system and changing test scores and grades. News stories speculated that he made the alterations to improve his chances of being admitted to a prestigious college.

David Lightman, the hero of *War Games*, also hacked his school's computer to change grades for himself and his friend;[2] for him, that was an aberration. Similar to his real-life counterparts, Lightman's primary interest was exploring computer technology, but he was not above exploiting it for personal advantage on occasion. By the beginning of the twenty-first century, that dynamic seemed to have reversed itself. News stories about adolescents who used their computer skills to explore systems had been replaced by stories about teenagers who, in similar ways to those of Khan, used their computer skills to exploit systems for personal advantage.

The reversal of that dynamic is not a sign that American adolescents are more unprincipled than they used to be. It is a function of the fact that computer technology is vastly more advanced than it was a quarter of a century ago. In the *War Games* era and for more than a decade afterward, computer technology was functionally analogous to automobile technology in the early part of the twentieth century. Those who owned cars back then had to know more than how to drive one. They had to know how to maintain a vehicle and how to fix it on the frequent occasions when it broke down.[3] The same was true for personal computer users in the 1980s and early 1990s. The operating systems in use at the time required a level of hands-on expertise and tinkering that was analogous to the mechanical expertise that was a basic survival skill for early car owners.[4]

At the beginning of the twenty-first century, the computer-automobile technology analogy is still valid but for different reasons. Modern vehicles are so reliable and so sophisticated that their owners no longer need mechanical expertise; all we do is drive. The same is true for twenty-first century computer technology: The operating systems that have been in use for roughly a decade are so self-contained and so sophisticated that we do not need the expertise that was *de rigueur* until relatively recently. Similar to modern car owners, all we do is use the technology.

That may account for the decline, if not the disappearance, of sport hackers. The generations that are growing up with modern computer technology are accustomed to using computers to do things instead of using them to learn how computers operate. Another factor that no doubt contributes to the decline in sport hacking is the Internet. As we saw in earlier chapters, the original hackers spent a great deal of time gaining access to networks and figuring out what they could do with them once they got access. Today, networked access is a given. Instead of having to use their computer skills to access a network, our David Lightmans use their skills and the Internet to do other things, such as changing grades, perpetrating hoaxes, and even committing cybercrimes.[5]

As we will see in Chapter 8, when law enforcement officers deal with cybercrime, they often confront an issue that historically seldom arose with crime: perpetrators who are in a foreign country. That issue frequently arises when law enforcement officers deal with the professional hackers who use their computer skills to commit the cybercrimes we surveyed in Chapters 4 and 5. Some professional hackers operate from inside the country whose citizens they victimize (e.g., from inside the United States). Many, though, do not. Conversely, although most of the declining pool of sport hackers are residents of the country whose systems they attack, some are not. We will return to the issues transborder cybercrime raises in Chapter 8.

INSIDERS

As we saw in Chapter 2, hacking began with insiders because they were the only ones who could exploit mainframe technology for improper purposes. In Chapter 4, we saw how that kind of insider hacking evolved into the current crime of exceeding one's authorized access to a computer or computer system. In Chapter 4, we reviewed some insider hacking cases, all of which involved more or less disgruntled employees.

Insider attacks have become a serious threat to computer security. The U.S. Secret Service conducted two studies of the insider threat. One focused on the banking and finance industry, and the other examined critical infrastructure sectors.[6] The researchers defined insiders as "individuals who were, or . . . had been, authorized to use the information systems they eventually employed to perpetrate harm."[7] They found that while there were similarities among the insiders within each group, there were notable differences between the banking and finance insiders and the insiders who worked in critical infrastructure sector positions.

The banking and finance industry study found that attacks "were not technically sophisticated or complex. . . . [T]hey typically involved exploitation of non-technical vulnerabilities such as business rules or organization policies . . . and were carried out by individuals who had little or no technical expertise."[8] Most attacks were planned in advance and were committed out of a desire for "financial gain, rather than a desire to harm the company."[9] A few were revenge for being fired.[10] Surprisingly, the attackers did not share a common profile. Most did not hold technical positions, did not have a history of launching technical attacks, and were not perceived as problem employees.[11] They ranged from 18 to 59 years old, and 42 percent were women.[12] Many of them were considered excellent employees. A man who "committed credit card fraud after 10 years of outstanding service in the banking field" was "well-paid and well-respected as a top salesman for the territory he managed."[13] Ultimately, this study concluded that the insider threat in the finance industry is a particularly complex phenomenon because it involves "an interaction among organizational culture, business practices, policies, and technology, as well as the insiders' motivations and external influences."[14]

The findings in the complex infrastructure sector study differed in several respects from those in the finance industry study.[15] For one thing, 86 percent of the insiders worked in technical positions: systems administrators (38%), programmers (21%), engineers (14%), and information technology specialists (14%).[16] Most (77%) were or had been full-time employees of the organization they attacked; 8 percent were or had been consultants and 8 percent were or had been temporary workers.[17] Age was again irrelevant; the critical infrastructure insiders were from 17 to 60 years old and were racially and ethnically diverse.[18] Ninety-six percent of them were males.[19] The most striking difference between these insiders and the banking and finance insiders was in the motives for the attack: 84 percent of critical infrastructure insiders were motivated "at least in part by a desire to seek revenge."[20] Ninety-two percent of the attacks were triggered by a "specific event or series of events" that included "employment termination (47%), dispute with a current or former employer (20%), and . . . demotion or transfer (13%)."[21] Similar to the banking and finance insiders, these insiders planned their attacks in advance. However, unlike the banking and finance insiders, most (80%) of the critical infrastructure insiders had been cited for "tardiness, truancy, arguments with coworkers, and poor job performance."[22]

The critical infrastructure insiders seem to have done more damage: "Eighty-one percent of the organizations experienced a negative financial impact as a result of the insiders' activities. The losses ranged from a reported low of $500 to a reported high of 'tens of millions of dollars.' "[23] Twenty-six percent of the organizations also suffered a "negative impact to their reputations."[24] Among other things, these insiders

- severed communication with affected organizations due to networks, routers, servers, or dial-up access being shut down;
- blocked sales due to blocked sales applications or deleted sales records;
- blocked customer contact due to modified customer passwords;
- damaged or destroyed critical information assets, such as proprietary software, data, computing systems, and storage media necessary to the organization's ability to contract work, produce product, or develop new products;
- damaged supervisory integrity, including exposed personal or private communications embarrassing to a supervisor.[25]

Because the vast majority of critical infrastructure insider attacks were triggered by a desire to seek revenge for a work-related event, these researchers concluded that the most effective way to address this type of attack is for organizations to implement policies that address "negative employment-related events."[26]

Although the Secret Service studies may seem too narrowly focused to allow us to generalize about those who launch inside attacks, the banking, finance, and critical infrastructure organizations involved in the studies actually represent a wide range of activities.[27] More importantly, they examined the two basic types of inside attacker: financial workers motivated by greed; and aggrieved employees who, unlike aggrieved employees in the past, have the skills and tools they need to revenge themselves on the employers whom they believe have treated them unfairly.

What the financial insiders are doing is not new. Insiders have been embezzling funds from financial institutions for centuries. Computer technology may make it easier for someone to embezzle funds or conceal the embezzlement, but neither the conduct nor the crime that results from the conduct is something we have not dealt with in the past. Financial insider attacks replicate history in another respect: Banks historically refused to prosecute embezzlers for fear the public would lose confidence in an institution if they learned it was susceptible to embezzlement.[28] They usually fired the embezzler and ignored the crime. The same thing happens with financial insider attacks. Banks and other financial institutions often do not report their crimes to law enforcement, preferring to dismiss them and avoid embarrassing publicity.[29]

What the other insiders are doing is new in one respect: the amount of damage the insider can cause. In the past, disgruntled employees stole office supplies, padded their expense reports, and took similar measures to exact revenge on the companies they believed had treated them unfairly. Today, every large organization necessarily hosts a cadre of insiders who can, if they so desire, cause tremendous damage to the company. Businesses and other organizations therefore are facing a serious new problem. While the insiders' motives are not new, the tools available to them are new. Because the tools an aggrieved employee can use to harm his employer tend to be the same tools he uses in his work, it is very difficult, if not impossible, to prevent attacks by dedicated insiders.

Because insiders, by definition, attack computer systems owned by their employers, they usually reside in the country where the systems they attack are located. That may change as offshoring and other trends increase the frequency with which people who live in one country are employed by a business or organization that is either physically or nominally "located" in another country.

FRAUDSTERS[30]

As we saw in Chapter 5, fraud is one of several financially motivated crimes that have migrated online. As we also saw in Chapter 5, those who commit online fraud can be in the United States but often operate from abroad.

As we will see in Chapter 8, cyberspace gives criminals the ability to target victims who are halfway around the world. This not only increases the pool of available victims, it also makes it easier for the online perpetrators to avoid being identified and apprehended by law enforcement. We will take up the law enforcement implications of transnational cybercrime in Chapter 8. Our focus here is on the people who commit cybercrimes, especially fraud.

In March 2009, the computer security company Finjan issued a report on its investigation of an online fraud operation based in the Ukraine.[31] The Ukrainian fraudsters implemented a scheme that was simple and ingenious: They hired rogue technical experts to inject specific, carefully chosen keywords into hundreds of legitimate news and shopping Web sites. Some of the keywords were misspellings of popular search terms, such as "Obbama" instead of "Obama." Others were "trendy keywords taken from the Google Trends system."[32]

Once seeded into a Web site, the keywords were picked up and indexed by search engines such as Google, which meant the search engines sent people to the altered Web sites. When someone's browser took him or her to one of the altered Web sites, scripts the experts had embedded into the altered Web pages sent him or her to an external site that sold fake antivirus software. When the victim arrived at that site, a barrage of pop-up messages appeared, warning that his computer was infected with viruses and other malware. The messages told the victims they needed the antivirus software being sold on the site to eliminate the infection. The antivirus software, of course, was worthless; it could not have removed any malware that might have been on a purchaser's computer.

The Finjan researchers surreptitiously monitored the scam for 16 days. During that period, more than 1.8 million people were redirected to the fake antivirus site, and 7–12 percent of them bought the fake software, which sold for $20 to $50.[33] According to the Finjan report, if these returns were extrapolated " '[b]ased on a normal work week, this would put [the operators of the scam] in the $2 million-plus annual income bracket'."[34] It also noted that the experts the operators of the scam hired to alter legitimate sites and drive traffic to the fraud site were paid "about $10,800 . . . a day for their work."[35]

Although this may seem an isolated instance of cyber-fraud, it in fact exemplifies the basic online fraud dynamic.[36] What we see today is a twenty-first-century version of the nineteenth-century snake oil peddlers who sold fake remedies in the Old West. A snake oil peddler rolled into a town, set up shop, put on a great show for potential customers, sold his worthless product to as many people as possible, and then left town before the victims could figure out they had been had.[37]

Online scams such as the one described above transpose that dynamic into a new context. Instead of going to a town to find potential victims, the fraudsters trick the victims into coming to a Web site they control. Similar to a snake oil peddler, the fraudsters make sure that the Web site puts on a great show, whether it is pitching software or drugs or some other product. Similar to their historical counterpart, online fraudsters sell their bogus product or service to as many victims as possible and then close up shop and disappear to make it as difficult as possible for law enforcement to find them, on the off chance that law enforcement might try to find them.[38]

The impetus for all of this is the Willie Sutton principle we examined in earlier chapters: the premise that criminals will "go where the money is." To-day, the money is increasingly online for several reasons. One is that we are spending more time online and conducting more of our activities online. As we become used to shopping, investing, and banking online, we become more confident in our ability to handle the online world and correspondingly less hesitant about trusting certain Web sites or opportunities.[39] A second reason, I believe, is that many of us implicitly assume that what happens online is not "real" and therefore cannot harm us. People who might never trust a stranger who walked up to them on the street and offered them a chance to make millions by helping him smuggle money out of Morocco do exactly this when the stranger contacts them online.

Finally, there is another, even more important reason why the Willie Sutton effect is so pronounced in cyberspace: Fraudsters can go where the money is in a way they could not when we lived our lives exclusively in physical space. A century ago, it would have been functionally impossible for someone in the Ukraine to defraud people in the United States, England, France, and all the other countries whose citizens fell prey to the fake antivirus software scam. There were mail fraud scams 100 and more years ago, but they inevitably tended to target people in the same country, if not in the same general area. What that meant is that U.S. citizens had to worry about being defrauded only by other U.S. citizens (unless they traveled abroad and fell prey to a foreign scam artist). Cyberspace changes that; it gives aspiring scam artists in any country the ability to target victims in wealthy countries such as the United States and United Kingdom.

It is only logical that given a choice between a victim who has little money and a victim who has (or is perceived to have) a lot of money, a fraudster will target the latter. Those who were responsible for the Ukraine antivirus scam presumably live in Eastern Europe, which is the point of origin for a great deal of the world's cybercrime. It is also an area in which jobs tend to be scarce and wages low, both of which exacerbate the Willie Sutton effect. If a talented hacker has a choice between working as a low-paid but honest furniture mover or becoming a wealthy online fraudster, he may choose the dark path, especially if, as we will see in the next chapter, he runs little risk of being caught and prosecuted for his crimes. The consequences of that choice, which is being made all over the globe, create and shape much of the cybercrime we see today.

STALKERS

Unlike fraudsters (who are consistently motivated by greed), online stalkers are driven by various motives. Those who study stalking have developed taxonomies in an effort to parse out what drives those who in effect persecute other. Because stalking emerged as a real-world crime,[40] many of the taxonomies tend to focus on conduct that takes place in physical space, such as following the victim or damaging his or her car or other tangible property.

I have, though, found a taxonomy I think captures the motives that are common to online stalkers, such as those we examined in Chapter 5. This taxonomy divides stalkers into four categories: ex-partner stalking, infatuation stalking, delusional fixation stalking, and sadistic stalking.[41]

The creators of the taxonomy believe ex-partner stalking is the most common of the four categories of stalking. They note that this type of stalking is likely to involve the use of threats and that the stalker's motivations derive from issues of power, control, and freedom.[42] The Joelle Ligon case was an extreme instance of ex-partner cyberstalking.[43] An ex-boyfriend used the Internet to torment Ligon for six years. Among other things, he posed as Ligon in chat rooms, where he solicited men for sex and gave them her phone numbers. In an effort to get away from him, Ligon moved from Virginia to Seattle, but he followed her. He e-mailed her Seattle co-workers, claiming to be a representative of a group that enforced honor codes for colleges, including Ligon's alma mater. The e-mails claimed Ligon got her college degree under false pretenses and had a history of sexual deviance and drug use (none of which was true). After trying unsuccessfully to interest state prosecutors in the case, Ligon finally convinced federal prosecutors to charge her stalker with online harassment.

That brings us to the second category in the taxonomy. The taxonomy's authors believe infatuation stalking occurs less often than ex-partner stalking but is far from uncommon.[44] In this type of stalking, the victim is not the target of the stalker's anger and resentment but is the focus of a romantic fantasy. The stalker obsessively pursues the object of his or her desire, often sending him or her small gifts or messages. The stalker may also obsess about knowing where the victim is and what he or she is doing at any particular time. According to the creators of the taxonomy, infatuation stalkers are not likely to be dangerous and/or to threaten their victims, either overtly or implicitly.

The only reported case I can find that seemed to involve infatuation stalking is a civil case. In this case, a female student became a professor's research assistant. According to the civil complaint the student ultimately filed, the professor became increasingly infatuated with her over the semester, "telling her routinely that he loved her and asking questions about her . . . sex life."[45] When she resigned as his research assistant, he sent her an e-mail that said, " 'Don't marry someone you can live with, Marry someone you can't live without.' "[46] After university authorities declined to discipline the professor, she filed a sexual harassment suit against him. I cannot find what the outcome of the suit was, although I suspect it was settled. Although I have not been able to find other reported cases dealing with similar conduct,[47] I suspect this kind of stalking is quite common, especially online. I think we hear little about it because, as the creators of the taxonomy noted, infatuation stalkers are more of an annoyance than a threat. As a result, their victims are probably able to deal with the problem themselves, instead of having to go to the authorities for help.

Stalkers who fall into the third category, on the other hand, can be dangerous. In delusional fixation stalking, the stalker is so fixated on the victim that he or she believes they are in a relationship when, in fact, they may never have met.[48] This type of stalking often involves a status imbalance between the stalker and the victim. The victim often has some type of elevated or noteworthy status, such as a professor or other professional, a local or national celebrity, or a local person who is not famous but is held in high esteem in the community. This type of stalking is often characterized by "the incessant bombarding of the" victim with phone calls, e-mails, and other communications.[49]

A story from the United Kingdom illustrates delusional fixation stalking. Alexis Bowater, a "TV newsreader" for a British broadcasting company, was "bombarded . . . with abusive and sexual emails" from a 24-year-old man she had never met.[50] Over a period of two years, the anonymous stalker repeatedly sent his pregnant victim e-mails that were threatening and of " 'an extremely explicit sexual nature.' " Police were finally able to identify the man, and he eventually pled guilty to charges arising from the stalking. In another case from the United Kingdom, a 42-year-old student at a university fixated on one of her professors, sending him so many e-mails he had to "close down the account because it became clogged."[51] The professor finally got a restraining order against her, but she ignored it. His stalker was finally convicted of violating the restraining order.

These two cases illustrate not only the dynamic that defines delusional fixation stalking but another aspect of it as well. The authors of the taxonomy divide delusional fixation stalking into two types: dangerous and less dangerous.[52] The 24-year-old who stalked the newsreader fell into the first category; the 42-year-old who stalked the professor fell into the second category. Both exhibited the core characteristics of this type of stalking (i.e., fixation on the victim, assuming a relationship that did not exist, bombarding the victim with unwanted communications), but the tenor of the messages each sent was quite different. The newsreader received e-mails that alternated between threats to harm her and her baby and graphic sexual fantasies. The e-mails the professor received contained "confused ramblings and often included inappropriate suggestions." The content of the first stalker's communications reasonably caused his victim to fear for her safety and that of her unborn child. The content of the other stalker's communications aggravated and infuriated her victim but apparently did not cause him to fear either for his safety or for the safety of his family. Although these cases arose in the United Kingdom, anecdotal evidence indicates that both types of delusional fixation stalking occur in the United States and in other countries as well.

All of this brings us to the fourth and perhaps most disturbing category in the stalking taxonomy: sadistic stalking.[53] The authors of the taxonomy note that this type of stalking often begins with an initial "low-level acquaintance" between the stalker and the victim that ultimately escalates until the stalker seeks to exert control "over *all* aspects . . . of the victim's life."[54] They explain that the sadistic element of this type of stalking lies in the stalker's desire to obtain "evidence of the victim's powerlessness" in order to validate his feeling of being in control.[55] The victim becomes the "obsessive target" of the stalker and usually has no idea why he has targeted her. This type of stalker is likely to expand the scope of his activities to include the victim's "family and friends . . . in a bid to isolate the victim and further enhance" his feeling of control.[56] The communications the stalker sends to the victim tend to be a "blend of loving and threatening" content, the purpose of which is to "destabilize and confuse" the victim.[57]

The best example of sadistic cyberstalking I know is a case that arose in Los Angeles in 1998.[58] Gary Dellapenta, a 50-year-old security guard from North Hollywood, tried to develop a romantic relationship with a woman from his church, but she made it clear she was not interested. Some time afterward, she began receiving calls and visits from strange men who told her they were ready to fulfill her fantasy of being raped. In all, six men showed up at her home, all with the same purpose. Some arrived when she was there but left when she said there had been a mistake. When she spoke to two of the men on the phone, she learned why they thought she wanted them to rape her: They had been in an online chat room with someone who used the victim's name and address. The person who posed as this woman in the chat room sent messages to the men, telling them "she" fantasized about being raped and inviting them to fulfill her fantasy. "She" gave them the woman's home address and phone number and even the security code to her alarm system.

When the victim realized what was happening, she recruited her father, who went online to find out where the messages were being posted. He found them in chat rooms hosted on two sites that offered users anonymity. The father began participating in the chat rooms and soon found himself corresponding with the person who was pretending to be his daughter. As with the other men, the person sent to the woman's father her home address, phone number, and the code to disable her alarm system. At that point, the father and daughter went to the police, who were able to identify Dellapenta as the person who assumed the daughter's identity in the chat rooms. Officers searched the home he shared with his mother, seized Dellapenta's computer, and found the evidence they needed to charge him with cyberstalking. Dellapenta eventually pled guilty to the charge and was sentenced to serve six years in prison for what he had done.[59]

Although the technology Dellapenta used to target his victim was primitive compared to what we have today, the psychological tactics he used and the motives that drove him perfectly illustrate sadistic stalking. We can only imagine the terror his victim felt when men bent on rape began showing up at her home or calling her. We understand why that was happening, but she did not, at least not while it was happening. We can imagine the sadistic delight Dellapenta must have taken in his power to manipulate his victim, to destroy any sense of security she had in what should have been her haven—her home.

SUM

As this survey of selected cybercrimes illustrates, computer technology makes it possible to commit traditional crimes (e.g., theft, fraud, extortion, defamation) online. At the moment, most cybercrime consists of traditional crimes being committed in nontraditional ways because most cybercrime is, as we saw in earlier chapters, financially motivated. For financial crimes, the cybercriminal's motive and the harm he inflicts are essentially indistinguishable from the motives and harms inflicted by his real-world counterparts. All that differs is the methodology used by the perpetrator in committing the crime.

As this survey of cybercrime also illustrates, however, there is a residuum of cybercrime that differs markedly from the crimes we so far have seen being committed in the real, physical world. Dellapenta's cyberstalking is an example: In the real world, he could never have posed as his female victim, at least not with the credibility he enjoyed online. The cyberworld gave Dellapenta the ability to inflict new and devastating harm on his victim because he was able to turn the victim's "self" against her; that is, he was able to make it appear that what was happening to her was something she, herself, had orchestrated. The power to do that—to assume and exploit someone else's identity—may have existed in some minimal form prior to the Internet, but cyberspace magnifies that power and makes it available to anyone with a basic set of computer skills and a skewed mind-set.

These and other cybercrimes are the result of a phenomenon we examined in earlier chapters: Cyberspace empowers criminals in new ways—ways that, as we will see in the next three chapters, make it difficult for law enforcement to react effectively to cybercrime.

Cyber-*Law and Order*: Investigating and Prosecuting Cybercrime

INTRODUCTION

Cybercrime creates a number of challenges for law enforcement. Rather than trying to address all of the challenges in a single chapter, we will use this chapter and the next two chapters to review how cyberspace complicates the process of identifying and apprehending cybercriminals. In this chapter and Chapter 10, we will examine the greatest challenge law enforcement faces: transnational cybercrime. This chapter touches on the prosecution of cybercriminals only insofar as prosecution depends on successfully investigating a cybercrime and apprehending the perpetrator(s). We will examine the challenges prosecutors face in more detail in Chapter 9.

As we saw in earlier chapters, cybercriminals in one country often target victims in a different country. As we will see in this chapter, that complicates law enforcement's task because police agencies are territorially based. Every law enforcement agency is located in, and derives its authority from, a particular nation-state. This, in turn, means that a law enforcement agency from one country—the United States' Federal Bureau of Investigation or France's National Police—has no legal authority to conduct a criminal investigation in the territory of another country. Our world is, in effect, composed of a series of sovereign boxes; each nation-state is a distinct entity that exercises absolute sovereign authority over the territory it controls. Because police officers operate within a specific box (i.e., within the territory of a specific nation-state), it is usually very difficult or even impossible for them to apprehend cybercriminals who are located in another nation-state.

In the first two sections that follow, we will examine cases in which officers pursued cybercriminals who were in a different country. In the next section, we will examine the legal options available to law enforcement officers in pursuing criminals into another country. We will return to this issue in Chapter 10, when we examine the treaty that is intended to improve law enforcement's ability to conduct transnational cybercrime investigations.

The cases both involved cybercriminals who attacked targets in the United States (and, in one instance, elsewhere) from outside U.S. territory. The perpetrators in each case were very different, as were their motives for attacking U.S. targets.

CASE #1: INVITA

The Invita case is the more recent of the two. As far as law enforcement was concerned, it began when the FBI was called to investigate a series of intrusions "into the computer systems of businesses in the United States" that came from Russia.[1] The intrusions targeted

Internet Service Providers, e-commerce sites, and . . . banks. . . . The hackers used their unauthorized access to the victims' computers to steal credit card . . . and other . . . financial information, and . . . tried to extort money from the victims with threats to expose the sensitive data to the public or damage the victims' computers. The hackers also defrauded PayPal through a scheme in which stolen credit cards were used to generate cash and to pay for computer parts purchased from vendors in the United States.[2]

According to some sources, the attackers "broke into the computers of at least" 40 U.S. companies, including the Nara Bank of Los Angeles and the Central National Bank in Waco, Texas.[3] They sometimes broke into systems and then tried to coerce the owners of the systems into hiring them as "security consultants"; the coercion came in the form of threats to release data they had obtained from the system unless they were hired as "consultants." One company hired the cybercriminals as "consultants," only to have them use its computer system as the vector for attacking systems belonging to other companies.[4] When one company did not immediately pay the cyber-attackers the $500,000 "consulting" fee they demanded, the cyber-attackers launched a DDoS attack that took the company Web site offline.[5]

The president of that company went to the FBI shortly after the attackers initially contacted him. FBI agents suggested he drag out his negotiations with the hackers and use the process to gather as much information as possible about them.[6] He agreed and spent months negotiating with the hackers, who used e-mail and what they claimed was a stolen satellite phone to contact him. After the negotiations had dragged on for some time, one of the hackers e-mailed the company president and told him to forget about the extortion fee. The still-unidentified hacker said he would forego the fee if he could get a visa to come to the United States and be given a job when he arrived. He said he wanted to bring his wife and " 'little child' " to the United States.[7] The president put the hacker—now known only as "Victor"—in touch with an FBI agent to see if they could work out a deal by which the hacker would be given immunity from prosecution in exchange for assisting federal law enforcement with this and other investigations.

The deal fell through, but in the meantime, more than "a dozen U.S. Attorneys and FBI agents" from four states were holding "brainstorming conferences" on how to stop the hackers, who were seen as a serious threat to U.S. businesses.[8] Federal authorities had already tried, and failed, to apprehend one of them through traditional channels. The hacker not only identified himself as "Alexey Ivanov" to his extortion victims, he sent his resume and photograph to a number of them, apparently as part of a search for legitimate employment in the United States.[9] Because Ivanov's resume and certain aspects of the attacks indicated that he was in Russia, the U.S. Justice Department sent a request through diplomatic channels to Russian authorities, asking them to detain Ivanov and question him about the attacks. The Russians did not respond to the initial contact or to a repeated request. Because the United States does not have an extradition treaty with Russia, that country was not obliged to turn Ivanov over to the United States for prosecution, had the United States made such a request.[10] Because U.S. law enforcement had no legal authority to arrest Ivanov in Russia, the federal prosecutors and agents decided to use a "sting" operation to get him to come to the United States.

The sting took the form of a job interview: FBI agents created a fake company called "Invita" and sent Ivanov a "flattering letter . . . telling him they had heard good things about him and were considering him" for a position with their company.[11] The letter told Ivanov he would have to come to the Invita offices in Seattle to interview for the job. Ivanov replied, agreeing to come for the interview and asking if he could bring his " 'business partner' " Vasiliy Gorshkov with him. The company responded that he could bring

Gorshkov, but Invita would pay only Ivanov's travel expenses; Gorshkov would have to pay his own way.[12]

Gorshkov agreed, and in November 2000, the men flew from Chelyabinsk, Russia, to Seattle. An undercover FBI agent picked them up at the airport and brought them to the Invita office, where they chatted with FBI agents who were posing as Invita employees. The Invita people then asked the Russians to demonstrate their hacking skills, using two Invita computers. The hackers did not know the FBI had installed loggers—programs that record what is typed on a keyboard—on the computers. As the Russians hacked, the loggers recorded what they typed. The information recorded included the user names and passwords they used to access the tech.net.ru server—their *kontora*'s, or unofficial company's, server in Russia.[13] (The server stored tools they needed for the hacking demonstration.) After the demonstration was over, the two were told they would be taken to the apartment that had been rented for them. On the way, FBI agents stopped the car and arrested both of them.[14]

Without getting a search warrant, Invita FBI agents retrieved the user names and passwords the loggers recorded and used them to access the tech.net.ru server and download 250 gigabytes of data.[15] The agents did not tell Russian authorities what they were doing, in violation of a 1997 agreement to which both the United States and Russia were parties.[16] Gorshkov and Ivanov were indicted for violating federal cybercrime law and prosecutors prepared to use evidence from the tech.net.ru server at their trials.[17]

Gorshkov moved to suppress all of the evidence, arguing that it was obtained in violation of the U.S. Fourth Amendment because the FBI agents did not obtain a search warrant before accessing the Russian server. He lost. The federal judge to whom his case was assigned held that the Fourth Amendment did not apply to the agents' actions. As the court noted, the U.S. Supreme Court has held that it applies only to searches and seizures "of a non-resident alien's property outside the United States."[18] Both Gorshkov and Ivanov were Russian citizens and, as such, nonresident aliens of the United States. The federal judge found that the search of the Russian computer took place entirely "in" Russia, not in the United States. Given that, the Fourth Amendment did not apply to the agents' accessing the tech.net.ru server and downloading its contents.[19]

Gorshkov also argued that the evidence should be suppressed because the FBI agents' actions violated Russian law. Article 272 of the Criminal Code of the Russian Federation makes it a crime to access a computer without being authorized to do so and to copy information stored on it.[20] The agents who accessed the tech.net.ru server did so without authorization; neither Gorshkov nor Ivanov gave their permission for agents to access their server. The FBI agents were able to access the server only because their loggers captured the log-in information necessary to do so. Once they gained access to the server, they proceeded to copy information being stored on it. Notwithstanding all that, Gorshkov lost again. The federal judge held that Russian law did not apply to the FBI agents' "actions in this case."[21]

Ivanov pled guilty to "multiple counts of conspiracy, computer hacking, computer fraud," and other federal crimes and was sentenced to four years in prison.[22] Gorshkov went to trial and was convicted on 20 counts of committing the same crimes. He was sentenced to three years in prison.[23]

In 2002, almost two years after FBI agents accessed the tech.net.ru server, Russia's Federal Security Service—a police agency—charged one of the Invita agents with hacking in violation of Russian law.[24] The charge was apparently symbolic—a way of asserting Russian sovereignty over persons and things in the territory that Russia controls. In announcing the charge, a spokesperson explained that " '[i]f the Russian hackers are sentenced on the basis of information obtained by the Americans through hacking, that will imply the future ability of U.S. secret services to use illegal methods in the collection of information in Russia and other countries'."[25] The Federal Security Service sent the criminal complaint to the U.S. Department of Justice and asked that the FBI agent be surrendered for prosecution in Russia; the United States has apparently never responded.

CASE #2: ROME LABS

The second case began when computer systems administrators at the Rome Air Development Center (Rome Labs) at Griffiss Air Force Base in New York discovered that hackers had installed sniffer programs on the Rome Labs networks.[26] Password sniffer programs collect the passwords of people who log into a computer system, which suggested that the hackers had the ability to access the sensitive databases of Rome Labs. As a Senate report later noted, Rome Labs was the "Air Force's premier command and control research facility. Its projects include artificial intelligence systems, radar guidance systems, and target detection and tracking systems."[27]

The Rome Labs administrators contacted the Defense Information Systems Agency, which notified the Air Force Office of Special Investigations (AFOSI). The AFOSI agents and computer security experts went to Rome Labs and began investigating the intrusion. They found that in addition to installing the sniffer programs, two unknown individuals had hacked into seven Rome Labs systems and "gained complete access to all" the information on the systems.[28] The AFOSI agents also found that one of the hackers was using the "access code of a high-ranking Pentagon employee" to access the Pentagon computer systems; the code gave the hacker the ability to "delete files, copy information and even crash the system."[29]

The investigation lasted for weeks. The AFOSI agents determined that the hackers, who called themselves "Datastream Cowboy" and "Kuji," were using the Rome Labs systems to attack targets in the United States and in other countries. Although the agents could monitor some of their activity, the hackers were untraceable because they wove "a path through computer systems in South Africa, Mexico and Europe before launching their attacks."[30] Finally, the agents used online informants to identify "Datastream Cowboy" as a 16-year-old who lived in the United Kingdom and liked to attack military targets. Datastream Cowboy was naïve enough to give one of the informants his home telephone number.

Armed with that information, agents contacted New Scotland Yard's computer crime unit and asked them to trace the number to a home address. The British agents rather quickly traced it to a "house in a cul-de-sac, part of the anonymous north London suburbs."[31] The AFOSI agents flew to London and staked out the address with British police officers. They wanted to be sure Datastream Cowboy was online when they entered the home to arrest him and execute a search warrant. On May 12, 1994, the officers on the stakeout got a call telling them he was online; they went to the home, knocked on the door, swept inside after a man answered, and went upstairs to a "loft-room" where they found Datastream Cowboy "tapping frantically away on the keyboard" of his computer.[32] New Scotland Yard officers arrested 16-year-old Richard Pryce, a music student. He admitted to breaking into the Rome Labs systems and other U.S. military systems.[33]

It took two more years before a New Scotland Yard agent was able to track down Kuji. In June 1996, British agents decided to "sift through . . . the mass of information" on Pryce's hard drive again This time, they found the name Kuji next to a telephone number.[34] The number led them to 21-year-old Mathew Bevan, "a soft-spoken computer worker" who was the son of a police officer.[35]

Bevan and Pryce were both charged with multiple counts of violating the United Kingdom's Computer Misuse Act and with a single count of conspiracy. The conspiracy charges were later dropped, and in March 1997, Pryce pled guilty to 12 counts of violating the Computer Misuse Act. All charges against Bevan were dropped in November 1997, "after the Crown

Prosecution service decided it was not in the public interest to pursue the case."[36]

OPTIONS: FORMAL OR INFORMAL

When cybercrimes involve victims in one country and perpetrators in another, law enforcement officers cannot rely on the procedures they normally use to find evidence and/or apprehend domestic perpetrators. A U.S. arrest warrant or search warrant is worthless in any other country, in the same way that a French warrant has no legal effect in the United States.

The problem of collecting evidence and apprehending perpetrators in another country is not unique to cybercrime. Criminals have historically fled the jurisdiction where they committed their crimes in an effort to avoid being prosecuted and punished. What is different about cybercrime is the frequency with which this scenario occurs. It used to be an aberration, but now it is increasingly becoming the norm. Unfortunately, law has not kept up with this trend.

As I have already noted, cross-border crimes create two kinds of challenges for law enforcement officers. One challenge is collecting evidence from abroad, and the other is obtaining custody of a suspect who is abroad. To understand the challenges, we need to review the options that are available to officers in each scenario.

Cybercrime investigators have two alternatives they can use to obtain evidence from abroad. One alternative is to rely on the formal devices that have historically been used to gather evidence in transnational criminal cases. The other option is informal cooperation. We will examine both options in the next section.

Cybercrime investigators also have two alternatives they can use to gain custody of a suspect who is in another country. One alternative is to rely on extradition, the formal device that is used to transfer a suspect from one country to another. The other option involves informal, unilateral action by the country seeking the suspect. We will examine both of these options in the second section that follows.

COLLECTING EVIDENCE

As the U.S. Department of Justice notes, the formal devices officers can use to obtain evidence from abroad include letters rogatory, treaty requests, and request for assistance under executive agreements.[37]

A letter rogatory is a request from a court in one country (e.g., the United States) to a court in another country. The letter asks the foreign court to perform a judicial act, such as authorizing local authorities to collect evidence located in that country.[38] The investigator seeking the evidence must draft the letter rogatory, making sure that what he or she is requesting will be clear to the judge in the foreign country. Because different countries want different things in a letter rogatory, officers usually consult the Department of Justice's Office of International Affairs (OIA) to find out what the letter should include. A letter rogatory usually includes the name and affiliation of the investigating officer; enough facts for a foreign judge to understand that a crime has been committed and the evidence sought that relates to that crime; the nature of the assistance sought; the text of the statutes violated; and a promise of reciprocal assistance.[39] The promise consists of the United States agreeing to provide similar assistance to officers conducting an investigation on behalf of the foreign country.[40] That promise is essential because letters rogatory are based on comity (i.e., congenial relations between the two countries).[41]

After drafting the letter rogatory, the officer will have to get a U.S. judge to sign it and then must have it authenticated by whatever device is appropriate under international law. Here, again, the officer will need to consult with the OIA to find out what method of authentication is needed and how he goes about obtaining it. The next step is having the letter rogatory translated (unless it is going to an English-speaking country). The final step is for the officer to deliver the letter rogatory (translated, if necessary) to the OIA, which will send it to the Department of State or to the American embassy in the country whose assistance is being sought. The usual process is for the U.S. diplomatic representative to deliver the letter rogatory to the Foreign Ministry of the country to which it is directed. The Foreign Ministry then will send it to the Ministry of Justice, and the Ministry of Justice will refer it to the appropriate judge, who will execute it. When the evidence has been collected, it will be returned to the officer via the same process. If a letter rogatory is found to be deficient at any point prior to being implemented, it will be returned to the officer, who will be responsible for revising it to eliminate the defects.

As is probably evident from this description of the process, letters rogatory are a time-consuming method of obtaining evidence from abroad. The Department of Justice tells its prosecutors to assume "the process will take a year or more."[42] A year is an optimistic estimate; in reality, it can take years for a letter rogatory to be implemented, if it is implemented at all. Officers often wait years, only to learn that their letter rogatory has not and will not be implemented.[43]

Requests under a mutual legal assistance treaty (MLAT) are "generally faster and more reliable than letters rogatory."[44] In 2009, the United States had MLATs in force with 53 countries.[45] As one author noted, the MLAT process "is designed to work more quickly than letters rogatory since the MLATs impose an international legal obligation on the requested state to respond, whereas letters rogatory can only request a response."[46]

An officer seeking evidence from abroad first must find out if the United States has an MLAT with the country in which the evidence is located. He does this by consulting with the Department of Justice's OIA. If the United States has an MLAT with the country, the officer will need to find out what investigations it covers because MLATS deal with specific crimes (e.g., drugs). If the MLAT covers the crime he is investigating, the officer will draft a request for assistance from the other country. The OIA has models that are "tailored to the treaty under which assistance is being requested."[47] An MLAT request contains essentially the same information as a letter rogatory, except the promise of reciprocity will be omitted, and certain information (e.g., the name, address, and citizenship of all those affected by the request) will be added.[48] After the officer drafts the MLAT request, he submits it to OIA for review. Then OIA will either use it to prepare the final request or sent the draft back to the officer to be revised. Because U.S. MLATs designate the Department of Justice as the entity authorized to make an MLAT request, an OIA representative will sign the request, have it translated (if necessary), and send it to the entity in the foreign country that has the authority to execute it.[49]

Although MLAT requests may have a quicker turnaround time than letters rogatory, they are still a slow, cumbersome process. As a federal prosecutor noted, MLATs "take months or even years to produce the required" evidence.[50] Although such delays can be aggravating or problematic in traditional criminal investigations, they are likely to be devastating in cybercrime investigations. Letters rogatory and MLATS were developed to obtain physical evidence, which tends to be stable and enduring; the digital evidence involved in cybercrime investigations is fragile and tenuous. When an officer has to rely on a letter rogatory or an MLAT request to obtain evidence in a cybercrime case, he runs the risk that the digital evidence he seeks will be deleted before his request ever reaches the appropriate foreign authorities.[51]

The last formal device is a request under an executive agreement. An executive agreement is a compact made by a U.S. president with representatives of another country. Unlike treaties, it does not have to be approved by Congress.[52] Executive agreements can be an effective means of obtaining evidence from abroad, but they are not likely to be a useful resource for an officer conducting a cybercrime investigation. As the U.S. Department of Justice notes, most of the executive agreements in force "apply to investigations arising from illegal narcotics trafficking."[53] So far, anyway, none seems to apply to cybercrime investigations.

Because the formal methods are not likely to be effective in obtaining evidence in cybercrime cases, law enforcement officers rely on informal methods when they are available. We saw this in the Rome Labs case. The AFOSI investigators contacted New Scotland Yard officers, who cooperated with the U.S. investigation of the Rome Labs intrusions. British officers helped the Air Force agents track down Datastream Cowboy, and they were the ones who eventually identified Kuji. Because the suspects were prosecuted in the United Kingdom (an issue we will return to in the next section), the evidence the U.S. and UK officers collected was not turned over to U.S. prosecutors and used at trial. That does not, however, detract from the fact that officers from both countries worked closely together in a spirit of cooperation—with no legal compulsion—to track down the suspects and collect evidence of their crimes.

Currently, informal cooperation of the kind that existed in the Rome Labs case is the most efficient means by which law enforcement officers in one countrycan obtain assistance from officers and other authorities in another country. As we will see in Chapter 10, the Council of Europe promulgated a cybercrime treaty that is intended to improve formal cooperation among law enforcement in countries that sign and ratify the treaty, but only a few countries have done so. Unless and until most, if not all, of the nations of the world ratify the treaty, informal cooperation among law enforcement will be the most effective way of obtaining evidence from abroad in cybercrime investigations.

The single greatest advantage of informal cooperation is the speed with which evidence can be preserved and collected. The single greatest disadvantage of informal cooperation is that it depends on the investigating officer knowing how to contact his counterpart in the country in which the evidence is located. A few years ago, I was in Italy participating in a working group dealing with computer forensics, and I met an officer from Germany. Earlier that year, he was working on a cybercrime investigation of some magnitude (I believe it was a particularly horrendous child pornography case), and he traced activity in the case to somewhere in Montana. What he then needed was to have a search warrant executed in Montana to find the evidence that he believed was in a specific place and was essential if Germany was to be able to prosecute the people involved. He told me he called all around Montana, trying to find someone who would help him by getting the warrant and executing it. He failed and gave up on the case.

Informal cooperation therefore depends to a great extent on networking among cybercrime investigators. Some investigators are very effective at this, often because they have the resources to be able to attend conferences where they meet investigators from other countries. Many investigators are not effective at this because they simply do not have the opportunity to network with officers from other countries.

Informal cooperation also depends to a great extent on the relations that exist between the two countries. In the Rome Labs case, the investigators were from countries that have historically had very congenial relations. Therefore, it is not surprising that the British agents were willing to assist their American counterparts without the compulsion provided by a letter rogatory or an MLAT request. In other cases—when the relationship between the two countries is not particularly congenial and/or when the country whose assistance is being sought tacitly accepts the cybercriminals operating in its territory—a request for informal cooperation is very unlikely to be successful. Many organizations are working to improve both the level of informal cooperation among law enforcement officers in different countries and the efficacy of formal methods as ways to obtain digital evidence from abroad. We will return to that issue in Chapter 10.

ARRESTING SUSPECTS

As we have seen, officers have two ways to gain custody of suspects who are in another country: extradition, the formal device that has historically been used to transfer suspects from one country to another; and extra-legal unilateral action by the country seeking the suspect.

Extradition requires a treaty between the countries. As one author noted, " [w]ithout an extradition treaty, extradition is not considered a binding obligation to most countries."[54] The United States has extradition treaties with more than 100 countries, but that leaves many countries with which it does not have such a treaty.[55] As we saw earlier, the United States does not have an extradition treaty with the Russian Federation.

Even when the United States has an extradition treaty with a country, extradition is often "difficult to obtain, legally and practically."[56] Here, as with using a letter rogatory or an MLAT request to obtain evidence, the legal process is complicated and can be very cumbersome. As the Department of

Justice explains, extradition "involves four basic steps": contacting the Department of Justice's OIA; determining extraditability; deciding whether to ask for provisional arrest; and submitting the documents required to support the formal request for extradition.[57]

The officer seeking custody of a suspect in another country works with the OIA to determine if the United States has an extradition treaty with that country and, if it does, to initiate the process of obtaining extradition. The first step in initiating extradition is determining the extraditability of the suspect, a process that involves analyzing eight factors.[58] Although all eight factors play a role in determining whether a suspect can be extradited, citizenship is clearly the most important. As the Justice notes, "[m]any countries will not extradite their own citizens,"[59] an issue we will revisit in a moment. If the OIA decides that the suspect is extraditable, it will work with the investigating officer to assemble the complex documentation needed to support the request for extradition.[60]

Even if the suspect is clearly extraditable and the OIA request and supporting documentation are impeccable, the request may not be granted. As we saw in Chapter 4, the United Kingdom, a country with which the United States maintains very cordial relations, was resistant to the idea of extraditing Gary McKinnon, the British hacker charged with breaking into U.S. military systems. The explicit focus of the British resistance to extraditing McKinnon was, as we saw in Chapter 4, the erroneous belief that he faced decades in prison in the United States if he was convicted of the charges against him. The resistance and the erroneous belief that provided its ostensible predicate were the predictable products of the reluctance countries have historically exhibited when asked to extradite their own citizens. Indeed, the constitutions of some countries bar them from extraditing their own citizens for prosecution abroad.[61]

Historically, international law dealt with a country's refusal to extradite its citizens by applying the principle of *aut dedere aut judicare*, which says a country that is asked to extradite one of its citizens must either extradite or prosecute the person itself.[62] As we saw in Chapter 4, that is the argument many in Britain made in justifying the country's refusal to extradite Gary McKinnon to the United States. As we also saw in Chapter 4, it is not uncommon for a victim state—the United States in the McKinnon case— to consider prosecution by the person's home country to be an unsatisfactory outcome. When a country has been the victim of a crime (either directly or by having one of its citizens victimized), it often feels justice will not be done unless the perpetrator is prosecuted, convicted, and punished by the state whose laws he or she violated. The need to prosecute locally is a function of a traditional aspect of criminal law: publicly denouncing those who violate the sovereign's law. It is also, to some extent, a product of concern that the offender's own country will "go too easy" on that person.

Cases such as the McKinnon case, in which the perpetrator's country is willing to prosecute him for the crimes he committed abroad, are a source of tension between two countries. However, the tension will be alleviated if the perpetrator's country carries through on its promise, and the victim country sees that the perpetrator is going to be punished. The truly difficult cases are the ones in which the perpetrator's country will not or cannot extradite him and refuses to prosecute him for the crimes he committed abroad.

We saw a version of this scenario in the Invita case. There, the FBI identified two Russians as the hackers who were attacking targets in the United States. The United States could not ask the Russians to turn over the hackers for prosecution because there is no extradition treaty in effect between the United States and the Russian Federation. This meant that the formal device used to obtain a suspect from abroad was not available and, as a result, that the "extradite or prosecute" principle did not apply. That is, because Russia was under no obligation to extradite the hackers, it also was under no obligation to prosecute them. In this and similar scenarios, the victim country (the United States in this instance) has no official recourse. Its only options are to give up on prosecuting the offenders or to resort to extralegal unilateral action to obtain custody of them. In other words, a victim country in this situation has no option but to go outside the law.

In a sense, U.S. authorities chose that second option with the Russian hackers. As we saw, they tricked the Russians into coming to the United States, where they could be, and were, arrested. When a person is inside a country's territory, its law enforcement officers can arrest him. His presence on the country's territory gives that country the authority to make the arrest.[63] Thus, the Russian hackers effectively guaranteed their arrest by coming to the United States.

What, if anything, could the FBI have done if the hackers had refused to come to the United States to interview with the Invita company? Informal cooperation is not an option in this instance. Absent an extradition treaty, Russian authorities simply cannot turn their citizens over to another country for prosecution. The United States did, however, have another, albeit problematic, option: to kidnap the hackers from Russia and bring them back to the United States to stand trial. The U.S. Supreme Court has long approved the use of kidnapping to bring foreign suspects to the United States for trial.[64] As the Supreme Court explained in a relatively recent case, it has so far never departed from the rule announced in [1886] that the power of a court to try a person for crime is not impaired by the fact that he had been brought within the court's jurisdiction by reason of a "forcible abduction." . . . [D]ue process of law is satisfied when one present in court is convicted of crime after having been fairly apprized of the charges against him and after a fair trial in accordance with constitutional . . . safeguards. There is nothing in the Constitution that requires a court to permit a guilty person . . . to escape justice because he was brought to trial against his will.[65]

Although abduction is an option under U.S. law, it is rarely used. A Department of Justice manual tells prosecutors that "[d]ue to the sensitivity of abducting defendants from a foreign country," they may not "secure custody over persons outside the United States (by government agents or the use of . . . bounty hunters or private investigators) . . . without advance approval" from the department.[66] Because the U.S. policy of abducting suspects is controversial under international law, the Department of Justice presumably applies a very stringent test in deciding whether to approve abduction. So far, anyway, there appear to be no cases in which cybercrime suspects have been abducted and brought to the United States for prosecution.

Although abduction was a legal option in the Invita, case, it was not practical. The FBI would have had to send agents to Chelyabinsk, where the suspects lived. Once in Chelyabinsk, the agents would have had to find both suspects, take them into custody without being noticed by the local authorities, and then smuggle them out of Russia. It would be an essentially impossible task, with a potentially serious downside: If the FBI agents were caught, they could have faced kidnapping and other charges in Russia.[67]

SUM

Generally, the formal legal devices nation-states have historically used to obtain evidence and/or suspects from abroad are ill-suited to dealing with cybercrimes and cybercriminals. Informal cooperation among law enforcement officers can facilitate the exchange of evidence between countries, but informal cooperation is not an alternative means of obtaining custody of cybercrime suspects.

The deficiencies of the current system have become increasingly apparent over the last decade. The problem nations face is coming up with alternative approaches that can address these deficiencies while preserving, and respecting, national sovereignty. As we will see in Chapter 10, the Council of Europe developed and is in the process of implementing what is so far the only alternative strategy for facilitating transnational cooperation in cybercrime investigations.

U.S. Law Enforcement:
Agencies and Challenges

INTRODUCTION

Chapter 8 focused on the challenges cybercrime creates for law enforcement. We will begin by reviewing the criminal justice system in America: the division of authority between state and federal law enforcement agencies, the number of agencies, and the number of people those agencies employ.

The review focuses on the agencies that are responsible for prosecuting crime, as well as investigating it. The first section deals with the officers who investigate cybercrime; the next section deals with the lawyers who prosecute it.

After we survey the criminal justice system, we will consider why, and how, cybercrime is making life difficult for those charged with maintaining law and order. We will continue that process in Chapter 10, which examines the unique challenges transnational cybercrime creates for those charged with maintaining law and order.

CRIMINAL JUSTICE SYSTEM: INVESTIGATING

The United States is a federal system; that is, it is a system of government in which "sovereignty is constitutionally divided between a central governing authority" (the U.S. federal government) and "constituent political units" (the states).[1] The federal system in place today is the product of the U.S. Constitution, which was ratified and went into effect in 1789. From 1781 until 1789, the United States was a confederation, rather than a federal system.[2]

Under the Articles of Confederation, which was "the first constitution of the thirteen United States of America,"[3] each state retained "its sovereignty, freedom, and independence, and every power, jurisdiction and right, which [was] not . . . expressly delegated to the United States."[4] The country created by the Articles of Confederation was therefore "more akin to 'an alliance . . . of nation-states' than it was to a nation-state."[5] The Congress that operated under the Articles of Confederation was, as a result, "notoriously weak," much "too weak to enact and enforce laws of a national character."[6]

The government created by the Articles of Confederation was weak because the drafters of the articles were leery of a strong national government.[7] Their concern about a strong central authority derived, in large part, from the colonists' experience with the British Crown's "abuse of the criminal justice system to serve political ends."[8] Because "criminal regulation by the federal government" was a particularly sensitive issue, the Articles of Confederation "did not provide for any federal criminal law authority."[9] Criminal law was consequently a matter that was dealt with exclusively by the states.[10]

By the mid-1780s, it had become obvious that the Articles of Confederation government was too weak to ensure the country's survival as a sovereign entity. The states were constantly quarreling, and Connecticut and Pennsylvania briefly went to war with each other.[11] In an effort to improve the situation, Congress passed a resolution "calling for delegates from each state to gather in Philadelphia on the second Monday in May of 1787 for the purpose of revising the Articles of Confederation."[12] Instead of revising the Articles of Confederation, they wrote the Constitution, which creates a federal system of government that has far more authority than its predecessor, at least in certain respects.

The delegates to what became the Constitutional Convention devoted surprisingly little attention to a federal criminal law. Their inattention to this issue is surprising because many of the delegates, including Alexander Hamilton, realized that the failure of the Articles of Confederation to provide for a national criminal law was one of its "most palpable defect[s]."[13] Notwithstanding that, their debates on criminal law focused on only four crimes: piracy, crimes against the law of nations, treason, and counterfeiting.[14] The delegates' exclusive focus on these crimes seems to have been the product of two factors. One factor was a lingering hesitation to involve the new federal government too much in what were regarded as purely domestic matters; criminal law had, after all, always been handled at the local level. The other factor was that these four crimes implicate what are clearly national interests. The federal government is the direct victim of counterfeiting and treason, and piracy and crimes against the law of nations both implicate its authority to deal with threats from outside the territory of the United States.[15] "Consequently, there seemed to be a general consensus that these matters were appropriate for national governmental action and thus deserved explicit mention in the Constitution."[16]

The Constitution therefore explicitly gives the federal government the power to outlaw and punish these crimes and only these crimes.[17] Many believed Congress could not outlaw other crimes, but it did not agree. In 1789 and again in 1790, Congress outlawed crimes that were not explicitly mentioned in the Constitution.[18] In doing this, Congress primarily relied on its authority under Article I Section 8 of the Constitution, which gives it the power to make "all laws which shall be necessary and proper for carrying" out the powers "vested by this Constitution in the Government of the United States." In 1792, Congress relied on its Constitutional power to "establish Post Offices and post Roads" in making it a crime to steal U.S. mail.[19]

Aside from these and a few other enactments, Congress left responsibility for defining and enforcing criminal law to the states, which is where it remained until the twentieth century. Therefore, until the twentieth century, "criminal justice was overwhelmingly the business of the states, not the federal government."[20] Law enforcement officers were almost exclusively hired by state and local governments, and the federal government did not "have a prison it could call its own until 1891," when Congress authorized the construction of three federal facilities.[21]

That began to change in the early decades of the last century, as Congress began using the Commerce Clause to criminalize various activities.[22] In 1910, Congress used the Commerce Clause to make it a federal crime to transport a "woman or girl" in interstate commerce "for the purpose of prostitution."[23] In 1919, Congress relied on the Commerce Clause in making it a federal crime to transport stolen vehicles across state lines (the Dyer Act).[24] In the 1930s, Congress used it to criminalize a wide variety of conduct, such as transporting a kidnap victim across state lines (the Lindbergh Act), fleeing across state lines to avoid being prosecuted for any of a list of enumerated felonies (the Fugitive Felon Act), and transporting stolen property across state lines (the National Stolen Property Act).[25]

The trend accelerated, and by the end of the twentieth century, there had been a massive expansion of federal criminal law and law enforcement.[26] The expansion of federal authority was the product of a technology introduced at the beginning of the century—the automobile. As one author noted, "[l]aws like the Dyer Act were necessary because even though auto theft could be punished ... under state criminal law, the jurisdiction where the theft occurred was powerless to pursue the thief across state lines. ... By crossing the state line, the thief could defy ... local authorities."[27] Crossing state lines frustrated local prosecution because a state's jurisdiction to prosecute "stops at the border. ... The penal code of North Dakota means nothing once you cross the frontier into South Dakota."[28] Congress decided the way to address this problem was to give the federal government the power to prosecute offenders who used automobiles or other technology to exploit state boundaries and evade prosecution by local authorities. As a result, Congress progressively expanded the scope of federal criminal law during the twentieth century. By the beginning of the twenty-first century, there were more than 3,000 federal crimes.[29]

The expansion of federal criminal law required federal law enforcement agencies. Until 1865, the federal government relied on "private guards and detectives for its occasional police work."[30] During the Civil War, it used the Pinkerton Detective Agency to spy on the Confederacy and to protect President Lincoln from assassination.[31] Congress created the Secret Service after the Civil War to deal with a "crisis of false currency" that followed the war.[32] In 1867, the investigative authority of the Secret Service was expanded to include "frauds against the government," and in 1913, it became responsible for protecting the president.[33] The Secret Service was the only federal law enforcement agency until 1908, when a Bureau of Investigation was created as part of the U.S. Department of Justice. Its investigative responsibilities expanded with federal criminal law, and by 1935, it had become the Federal Bureau of Investigation (FBI).[34]

The Secret Service and the FBI are not the only federal law enforcement agencies. The Bureau of Alcohol, Tobacco and Firearms (ATF) was created in 1968; its origins go back to the Bureau of Prohibition, which enforced federal alcohol law in the 1920s and 1930s.[35] The Drug Enforcement Administration (DEA) was created in 1973, but its origins go back to the Federal Bureau of Narcotics, which enforced federal drug laws in the 1930s and for several decades afterward.[36] The other major federal law enforcement agency is U.S. Immigration and Customs Enforcement (ICE), which was established in 2002. ICE consolidated the functions of several preexisting agencies, including the U.S. Customs Service, the Immigration and Naturalization Service, and the U.S. Federal Protective Service.[37] Other federal agencies have at least some responsibility for enforcing federal criminal law,[38] but these five play the most important role in that process.

Federal agencies play only a small part of law enforcement in the United States. The Congressional expansion of federal criminal law did not alter the Constitutional allocation of responsibility for dealing with crime; the investigation and prosecution of crimes is still handled primarily by the states. Thus, there is a large network of state and local law enforcement agencies. In 2004, there were 17,876 state and local agencies in the United States, which were staffed by 731,903 full-time officers.[39] Organizationally, state and local agencies are divided into three tiers: local (municipal police); county, parish, or borough (sheriff); and state (state police, state patrol, or highway patrol).[40] Local and county officers tend to have general police power; they can investigate any crime committed within the territory over which their agency has jurisdiction.[41] State police tend to have similar power,[42] but their involvement in an investigation may depend on the local agency's involvement and preferences.

Because state and local enforcement is the default, the number of federal officers is much smaller. In 2004, there were 106,354 federal agents, 40,408 of whom were assigned to criminal investigation and law enforcement duty.[43] FBI agents accounted for 12,414 of these agents and ICE for another 10,691;[44] the other agencies described here are much smaller. The DEA has 5,235 agents, the Secret Service has 3,200, and the ATF has 2,400.[45] Each of these agencies is responsible for investigating the crimes that come within its distinct mandate. For example, the DEA concentrates on drug and drug-related crimes.

Because the crimes federal agencies investigate are committed, for the most part, within the United States, local, county, and/or state agencies can have concurrent jurisdiction over those crimes. When that happens, the federal agency will claim priority if the crime involves matters of particular federal concern, such as counterfeiting and terrorism. "Beyond this sphere, in the areas traditionally policed by the States, the line between what goes federally and what is left 'stateside'" is usually a matter of negotiation between federal and state authorities.[46] One of the issues that can factor into such a negotiation is resources. Federal agencies can usually devote more time, money, personnel, and expertise to a case than can their state counterparts.[47] We will return to that issue later in this chapter.

CRIMINAL JUSTICE SYSTEM: PROSECUTING

The structure of the agencies responsible for prosecuting those suspected of committing crimes mirrors the law enforcement structure examined in the preceding text. Prosecutors in the Unites States work for a state in a county, parish, or borough[48] prosecutor's office; in a state attorney general's office; or for the U.S. Department of Justice.

Every county, parish, or borough has a chief prosecutor who is elected or appointed; most are elected.[49] The chief prosecutor's office has jurisdiction over crimes committed in the county, parish, or borough that elected him or her.[50] Depending on the state, chief prosecutors are called district attorneys, county attorneys, county prosecutors, or state's attorneys.[51] There are 2,344 chief prosecutors in the United States;[52] each hires staff attorneys (assistant district attorneys, assistant county attorneys, and so on) to assist him or her. Most have a small staff; in 2005, half of the prosecutors' offices in the United States "employed 9 or fewer people."[53] In large counties, the chief prosecutor can have hundreds of assistants.[54]

In the United States, the vast majority of criminal cases are prosecuted at the local level. As an American Bar Association study noted, "federal efforts account for only five percent of all prosecutions nationwide."[55] Chief prosecutors and their staff attorneys are responsible for the prosecution of all local crimes, from shoplifting to homicides. In 2005, they handled "[o]ver 2.4 million felony cases and almost 7.5 million misdemeanor cases."[56]

Because the federal government is a single, unitary system, federal prosecutors work for the U.S. Department of Justice, which has jurisdiction over any federal crime committed in the territory of the United States and, in certain circumstances, outside the United States. The attorney general heads the Department of Justice, but the prosecution of specific cases is handled by appointed individuals known as U.S. attorneys. Similar to their state counterparts, U.S. attorneys are based in and have responsibility for a specific geographical area.

The assignment of U.S. attorneys to the various parts of the country tracks the system used for organizing the federal courts. Congress long ago divided the United States into federal judicial districts: There is at least one judicial district in each state; many states have two, and a few (such as California and New York) have three or more.[57] There are currently 93 U.S. attorneys, each of whom is assigned to a specific judicial district.[58] Similar to their state counterparts, each U.S. attorney has staff attorneys; federal prosecutors below the rank of U.S. attorney are known as assistant U.S. attorneys (AUSAs). In the same way as assistant district attorneys, AUSAs prosecute the cases that arise in the judicial district to which they are assigned; they usually do not specialize in any particular type of crime.

There are, however, AUSAs who do specialize. Because it recognized that cybercrime presents novel and difficult legal issues, the Department of Justice created a special program to train cybercrime prosecutors. The Computer Hacking and Intellectual Property (CHIP) Program began in 2001, with 48 CHIP AUSAs who were assigned to U.S. attorneys' offices in 10 cities.[59] By 2009, 240 CHIP AUSAs were assigned to U.S. attorneys' offices; each office had at least one CHIP AUSA. The CHIP AUSAs are responsible for prosecuting cybercrime cases and serving as that judicial district's expert on digital evidence and computer investigations.[60] Their role is to support the cybercrime prosecutor at the local federal level (i.e., in each judicial district).

The Justice Department also created a special unit of cybercrime prosecutors who work for the attorney general, instead of for a U.S. attorney. The Computer Crime and Intellectual Property Section (CCIPS) was founded in 1991 as a Computer Crime Unit in the Department of Justice's General Litigation Section. In 1996, it was renamed CCIPS and became a section of the Department of Justice's Criminal Division.[61] The AUSAs in CCIPS therefore report to a deputy assistant attorney general, who, in turn, reports to the assistant attorney feneral. By 2009, there were approximately 40 CCIPS AUSAs. Although these AUSAs prosecute cases, CCIPS' primary responsibility is "developing the Department's overall computer and intellectual property offense enforcement strategies" and "coordinating computer crime . . . investigations . . . that may significantly impact more than one district and/or other countries."[62] The CCIPS' role is to focus on the national and international aspects of cybercrime. Its AUSAs develop U.S. law and policy in this area and work with officials from other countries on cybercrime investigations and on reconciling their cybercrime law with U.S. law. We will return to that issue in Chapter 10.

CRIMINAL JUSTICE SYSTEM: CHALLENGES

The United States, similar to most countries,[63] has a two-tiered, geographically based system of law enforcement. The tasks of investigating and prosecuting crime are primarily carried out at the local level. However, as in many countries, there is also a national system that deals with cases that are of particular interest to the national government and/or are difficult for local personnel to pursue effectively. The systems we have in place today evolved from systems that developed when travel and technology were far more primitive and crime was consequently a parochial phenomenon.

These systems have worked well because, as we will see in the next chapter, crime has historically been local crime; even today, most crime is local. The efficacy of the systems began to erode about a century ago when modern transportation made it easier for criminals to evade prosecution by fleeing the jurisdiction in which they had committed a crime. As we saw earlier, criminals in the United States, such as the gangs of the 1930s, used automobiles to avoid local police. They could rob a bank in Texas and flee to Oklahoma, where they were safe from Texas law. In the same way as today's cybercriminals, the 1930s gangsters appreciated the advantages technology gave them. In 1934, Clyde Barrow, of the Bonnie and Clyde gang, wrote a letter to Henry Ford, thanking Ford for his "steel-bodied V-8 automobiles" because they made it so much easier for the gang to elude police after they committed a robbery.[64]

As we saw earlier, U.S. authorities responded to the challenges the automobile created for local law enforcement by expanding the role of federal law enforcement, an approach that has proven satisfactory in the intervening years. Now, law enforcement faces a new set of challenges created by technology that is much more complex and much less straightforward in its implications than was motor vehicle technology. Motor vehicle technology enabled a criminal to move from one jurisdiction into another after he or she committed a crime in the first jurisdiction. As we saw in earlier chapters, computer technology enables cybercriminals to operate simultaneously in one, two, or multiple jurisdictions. It essentially creates a virtual world that overlays the physical world.

The existence of that virtual world means law enforcement officers and prosecutors confront challenges that are far more difficult to resolve than apprehending perpetrators who flee from one U.S. state to another. As we have seen, a cybercriminal who attacks a victim in the United States can be essentially anywhere in the physical world. As we will see in the next chapter, this fundamentally alters the assumptions that shaped our approach to law enforcement and makes that model increasingly ineffective in dealing with cybercrime.

Although transnational cybercrime creates distinct challenges for law enforcement, other challenges are common to any type of cybercrime. Cybercrime cases involve digital evidence, which is far more insubstantial and elusive than the tangible evidence most police officers and prosecutors are accustomed to handling. Police officers are responsible for collecting evidence, including digital evidence; untrained officers can damage, destroy, or overlook digital evidence.

A number of years ago, a computer forensics expert who had worked for the federal government but now had his own business told me this story. The FBI agents in a state I shall not name executed a search warrant in a computer hacking case. They seized the suspect's computer and brought it to the FBI office in that city, where it was put on a table in a general area of the office. Someone—maybe an agent—plugged in the computer, and agents and other office personnel used it to play computer games. The computer forensics expert, who worked for the federal government at that point, walked into the office and saw someone using the suspect's computer to play games. When he asked what was going on, he was told people had been using it to play games for several days. At that point, the computer forensics expert asked to see the agent handling the case. When the agent showed up, the expert told him he should forget all about prosecuting the case because leaving the computer out for people to use had fatally contaminated the evidence.[65] The expert said there was no way he could analyze the computer and then testify with any confidence that whatever evidence he found had been put on the computer by the suspect, rather than by someone else. He said after he told the same thing to the AUSA who was handling the case, the prosecutor abandoned the investigation.

That story is an old story, in cybercrime time. Nothing like that would happen today, certainly not in the federal system and probably not in any state law enforcement agency. One reason for that is the increasing pervasiveness of computers. Similar to all of us, police officers and prosecutors use computers at work and at home. Consequently, they are more aware of the nuances and implications of computer technology than prosecutors and investigators were even a decade ago.

However, that does not mean every officer or prosecutor who uses a computer is adept at dealing with digital evidence. A few are; most are not. Many officers may not even realize digital evidence is important. In 2008, an assistant district attorney in a county in a state I will not identify told me this story: The prosecutor's office, which is in a medium-sized city, was investigating drug-dealing by a local street gang. This assistant district attorney got a warrant that authorized a search of the gang's headquarters, which was in an old house. The warrant authorized a search for drugs and evidence related to drug-dealing. The officers who executed the warrant seized a large quantity of drugs and drug paraphernalia but did not bother to seize the four laptop computers they found in the headquarters. Those officers did not associate the laptops with evidence of drug-dealing, even though drug dealers have been using computers and spreadsheets for years.

Problems such as that can be addressed with a basic level of officer training, and training is being offered. Unfortunately, as we saw earlier, there are hundreds of thousands of state and local law enforcement officers in the United States. Training that many officers in even the basics of digital evidence is an expensive undertaking.[66] Furthermore, the expense is compounded by several other factors. One is that prosecutors need to be trained along with police. Prosecutors do not necessarily need to be trained in how to find and preserve digital evidence, but they do need to be trained in how to understand it and how to use it in court. The costs of training prosecutors in the intricacies and use of digital evidence therefore must be added to the costs involved in training law enforcement officers to collect and preserve digital evidence.

Another factor that increases the cost of training law enforcement officers and prosecutors is that digital evidence is not static. It is a relatively simple matter to train law enforcement officers to take someone's fingerprints or DNA. It is also relatively simple to train law enforcement officers to identify and preserve physical evidence, such as spent cartridges. All of that evidence is stable. Fingerprints, DNA, and spent cartridges do not evolve into new iterations, but digital evidence does. The computers we use today are much more powerful and sophisticated than the ones in use a decade ago, and computer technology is evolving at what seems to be an accelerating pace. This means that what officers and prosecutors learned about computer technology last year may not be adequate if they are to do their jobs effectively this year. That means officers and prosecutors need to be trained on a continuing basis if they are to keep abreast of new developments in technology.

It also means that some police officers (i.e., those who work in the area of cybercrime) and some prosecutors need to be equipped with the latest technology. This is particularly true when it comes to the technology police computer forensics experts use to analyze computers and other technology that has been seized as potential evidence. However, this training is both expensive and unprecedented. In the past, a new police officer was outfitted with a badge, a radio, a gun, and maybe a police vehicle. Most of those things would eventually need to be replaced, but they would last for years before the items quit working or became outmoded. That, of course, is not true of computer technology. Hardware and software change constantly, and cybercriminals are likely to have the latest versions of each. If police and prosecutors are to compete, they need to have the same technological advantages as the cybercriminals, but that is difficult.[67]

It is difficult for at least two reasons. One reason is that police departments and prosecutors' offices have limited budgets that were not designed to accommodate the need to deal with cybercrime. Expanding the budgets to accommodate the needs of cybercrime investigators and prosecutors is unlikely, given the economic uncertainty this and other countries confront. Another factor may be at play also: skepticism as to whether the officers and prosecutors who deal with cybercrime really need to keep upgrading the hardware and software they use. Here, again, we may have a parallel with the impact automobiles had on early twentieth-century law enforcement.

Early twentieth-century officers often were not provided with motor vehicles. In 1917, for example, Hinton Clabaugh, supervisor of the U.S. Department of Justice office in Chicago, did not have cars for his agents.[68] Instead, the Department of Justice agents used streetcars in their "high-speed" pursuits of criminals who were fleeing in automobiles.[69] Clabaugh's problem was, of course, budgetary; Congress refused to appropriate funds for the equipment the agents needed.[70] Local police met with similar problems. In 1909, Louisville Police Chief J. H Haager said citizens " 'seemed to view it as a display of extravagance' " when his department bought its first motor vehicle.[71]

Over the years, people came to accept that police needed cars and the money to buy them. Motor vehicles eventually became a basic tool of law enforcement. In some instances, citizen-approved funding was supplemented by other means. In 1917, Chicago businessmen donated 75 automobiles to the Department of Justice, suggesting that they be distributed for federal agents' use in various cities, which they were.[72] Some have suggested that private funding could be used to support the technology needs of state law enforcement officers and prosecutors, but this suggestion usually meets with resistance. The concern seems to be that the citizens who fund the technology will in effect be "buying preferential law enforcement."[73]

The other reason it is difficult for law enforcement agencies and prosecutors' offices to get the funds they need to train and equip cybercrime investigators and prosecutors is the persistence of real-world crime. Cybercrime does not displace real-world crime; it is new crime that is added to the traditional crime that police and prosecutors must still handle. This means that the funds for cybercrime training and equipment would have to be added to the funds that are already being allocated to law enforcement agencies and prosecutors' offices. The prospect of obtaining additional funding for cybercrime investigations and prosecutions is highly unlikely, given the current economic climate and, perhaps, a failure to understand the importance of adequately funding the battle against cybercrime. This state of affairs creates a dilemma—or, more precisely, a Hobson's choice—for police and prosecutors. Unless and until their budgets are increased, they must decide how to allocate their limited resources. Which should be given priority—the complex virtual world crimes or the real-world crimes?

That is a difficult question to answer, primarily because although the two types of crimes both inflict harm, the harms they inflict differ in at least one notable respect. So far, cybercrime has not involved the infliction of death or physical injury to persons or property. Responding to the infliction of these very serious harms has always been the highest priority of the criminal justice system, and for good reason. These are the most serious harms one human being can inflict on another. Given the severity of the harm at issue, it is reasonable and appropriate for police and prosecutors to concentrate their efforts on finding and sanctioning those who inflict such harm. As we will see in the next chapter, this is how societies discourage people from engaging in this type of activity.

Obviously, we want law enforcement agencies and prosecutors' offices to make these crimes their first priority, but what about the other real-world crimes? Should real-world theft be given priority over online theft? Should arson be given a higher priority than hacking? Both are property crimes; however, in one instance, the property is tangible, whereas in the other instance, it is not. Does that matter? Should it matter?

When I think about these issues, I recall a conversation I had with a police officer a couple years ago. This officer worked for a small police department in large town/small city that was the county seat of a prosperous county in the Midwest. The officer—we'll call him Officer Jones—had developed and was operating an online sting aimed at adult males who use the Internet to solicit underage girls for sex. The sting was incredibly successful, as they always are. There seems to be an inexhaustible number of male adults who go into chat rooms and other online forums, looking for minors with whom to have sex.[74] Officer Jones and the other officer with whom he worked would take turns logging into likely chat rooms or other Web sites and pretending to be a girl who was, say, 13 or 14 years old. Officers tell me that once they do this, the "girl" is bombarded with messages from what are apparently adult men, who want to eventually set up a meeting to have sex with the girl. In this sting, as in others, officers would be waiting at the motel or other place where the "girl" arranged to meet a particular man, and they would arrest him when he appeared. The usual charge for this kind of conduct is soliciting a minor for sex or luring a child for the purposes of sex.[75] The cases are ridiculously easy to prosecute because the officers have a record of the conversation between the "girl" and the defendant. As a result, most of the men caught in these stings plead guilty rather quickly.

After they had been operating the sting for a year or so, Officer Jones ran into a police officer from a nearby city, which had a much larger police department. The other officer was (we'll say) Officer Smith, who was in charge of the Sex Crimes Unit of the city police department. The Sex Crimes Unit handled crimes against minors, among other things. Officer Jones said he told Officer Smith about the sting he and the other officer were running in the county seat, and he offered to show Officer Smith how to have his officers start their own version of the sting. According to Officer Jones, Officer Smith turned him down, saying "I have people being hurt in the real world. I don't have time to fool around with that online stuff."

Officer Jones was astonished and appalled at Officer Smith's reaction, but I think I understand it. If you were Officer Smith and your department was struggling to deal with the always tragic and often horrifying sexual victimization occurring in your city, would you want to divert part of your scarce resources to an online sting? Many—such as, presumably, Officer Smith—do not believe these stings accomplish very much in the way of crime control. They argue, with some justification, that there is reason to believe these men pose a small risk of actual danger to minors because most minors avoid the sites they frequent, and those who do visit them generally tend not to set up meetings with strange men. Others quite justifiably point out that the men in these stings do everything they can to have sex with a minor, which shows that they are, or can be, dangerous to children. I do not know which side is right, but I suspect I would have the same reaction as Officer Smith. On the one hand, I have actual victimization; on the other hand, I have the manufacture of what is essentially fictive victimization. If I could pursue both, I probably would, but I cannot. Similar to Officer Smith, then, I think I would opt for focusing my resources on the harms being inflicted in the real world.

Officer Smith's reaction is quite justifiable, especially in this context. The calculus becomes much more difficult if we consider other types of cybercrime, particularly the financial cybercrime that saps millions, perhaps billions, of dollars from financial institutions and online businesses.[76] Although financial losses of any magnitude cannot compare in severity to physically harming a human being, they cannot be dismissed either. As we will see in the next chapter, the way we control crime is to discourage people from committing it; the way we discourage people from committing crime is to apprehend, convict, and punish them. If criminals know they have little, if any, chance of being caught, they essentially have no reason not to commit crimes. If they can make money by committing crimes, they have a strong incentive to break the law.

We do a good job of controlling crime of all kinds in the real world, but we are doing a terrible job of controlling crime in the online world. The lack of resources for law enforcement officers and prosecutors is one of the factors that contribute to our lack of success in dealing with cybercrime, but it is far from the only factor. Indeed, there is no one factor, and no one person or entity, that is to blame for our failure in this regard. As we will see in the next chapter, our inability to combat cybercrime is primarily a function of the fact that our world has changed in ways that may require us to revise how we approach law enforcement and prosecution.

Global Law Enforcement: Few Agencies, Even More Challenges

INTRODUCTION

In Chapter 9, as in earlier chapters, we have seen that cybercrime creates new challenges for law enforcement. To understand why those challenges arise and how we can address them, it is necessary to understand the origins and structure of the system we currently use to enforce criminal law. To do that, we need to understand why we have criminal law and why we use professional police officers to enforce it. As we will see, although criminal law has always been an aspect of human society, that is not true of the police.

THE NEED FOR ORDER

Humans are social animals. We can live alone, but as a species, we prefer to live with others of our kind. Humans, therefore, have always lived in groups that have evolved in complexity over the millennia. Tribes evolved into city-states; city-states evolved into empires; and empires eventually evolved into the nation-states that dominate our world.[1] Each of these entities was a society; that is, each was a more or less complex socioeconomic infrastructure composed of individuals who were bound by social, cultural, and economic ties. Similar to other social animals, humans congregate in societies because organized social life helps to ensure our survival as individuals and as a species. In our societies, we divide the tasks that are essential for our survival —providing food and shelter, fending off danger from other societies, and ensuring the birth, survival, and education of children—in ways that enable us to carry out those tasks more efficiently and effectively.

Therefore, societies must ensure their citizens are willing and able to carry out these and other essential tasks. To do that, societies must maintain order, both internally and externally. As I have already noted, they maintain external order primarily by fending off threats from other societies.[2] For millenia, societies have relied on special cadres of their citizens—the military—to deal with other societies. The military—armies, navies, and now air forces—is responsible for ensuring that a society is not susceptible to threats from "outside." Viable, stable societies require an environment in which the external threats have been either nullified or controlled. Such an environment is essential for the society to concentrate its resources on fulfilling the tasks that are essential for it to survive and prosper.

Our concern, though, is with "inside" threats—the need to maintain internal order. We have not explicitly dealt with this issue, but the need to maintain internal order has been implicit in our review of cybercrime. A society must maintain internal order if it is to endure. "Order" refers to the need to coordinate activities among the citizens of a society in a way that ensures the satisfactory performance of the functions previously noted , which are necessary for the survival of both the society and its citizens. Societies use two types of rules—civil and criminal—to maintain order. A civil rule specifies which actions are allowable and which are not. Civil rules define the structure of a society by defining the relationships that exist among the individuals who make up that society (e.g., employer-employee, wife-husband, priest-parishioner). Civil rules also allocate tasks among the members of the society and ensure that the tasks are performed.

Until recently, societies were bounded systems located in a specific area and composed of a defined populace (e.g., the people of Rome, the American public). Spatial and population constraints facilitate the operation of the civil rules because spatial and demographic isolation make it easier to socialize the members of a society so most accept and abide by its civil rules. In other words, the people who live in a society understand and accept the rules that apply in that society; most of them will not be familiar with the rules that exist elsewhere. Therefore, they will tend to accept the rules of their society as valid. Most of us, for example, know how we are expected to behave in various situations and conform our behavior to those expectations. We want to avoid the social disapproval we would incur if we violated those expectations.

Spatial and demographic constraints also make it easier to identify and suppress those who do not voluntarily abide by the civil rules. Societies cannot simply rely on civil rules to maintain order because humans are intelligent and can deliberately violate rules. Societies therefore use another set of rules—criminal rules—to rigorously discourage us from intentionally violating the rules that sustain order in our society. The goal here is not to ensure the performance of tasks that are essential for the survival of the society and its citizens; it is to prevent members of a society from preying on each other in ways that will lead to chaos. If the strong can rob, rape, and murder the weak as they please, the society will not be able to ensure that the functions essential for its survival and that of its citizens will be carried out in an effective fashion. It will have become a failed state, such as Somalia.[3]

Because a society must avoid this state of affairs or perish, societies use special rules and special sanctions in an effort to discourage serious rule violations. Criminal rules consequently impose criminal liability and severe sanctions—such as imprisonment or death—on those who deliberately do not abide by civil rules. Criminal rules are based on the assumption that sanctioning intentional rule violators helps to maintain order by discouraging future violations. This assumption incorporates two other assumptions: (1) sanctions deter violations by presenting us with a simple choice of "obey the rules or suffer the consequences," and (2) rule violators will be identified, apprehended, and sanctioned.

The first assumption seems to be valid, or valid enough; punishing those who violate rules seems a reasonably effective way of maintaining order in a society. The second assumption, though, can be problematic. Under that assumption, if criminal rules are to maintain order, there must be some system in place that ensures that rule violators are identified, apprehended, and sanctioned. In other words, there must be a credible threat of retaliation for violating criminal rules. Absent such a threat, they cannot effectively discourage deviance and maintain order.

KEEPING ORDER

For most of human history, societies relied on ad hoc means, particularly citizen enforcement, to maintain this threat of retaliation. The particular means on which societies relied depended on their level of organizational development. Early human tribes relied on "communal, collective security efforts."[4] As human social systems became larger and more complex, they tended to institutionalize this function. Egypt had an "early system of citizen police" by 1500 B.C. The ancient Greeks used a "system of 'kin policing,'" and the ancient Romans used civilian patrols and military forces to maintain internal order.[5]

The disintegration of the Roman Empire plunged Europe into chaos. Societies that had relied on the Romans resorted to older measures to maintain order. In what would become England, people relied on the "tything sytem" to control crime. Every male over the age of 12 was required to participate in a tything, which was a group of 10 families led by a tythingman. Each tythingman was responsible for raising the "hue and cry" when a crime was committed. The hue and cry summoned the male members of his tything to pursue the criminal. If the members of a tything failed to catch a fleeing criminal, the tything could be fined.[6] Each tything belonged to a group of 10 tythings, which was ultimately responsible to the shire-reeve (later sheriff) of that county.[7] When the Normans conquered England in 1066, they kept this system in place but expanded the role of the shire-reeve. Under the Norman system, the shire-reeve could summon "the tythingmen . . . of several hundred tythings" to respond to a hue and cry.[8]

A statute adopted in 1285 created watch patrols in the large towns of England that operated between sunset and dawn. All males between 15 and 60 served on the patrols, which were responsible for protecting property from fire, guarding the town gates, and apprehending anyone who committed a crime. If a watchman raised the hue and cry; the able-bodied males in the community were required to join the hunt for the criminal. Anyone who did not participate in the watch or join the hue and cry would be punished. The statute also "required every man between the ages of fifteen and sixty to maintain specified weaponry, which varied according to his wealth."[9]

This system was used in England for nearly 500 years and was brought to America by the English colonists.[10] It was effective for a time but eroded over the years. As men became more prosperous, they hired substitutes to serve in their place. Because they tended to prefer cheap substitutes, the watches were often staffed by men who were "too old to be of any value," which led to an increase in crime.[11] The rise in crime was exacerbated by the Industrial Revolution, which caused "a vast migration to urban areas" and created a concomitant need for better law enforcement.[12] Over the next few decades, London authorities experimented with using civic associations and private police to control crime, but none of the efforts was successful. During the same era, American cities were experiencing similar problems and trying similar solutions, again with little success.[13]

Modern policing emerged in 1829 when Sir Robert Peel created the London Metropolitan Police.[14] The Metropolitan Police was something new: an independent agency staffed by full-time, uniformed professionals whose sole task was to maintain order by reacting to crimes and apprehending perpetrators.[15] Peel's model spread across England, and by 1860, full-time police "had become standard in all large American cities."[16] This professional policing model eventually spread around the world and is the approach all modern societies use to control crime.[17]

REAL-WORLD CRIME AND THE LAW ENFORCEMENT MODEL

Because it was created to maintain order in a world in which the only crime was real-world crime, the professional policing model that began with Peel's Metropolitan Police assumes real-world crime. Real-world crime has four distinct characteristics that shaped the professional policing model of law enforcement. This section examines those characteristics and the impact of each on the professional policing model. The next section analyzes the extent to which cybercrime shares these characteristics.

The four characteristics of real-world crime are proximity, scale, physical constraints, and patterns. They all derive from the fact that real-world crime is committed in a tangible, physical environment.

Proximity is perhaps the most fundamental characteristic of real-world crime. In the physical world, the perpetrator and victim are necessarily physically proximate to each other when the perpetrator commits the crime. It is simply not possible to rape someone if the rapist and the victim are 50 miles apart. In a nontechnological world, it is physically impossible to pick someone's pocket, rob them, or defraud them out of their property if the thief and victim are in different cities, different states, or different countries. In real-world crimes, therefore, the victim and perpetrator are simultaneously present in a specific physical place when the crime is committed.

Scale is another important characteristic. Real-world crime tends to be one-to-one crime; that is, it involves one perpetrator and one victim. A crime begins when the victimization of the target begins, and it ends when it is finished. During the event, the perpetrator focuses all of his or her attention on consummating that crime. When it is complete, he or she can move to another crime and another victim. Similar to proximity, the one-to-one character of real-world crime derives from the physical constraints that reality imposes on human activity. A thief cannot pick more than one pocket at a time; a forger cannot forge more than one document at a time; and prior to the rise of firearms, it was very difficult for one to cause the simultaneous deaths of more than one person. Therefore, real-world crime tends to be serial crime.[18]

Real-world crime is also subject to the physical constraints that govern all activity in the real world. Every crime—even street-level drug-dealing or prostitution—requires a level of preparation, planning, and implementation if it is to succeed. A bank robber must visit the bank to familiarize himself or herself with its layout, security, and routine. This exposes the robber to public scrutiny, which can lead to him or her being identified and apprehended. While in the bank, the robber leaves trace evidence and is subject to observations that can result in him or her being identified and apprehended. As the robber flees after committing the robbery, he or she is again exposed to public view and again risks being identified and apprehended. In addition to taking these obvious risks, the robber probably had to secure a gun and a disguise before the robbery and probably needed help to dispose of the cash afterward. Each step takes time and effort and incrementally increases the risks involved in committing this or any other crime.

Patterns, the fourth and final characteristic of real-world crime, goes not to the commission of *a* crime, but to our ability to track *crimes*. For years, law enforcement experts have been able to identify the contours and incidence of the real-world crimes committed in a society. Victimization tends to fall into demographic and geographic patterns for two reasons. One reason is that only a small segment of a society's populace will persistently engage in criminal activity. Those who fall into this category are apt to be from economically deprived backgrounds and to reside in areas that share geographic and demographic characteristics. They will be inclined to focus their efforts on those with whom they share a level of physical proximity because they are convenient victims. Consequently, much of a society's routine crime will be concentrated in identifiable areas. The other reason why crimes fall into patterns is that each society has a repertoire of crimes—rules that outlaw behaviors ranging from more to less serious in terms of the harm each inflicts. Rape, for example, produces the harm of nonconsensual sexual intercourse. Theft results in a loss of property, murder results in a loss of life, and so on. More egregious crimes (e.g., murder, rape, arson) will occur much less often and much less predictably in societies that are successfully maintaining internal order than minor crimes. Murder, for example, is an extraordinary event in any society that is successfully maintaining internal order, but theft will be a much less extraordinary event, as will be "victimless" crimes such as drunkenness or prostitution.

These characteristics combined to shape the crime control strategy outlined in the preceding paragraphs. Proximity contributed a presumed dynamic. The victim and perpetrator are in physical proximity while the crime is committed; the perpetrator will then attempt to flee the scene and avoid being caught; the police will investigate the crime; and the perpetrator eventually will be identified and caught (usually). This dynamic originated in an era when crime was parochial, when victims and perpetrators tended to live in the same village or neighborhood. If a victim and perpetrator did not know each other, they probably shared community ties that made it possible to identify the perpetrator and apprehend him. There was a good chance he could be identified by witnesses or reputation. If a perpetrator and a victim did not share community ties (i.e., that is, if he was a stranger), this would likely contribute to his being arrested because he would "stand out" as someone who did not belong. Law enforcement dealt effectively with this type of crime because its spatial limitations meant investigations were limited in scope. If one of Peel's bobbies was investigating a murder, he could assume the perpetrator was from London and probably from the area of London in which the murder was committed. This quite logical focus on where a crime was committed persists. The law enforcement model in use today still assumes that the investigation of a crime should focus on the physical scene of the crime.

The model also assumes one-to-one victimization. and that along with another assumption gives rise to the premise that the amount of crime will be limited in a functioning society. The other assumption is that crimes are extraordinary events—that law-abiding conduct is the norm, and crime is unusual. This assumption derives not from the characteristics of real-world crime but from the need to maintain order. A society's civil and criminal rules work together to achieve this. The civil rules define the acceptable behaviors that are encouraged, and the criminal rules emphasize that certain behaviors will definitely not be tolerated. Individuals are socialized to accept the civil rules as prescribing the "correct" standards of behavior, and most conform to those expectations. Criminal rules reinforce this by emphasizing that the behaviors they condemn are not only "bad," they are outside the norm, unusual, and extraordinary. The combined effect of both sets of rules is that crime becomes extraordinary. In a functioning society, crime is usually a small subset of the total behaviors in that society, and that has implications for the efficacy of the professional policing model of law enforcement. The limited incidence of criminal behavior, coupled with one-to-one victimization as the default crime mode, means law enforcement officers can focus their efforts on a limited segment of the conduct within a given society. Crime, in other words, is manageable.

Finally, the law enforcement model incorporates the premise that crime falls into patterns. It assumes that crime will be limited in incidence and in the types of harms it inflicts. The model also assumes that an identifiable percentage of crime will occur in geographically and demographically demarcated areas. The combined effects of localized crime and the differential frequency with which various crimes are committed gives law enforcement the ability to concentrate its resources in areas where crime is most likely to occur, which enhances its ability to react to completed crimes. In other words, law enforcement can allocate its limited resources effectively.

CYBERCRIME AND THE LAW ENFORCEMENT MODEL

As we have seen, cybercrime does not require physical proximity between the victim and the perpetrator. Cybercrime is unbounded crime; the victim and perpetrator can be in different cities, different states, or different countries.[19] All a cybercriminal needs is a computer linked to the Internet. With this, he can attack a victim's computer, defraud someone, or commit any of a host of cybercrimes.

Cybercrime can, but does not necessarily, involve one-to-one victimization. Cybercrime is automated crime. With automation, perpetrators can commit thousands of crimes quickly and with little effort. One-to-many victimization, which is basically unheard of in the real world, is common in cybercrime, and that has important consequences for the current model of law enforcement. In that current model, police officers react to a crime by investigating a physical crime scene and finding evidence that enables them catch the perpetrator. The model assumes crime is committed on a scale that is limited enough for officers react effectively to individual crimes. Cybercrime violates this assumption in two ways. Although cybercrime is carried out by a small percentage of the population of a society (or the world, because cybercrime tends to ignore boundaries), this small group can commit crimes on a scale far surpassing what they could achieve in the real world, where one-to-one victimization and serial crimes are the norm. As a result, the number of cybercrimes will vastly exceed the number of real-world crimes, which erodes law enforcement's ability to react effectively to individual crimes. This erosion is exacerbated by another factor. As we saw in Chapter 9, cybercrime does not displace real-world crime; it is added to the real-world crimes that still occur with routine frequency. So far, cybercrime has not altered people's inclination to rape, rob, or kill in the real world. The combined effect of these two factors creates an overload. Law enforcement's ability to react to cybercrime erodes because the resources that are minimally adequate to deal with real-world crime are inadequate to deal with cybercrime plus real-world crime.

Cybercriminals also avoid the physical constraints that govern real-world crime. As we have seen, a cybercriminal can extract funds from a U.S. bank account and move them into offshore accounts with little effort and less visibility. The professional policing model, which is predicated on law enforcement reacting effectively to a crime, is far less effective against online crime because the police reaction usually begins well after the cybercrime has been successfully concluded. The trail, such as it is, is cold. Another problem is that because most or all of the conduct involved in committing the crime occurs in an electronic environment, the evidence is fragile and volatile. By the time police do react, some or all of the evidence may have been destroyed. Because cybercriminals are not physically present at the crime "scene," the assumption that they will have been observed while preparing for, committing, or fleeing from the crime is not valid. Indeed, officers may not be able to determine the location from which the perpetrator carried out the crime or who he is. Unlike their real-world counterparts, cybercriminals often remain anonymous. Even if police officers can identify a cybercriminal, gathering evidence and apprehending that criminal can be difficult, as we saw earlier, because the country that has the criminal may refuse to extradite him or her.[20]

Finally, we cannot identify offender-offense patterns comparable to those for real-world crime. This makes it difficult for law enforcement agencies to allocate their already-scarce resources effectively.[21] There are several reasons why we cannot identify cybercrime patterns:[22] One reason is that cybercrime is not well documented. Even if agencies track cybercrimes, they tend not to break them out into a separate category. For example, online fraud is often included in the general category of fraud. Another reason is that it can be difficult to parse cybercrime into discrete offenses. One example is a virus that causes billions of dollars of damage in more than 20 countries. Is that one crime (one virus), thousands of crimes (thousands of victims), or billions of crimes (billions of dollars lost)? Clearly, though, the most important reason is that we simply do not have accurate cybercrime statistics. We do not have accurate statistics because many cybercrimes go undetected, and many cybercrimes that are detected are not reported.[23] Cybercrime goes undetected for many reasons, two of which are that the security systems in place cannot detect them or that they are committed by trusted insiders who know how to hide their tracks.[24] As to reporting cybercrimes, commercial victims, at least, are not inclined to admit they have been attacked by a cybercriminal. For good reasons, they prefer not to reveal their vulnerability to their customers and shareholders.[25] Research shows there is yet another reason why victims, especially corporate victims, do not report cybercrime.

They do not report being victimized because they do not believe law enforcement will be able to apprehend the persons responsible.[26]

ASSESSMENT

We have a nineteenth-century law enforcement model and twenty-first century crime. The nineteenth-century model is problematic when it comes to cybercrime for the reasons already given and for another reason. It implicitly assumes crime is committed *in* a society—within a particular nation-state. That was true until relatively recently. Crime *was* committed within the territory of a nation-state. The functional requirement of physical proximity between the offender and the victim, coupled with the physical constraints of the real world, make that the default for traditional crime. Law enforcement is the responsibility of nation-states; it is a function of a nation-state's interest in maintaining order inside the territory it controls.

As we have seen, cybercrime can be domestic—the perpetrator and the victim can be in the same nation-state—but it does not have to be. Territorial constraints are irrelevant in cyberspace. It is as easy for a cybercriminal to target a victim halfway around the globe as it is to target the person next door.

Although the perpetrator's and victim's respective physical locations are irrelevant to the operational aspects of cybercrime, another factor—income disparity—encourages cybercriminals to target victims in other countries. Many of those who commit financial cybercrimes (e.g., extortion, identity theft, fraud) are from poorer countries where the standard of living is lower than in countries such as the United States. The Willie Sutton effect—criminals "go where the money is"—comes into play here, as in the real world. In the real world, of course, bank robbers such as Willie Sutton necessarily target their fellow citizens. In the cyberworld, they can easily prey on citizens from other, more affluent countries.

As a result, much of cybercrime is transnational cybercrime. As we saw in earlier chapters, it is very difficult for nation-states to deal effectively with crime that crosses national borders. Today's cybercriminals are replicating Bonnie and Clyde's manipulation of state borders[27] on a grander and more elusive scale. Instead of using an automobile to flee from one U.S. state to another, they use the borderless ambiguities of cyberspace to evade national police.

As we saw in the last chapter, the United States dealt with the Bonnie and Clyde problem by expanding federal law, which applies throughout all U.S. territory. Fleeing from Texas into Oklahoma is useless when the criminals are being pursued by federal law enforcement agents because those agents' jurisdiction is national. Logically, it seems a similar strategy should work for transnational cybercrime; that is, it seems a system of global law enforcement —the World Cybercrime Police—would be the optimum way to deal with transnational cybercrime. However, as we will see in the next section, although there are international efforts to combat cybercrime, a system of global enforcement is not a viable possibility, at least not for the foreseeable future.

GLOBAL INITIATIVES

A number of organizations are—and have been—trying to develop solutions for transnational cybercrime.[28] The efforts began in Europe. In 1983, the Organisation for Economic Co-operation and Development (OECD)[29] organized a group of experts who met to discuss the legal issues posed by transnational cybercrime. Based on the results of that meeting, the OECD commissioned a two-year study focusing on the possibility of harmonizing and internationalizing national cybercrime laws. In 1986, the OECD issued a report that summarized the results of the study. It surveyed existing cybercrime laws and recommended a set of offenses all countries should criminalize. The approach the OECD took in this initiative is the same approach that has been taken by other European efforts: combat transnational cybercrime by ensuring that as many nations as possible outlaw a basic set of cybercrimes. The OECD followed this report with a series of other efforts, all of which were designed to support this approach.

In 1985, the Council of Europe convened its own panel of experts, who spent four years studying the legal issues raised by transnational cybercrime. In 1989, they issued a recommendation (Recommendation 89[9]) that emphasized the need to ensure that countries around the world criminalized a basic set of offenses. The set of offenses the Council of Europe experts identified was similar to the offenses the OECD experts identified in their report. In 1995, the Council of Europe issued a recommendation to its member states that focused on the legal issues involved in investigating cybercrime. In 1997, the Council of Europe convened another group of experts and assigned them the task of drafting a cybercrime treaty that would harmonize national laws dealing with cybercrime offenses and investigations. In 2001, this effort produced a treaty known as the Convention on Cybercrime. We will examine the Convention on Cybercrime in Chapter 12, when we evaluate the various solutions that have been proposed for dealing with cybercrime.

In 1990, the United Nations adopted a resolution inviting governments to be guided by policies developed at a UN conference held earlier that year. The resolution called for UN member states to ensure that their criminal laws were adequate to deal with cybercrime. The United Nations followed this resolution with a cybercrime manual issued in 1995. It examined the general phenomenon of cybercrime, the law needed to control it, and the need for international cooperation in combating it. More recently, the United Nations has delegated the task of dealing with cybercrime to one of its agencies known as the International Telecommunications Union (ITU).[30] The ITU is a UN agency that is responsible for dealing with information and communication technology issues.[31] Similar to the OECD and the Council of Europe, the ITU focuses on the need for countries to have adequate, consistent cybercrime laws.

The theory underlying these and other similar efforts is that if countries adopt adequate, consistent cybercrime laws, it will become easier to conduct transnational cybercrime investigations and easier to have a cybercriminal extradited for prosecution. The G8 states have supported this approach in their statements and declarations on cybercrime.[32] (The Group of 8, or G8, is composed of Canada, France, Germany, Italy, Japan, Russia, the United Kingdom, and the United States and serves as a forum in which the member countries can discuss issues of mutual concern.) The same is true of the Asia Pacific Economic Cooperation (APEC), the Organization of American States, the League of Arab States, and other organizations.[33] Currently, there is no initiative that seeks to create a global cybercrime law enforcement agency. The assumption is that cybercrime is best handled by individual countries, each of which has adopted laws that allow it to prosecute cybercriminals and to cooperate with other countries in investigating cybercrimes and apprehending those who perpetrate them. In other words, the nations of the world tacitly assume that the best approach for dealing with cybercrime is the approach we use for crime, with some legislative improvements.

INTERPOL, the international police organization, has its own cybercrime initiative, but it, too, focuses on supporting law enforcement at the national level. Interpol's mission is to facilitate "cross-border police co-operation," and to that end, it "supports and assists all organizations . . . whose mission is to . . . combat international crime."[34] Interpol primarily acts as a resource for officers investigating cybercrimes by helping them obtain evidence and other information from abroad.[35] It also has regional cybercrime working groups that train officers from different countries in the processes of investigating cybercrime.[36] Although it makes useful contributions in this and other regards, INTERPOL does not have the resources to become a global cybercrime policing force.

Because the global efforts to deal with transnational cybercrime focus entirely on harmonizing national laws to facilitate cooperation among national police agencies, there is little, if any, likelihood that a World Cybercrime Police agency will be created in the foreseeable future. The strategy the United States used to deal with the Bonnie and Clyde phenomenon is a perfectly logical way to deal with transnational cybercrime, but in this context, it founders on a critical difference between the countries of the world and the states in a federal system the United States.

Each U.S. state is a sovereign in its own right, but it is also a subordinate entity in a larger federal system; therefore, as long as the federal government does not exceed constitutional limits on its authority, it can exercise authority over what have traditionally been matters of purely state concern.[37] The Bonnie and Clyde strategy works because the states and the federal government are all part of a single system. It does not work at the global level because each nation-state is an independent sovereignty. There is no larger, comprehensive system, and there is unlikely to be one.

Nation-states are protective of their sovereignty and therefore are unlikely to surrender any quantum of their authority to maintain order in their territory by agreeing to the creation of a World Cybercrime Police. Because such an agency would take jurisdiction over cybercrimes committed by and against the citizens of the various nation-states, it would deprive the nation-states of a portion of their sovereignty. The countries of the world are not prepared to do this, and I suspect that most of us are not prepared for it either. Although I see the tactical advantages of the global policing approach, I would have serious concerns about becoming subject to the authority not only of the U.S. local and federal police, but also to the authority of a police agency that is not part of my country. I suspect the citizens of other countries would have the same reservations, as well.

Because global policing is simply not a viable option now and for the foreseeable future, we are left with the national policing model as our only approach to cybercrime. This means cybercrime investigations will continue to be undertaken by the thousands, perhaps millions, of law enforcement agencies operating under the authority of the 195 countries of the world.[38] It also means that cybercrime investigations will continue to be plagued by the jurisdictional and other parochial issues that constitute the twenty-first-century version of the Bonnie and Clyde phenomenon. Many believe the efforts to encourage countries to adopt consistent cybercrime laws will resolve these problems. I do not. We will return to this issue in Chapter 12, where we examine the viability of this and other proposals for improving the enforcement of cybercrime law.

First, we need to consider a related issue: the inherent tension between policing and individual privacy. We take up that topic in the next chapter.

Privacy versus Security:
Which Trumps?

INTRODUCTION

There is an inherent tension between policing and privacy. As we saw in the
last chapter, police are charged with investigating crimes that have already
been committed, identifying the perpetrator(s), and apprehending him,
her, or them. As we also saw, an effective law enforcement reaction to completed crimes is essential to discourage enough people from committing
crimes that a society is able to maintain the level of internal order it needs
to survive and prosper. The need for an effective law enforcement reaction
also encompasses a related task: preventing crimes from being committed.
Police also work to identify crimes that are in the planning and preparation
stages so they can interrupt the would-be criminals before those criminals
can inflict actual harm on someone or something.[1]

Both of these tasks are based on the police's ability to collect information
about crimes that have been committed and crimes that will be committed.
As a society, we want our police to collect information and solve or prevent
as many crimes as possible. However, we also want them to stay within certain limits as they collect this information. We do not want the police to be
able to violate individual privacy, at least not unless they comply with certain
legal requirements. These requirements are intended to resolve the tension
between policing and privacy by allowing the police obtain information

when they can demonstrate a compelling need for it and by preventing the police from intruding into our privacy when they cannot demonstrate such a need.

This chapter examines the requirements U.S. law imposes on police in their efforts to collect the evidence of a crime. As we will see, these requirements come into play only when the police's investigatory efforts intrude or threaten to intrude on an area or an activity that is legally defined as "private." Our law, similar to that of other countries, is not concerned with regulating police conduct that is designed to obtain information that is public or is in a public area.

The United States is a very large, very complex nation-state. It encompasses a substantial geographical area and has a population of more than 300 million people.[2] It is also organizationally complex. As we saw in Chapter 9, the United States has a number of federal police agencies and more than 17,000 state and local police agencies. Because the United States is a federal system, there are federal laws plus a distinct set of laws for each of the 50 states plus the District of Columbia and five U.S. territories.[3]

If the laws adopted by each of the states and territories could trump the laws of the federal government and the laws of the other states and territories, the United States would descend into a state of legal cacophony. It would be nothing more than a loose confederation of independent sovereign states. As we saw in Chapter 9, that describes the United States under the Articles of Confederation, but the Constitution changed that.

Article VI of the Constitution declares that

[t]his constitution and the laws of the United States which shall be made in pursuance thereof . . . shall be the supreme law of the land; and the judges in every state shall be bound thereby, any thing in the constitution or laws of any state to the contrary notwithstanding.[4]

The Constitution also makes it clear that the federal government is to respect the states and the laws they adopt. The Tenth Amendment says the "powers not delegated to the United States by the Constitution, nor prohibited by it to the States, are reserved to the States." And Article IV of the Constitution says that each state is to give "full faith and credit" to the "public acts, records and judicial proceedings of every other state."[5]

Therefore, states can adopt their own laws as long as those laws do not infringe on the powers reserved for the federal government. Likewise, the federal government can adopt laws as long as those laws do not infringe on powers reserved to the states. This system has certain consequences for laws that define the privacy of U.S. citizens: As long as those laws are implementing provisions of the U.S. Constitution, including the amendments that have been added to it, they are valid because the constitution is the "supreme law of the land." This is true regardless of whether the laws in question are adopted by the federal government or by a state.

The federal government can adopt only those laws that are authorized either by the explicit language of the Constitution or by powers the Constitution delegates to the federal government. On the other hand, the states can adopt laws that go beyond the provisions of the Constitution, as long as they do not conflict with those provisions or are otherwise illegal. For example, a state could not adopt a law reestablishing slavery because the Thirteenth Amendment to the Constitution abolished slavery "within the United States or any place subject to" its jurisdiction. However, states can adopt laws that legalize gay marriage because marriage is not a matter the Constitution delegates to the federal government; therefore, marriage is an issue reserved for state law under the Tenth Amendment.[6]

That brings us back to privacy: The Constitution does not address the issue of privacy, but two of its amendments do. As we will see in the next section, the Fourth Amendment directly addresses police invasions of privacy. As we will see later in this chapter, the Fifth Amendment addresses privacy indirectly by giving us a privilege not to cooperate with law enforcement evidence-gathering under certain circumstances.

Our review of the limits U.S. law places on police intrusions into private places and private activities will focus almost exclusively on these two provisions for several reasons, the most obvious of which is that they are the only constitutional provisions to deal with privacy. There are also federal and state statutes that deal with privacy, but we will consider them only briefly, for two reasons.

One reason is that these statutes either implement the Fourth Amendment and Fifth Amendment, which means reviewing them would be superfluous, or they are state laws that provide citizens with more protection than either or both amendments. State statutes that provide more protection than the Fourth and/or Fifth Amendments apply only to police conduct that occurs in the state that has adopted such a law. Therefore, these state statutes are of limited applicability. More importantly, these statutes are enforceable only against law enforcement officers who are employed by that state; they do not apply to federal law enforcement officers or to law enforcement officers from other states.

The other reason we will focus primarily on constitutional provisions and only incidentally on state and federal privacy statutes is that statutes are much more fragile than constitutional provisions. It is not particularly difficult for Congress or for a state legislature to modify or even repeal a statute it adopted at some earlier time. Statutory law is inevitably unstable, in greater or lesser degrees. A statute is in effect only unless and until the legislature that adopted the statute decides to change it or eliminate it.

On the other hand, it is very difficult to modify the U.S. Constitution. The only way to modify it is by amending it (i.e., by adding to it), and amendment is far from easy. Under Article V of the Constitution, there are two ways it can be amended.[7] One way is for two-thirds of both Houses of Congress to propose an amendment; the other way is for the legislatures of two-thirds of the states to ask Congress to convene a Constitutional Convention for the purpose of considering an amendment.[8] Once an amendment has been proposed by either means, it does not become part of the Constitution until it has been ratified by at least three-quarters of the U.S. states.[9] All the amendments that have been proposed so far came from Congress; the second method has never been used.[10]

The amendments we will examine are both part of the Bill of Rights, a set of 10 amendments that went into effect in 1791, after they were ratified by three-quarters of the states that then existed.[11] The Bill of Rights was added to the Constitution because some of those involved in drafting the Constitution feared the strong federal government it creates might become a threat to individual rights. The Bill of Rights was intended to emphasize that the rights it addresses are protected under the U.S. Constitution and therefore are binding on both the state and federal governments.

FOURTH AMENDMENT: BACKGROUND

The Fourth Amendment provides as follows: "The right of the people to be secure in their persons, houses, papers, and effects, against unreasonable searches and seizures, shall not be violated, and no Warrants shall issue, but upon probable cause, supported by Oath or affirmation, and particularly describing the place to be searched, and the persons or things to be seized." In the first section that follows, we will examine the evil the Fourth Amendment was originally intended to address. In the next two sections after that, we will examine how the Fourth Amendment has been—and should be— applied to technology that did not exist when it was adopted.

As is the case with much of our law, the Fourth Amendment derives from English common law. Early common law punished "those who invaded a neighbor's premises,"[12] and by the sixteenth-century, English law criminalized burglary and trespass.[13] These laws were directed at private citizens because law enforcement searches of private property were almost unknown until the fifteenth century.[14] In the late fifteenth century, the king and Parliament began authorizing guilds to search property as a way of enforcing guild regulations.[15] Roughly a century later, the Court of the Star Chamber, which regulated printing, "decreed that the wardens of the Stationers' Company" had "authority to . . . search in any warehouse, shop, or any other place where they suspected a violation of the laws of printing to be taking place [and] seize the books printed contrary to law."[16] Other courts issued similar edicts authorizing searches targeting those suspected of heresy and political dissent.[17] This led to the evolution of the general warrant, which issued with no proof of individualized suspicion and in which no "names are specified . . . and . . . a discretionary power given to messengers to search wherever their suspicions may chance to fall."[18] As arbitrary searches became more common, "Englishmen began to insist that their houses were castles for the paradoxical reason that the castle-like security that those houses had afforded from intrusion was vanishing."[19]

In several cases from the mid-eighteenth century, English judges held that law enforcement officers could not arbitrarily search people's homes.[20] Most of the decisions resulted from an investigation into seditious libel.[21] Ordered to find the person who wrote a recently published seditious letter, officers armed with a general warrant searched five houses.[22] The people whose homes they searched sued the officers for trespass, and the British government defended them. To the delight of the British public, the plaintiffs won, and their verdicts were upheld on appeal.[23] Encouraged by their success, John Entick, the victim of a similar search, sued the officers who searched his home for trespass and won a verdict of £300.[24] The Court of Common Pleas upheld his verdict:

Our law holds the property of every man so sacred that no man can set his foot upon his neighbour's close without his leave. If he does, he is a trespasser. . . . The defendants have no right to avail themselves of the usage of these warrants. . . . We can safely say there is no law in this country to justify the defendants in what they have done; if there was, it would destroy all the comforts of society.[25]

The cases applied the same standard to private citizens and law enforcement officers. Either could be held civilly liable for trespass if he entered someone's property "without a lawful authority."[26] The difference was that a law enforcement officer could rely on a warrant, as well as on a property owner's consent, as authorization for an entry.[27]

During this era, the American colonists were waging their own war against writs of assistance, a variant of the general warrant.[28] The colonists challenged the writs in court but lost,[29] and the failure generated resentment that was a driving factor in the Revolution and in the adoption of the Bill of Rights.[30] The Fourth Amendment was a product of the same concerns that resulted in the law of trespass being applied to public actors: "to guard individuals against improper intrusion into their buildings where they had the exclusive right of possession."[31] It was meant to secure spatial privacy—to restrict law enforcement's ability to break down doors and rummage through rooms, boxes, chests, drawers, and so forth. Similar to its English analogue, the Fourth Amendment was meant to ensure that law enforcement officers could legitimately intrude into someone's private places only if they had a valid search warrant—one based on probable cause to believe this particular person was involved in specific criminal activity.

General warrants gave officers essentially unlimited discretion; they could search wherever they liked, as often as they liked. Fourth Amendment search warrants limit an officer's discretion by requiring "individualized suspicion." To search a person or place, an officer must be able to cite "specific, articulable facts" that indicate evidence of a crime will be found at that place or on that person.[32]

For more than a century, courts had little difficulty applying the provisions of the Fourth Amendment because the conduct in which law enforcement officers engaged was essentially indistinguishable from what British and American officers had been doing for centuries: searching places and people. Privacy was still a matter of places: the inside of a home, the bed of a horse-drawn cart, or the contents of someone's pockets. As we will see in the next section, privacy became much more problematic in the twentieth century as new technologies began to erode the linkage between privacy and a spatial area.

Before we take up modern technologies, I need to note an 1877 U.S. Supreme Court decision that dealt with an aspect of what I call portable privacy. The issue was whether items traveling through the U.S. mail are private under the Fourth Amendment.

The case is *Ex parte Jackson*.[33] It involved Mr. Jackson appealing his conviction for sending "a circular concerning a lottery" through the mail.[34] In 1876, Congress made it a federal crime to "deposit in the mails any letters or circulars concerning lotteries"; the legislation was prompted by concerns that honest citizens were being "swindled" by crooked lotteries.[35] Jackson argued that the statute criminalizing the use of the mail to send lottery materials was unconstitutional but lost on this issue. The Supreme Court held that Congress could prohibit the mail from being used to deliver certain types of material as long as the enforcement of the prohibitions complied with the Fourth Amendment:

[A] distinction is to be made between . . . what is intended to be kept free from inspection, such as letters, and sealed packages . . . and what is open to inspection, such as newspapers . . . and other printed matter, purposely left in a condition to be examined. Letters and sealed packages . . . are as fully guarded from . . . inspection, except as to their outward form and weight, *as if they were retained by the parties forwarding them in their own domiciles.*[36]

In the Jackson case, the Supreme Court took its first step toward portable privacy, that is, toward the principle that the Fourth Amendment does more than prevent police from breaking into our homes and searching them without a valid warrant. The court would return to this issue roughly 50 years later in a case involving telephones.

FOURTH AMENDMENT: TELEPHONES

Alexander Graham Bell invented the telephone in 1876. By 1877, there were more than 30,000 phones in use around the world; by 1886, more than 250,000 were in use.[37] By 1898, the Bell Telephone Company had installed one million telephones in the United States. The installation and use of telephones continued its rapid expansion over the next 20 years, and by the 1920s, telephones were a routine feature of life, even in many rural areas.[38]

Police quickly realized that eavesdropping on telephone calls could be useful in investigating crime. Wiretapping was not new. During the Civil War, the Union and Confederate armies tapped each other's telegraph lines to gain information about troop movements and battles.[39]

Police had begun tapping telephone conversations at least by the 1890s.[40] Law enforcement wiretapping continued for years and became the focus of a controversy in 1916, when the public learned the phone company had been helping the New York City Police eavesdrop on calls.[41] The police claimed there was nothing improper about this because at the time, people had to go through an operator to place calls: "Telephone conversations . . . cannot be private in the way that letters can be, since the employees of the telephone company cannot help hearing parts of conversations and may, if they are inclined, easily hear all."[42] Basically, the New York City Police—similar to other police departments—viewed operator-assisted phone calls as the oral equivalent of sending a postcard through the mail. Similar to a postcard, a telephone call placed through an operator was not, in fact, private.

By the 1920s, automatic switching systems had eliminated the need to rely on an operator to place a call.[43] With automated switching, we dial a number, and the phone company's technology connects the call, without human involvement. As automated switching became increasingly common, people began to assume phone calls were private, in the same way that sealed mail is private.[44] People therefore began to use phones more and more, and that brings us to Roy "Big Boy" Olmstead.

On January 16, 1920, the Eighteenth Amendment to the U.S. Constitution went into effect. Along with the National Prohibition Act, it outlawed the "manufacture, sale, transportation," and importation of "intoxicating liquors" in the United States.[45] Ironically, Prohibition gave rise to an increased demand for liquor in the United States, and a new profession arose: bootlegger. Everyone has heard of Al Capone, who made millions selling illegal alcohol, but almost no one knows about Roy "Big Boy" Olmstead, who would play an important role in shaping how the Fourth Amendment applies to telephone calls.

When Prohibition went into effect, Olmstead was a respected lieutenant in the Seattle Police Department.[46] As a police officer, Olmstead was involved in raids on the bootleggers, who cropped up almost as soon as Prohibition went into effect. He noted the bootleggers tended to have a lot of money and to get caught because their operations were not well organized. Attracted by the money, Olmstead decided to become a bootlegger and quickly became the head of a large, complex organization that smuggled alcohol into the United States from Canada. His gang operated unimpeded for four years because there were few Prohibition agents, and it was virtually impossible to catch smugglers in the Pacific Northwest: "There was too much border, too much water, and too many islands . . . to patrol effectively."[47]

By 1924, federal Prohibition agents were investigating what had become a very visible bootlegging operation that brought in $2 million a year at its peak.[48] In addition to using traditional investigative methods such as snitches, the Prohibition agents put wiretaps on a number of telephones being used by the Olmstead gang, including the telephone in Olmstead's home. Agents spent months listening to conversations between Olmstead and other members of his gang. They used what they had heard—and had transcribed by a stenographer—to get a warrant to search Olmstead's home. On November 24, 1924, they raided Olmstead's home and seized the organization's records." On January 25, Olmstead and 89others were indicted on two counts of violating federal Prohibition laws.

Olmstead went to trial and was convicted. He appealed a single issue all the way to the U.S. Supreme Court: "whether the use of evidence of private telephone conversations between [Olmstead] and others, intercepted by means of wire tapping, amounted to a violation of the" Fourth Amendment.[49] In its opinion, the Supreme Court described how the wiretapping was carried out:

Small wires were inserted along the . . . telephone wires from the residences of four [conspirators] and those leading from the chief office. The insertions were made without trespass upon any property of the defendants. They were made in the basement of the large office building. The taps from house lines were made in the streets near the houses.[50]

Olmstead argued that what the Prohibition agents did was a search because they listened in on conversations that occurred in private places: his home and those of three other members of his gang plus the office the gang used as its headquarters. Olmstead was arguing that the agents effectively did the same thing the British officers did when they searched Entick's home; they violated the sanctity of homes and another private place without having first obtained a search warrant.

Olmstead's argument may strike us as compelling, but most of the members of the court that heard his appeal were born and educated in the nineteenth century and therefore did not understand how technology can alter traditional conceptions of privacy. These Justices held that the use of technology was irrelevant because the "Fourth Amendment is to be construed in the light of what was deemed an unreasonable search . . . when it was adopted."[51] They went on to hold that because the Prohibition agents had not physically entered the homes or the office, there was no search:

[O]ne who installs in his house a telephone instrument with connecting wires intends to project his voice to those quite outside, and . . . the wires beyond his house, and messages while passing over them, are not within the protection of the Fourth Amendment. Here those who intercepted the projected voices were not in the house of either party to the conversation.

We think, therefore, that the wire tapping here . . . did not amount to a search . . . within the meaning of the Fourth Amendment.

Justice Louis Brandeis dissented. Similar to his colleagues, Brandeis was a product of the nineteenth century; unlike them, he was able to grasp the significance of this new technology. In his dissent, he wrote that when the Fourth Amendment was adopted, the only way the government could "secure possession of [the] papers and other articles incident to [someone's] private life" was by "breaking and entry" into the person's home or office.[52] He explained why the majority of the court was wrong when it insisted that the Fourth Amendment was set in stone, that is, was to be interpreted as if the world had not changed in the years since it was adopted:

[I]n the application of a Constitution, our contemplation cannot be only of what has been, but of what may be. The progress of science in furnishing the government with means of espionage is not likely to stop with wire tapping. Ways may . . . be developed by which the government, without removing papers from secret drawers, can reproduce them in court, and by which it will be enabled to expose . . . the most intimate occurrences of the home. . . . That places the liberty of every man in the hands of every petty officer.

Justice Brandeis would have applied the Fourth Amendment to the wiretapping in the Olmstead case, which would have meant the evidence would have been suppressed; unfortunately, he did not prevail. Olmstead went to jail and for the next almost 40 years, telephone conversations were not protected by the Fourth Amendment.

In 1965, the FBI was investigating Charles Katz, a bookie who operated in Los Angeles, for violating federal gambling law.[53] As the agents surveilled Katz, they realized he always used one of three phone booths in the 8200 block of Sunset Boulevard to make calls concerning bets; the agents put microphones and recording devices on the top of all three phone booths and spent a week intercepting and recording all the calls he made. The intercepted calls were used to convince a grand jury to indict Katz on federal gambling charges. They were also used to convict him of those charges at his trial.

Prior to trial, Katz moved to suppress the transcripts of the intercepted calls, arguing that the interceptions were illegal searches under the Fourth Amendment. Because the Olmstead court had held wiretapping was not a Fourth Amendment search, the FBI agents had not gotten a warrant before installing the microphones and recorders. The trial court denied Katz's motion, and the Ninth Circuit Court of Appeals upheld the denial. Similar to the majority of the Olmstead Justices, these judges all held that there was no search because the agents put the recording devices on the outside of the phone booths. Because the agents did not trespass into the phone booths when Katz was in them, these judges held that there had been no Fourth Amendment searches.

The Supreme Court agreed to hear Katz's appeal and reversed the decision of the lower courts. The Katz court began its opinion by noting that the lower courts' focus on whether there had been a trespass into a physical space focused on the wrong issue because "the Fourth Amendment protects people, not places."[54] It also explained that "[w]hat a person knowingly exposes to the public, even in his own home or office, is not a subject of Fourth Amendment protection, . . . but what he seeks to preserve as private, even in an area accessible to the public, may be constitutionally protected." In a concurring opinion, Justice Harlan explained how courts are to determine whether something is, in fact private, under the Fourth Amendment:

[T[here is a twofold requirement, first that a person have exhibited an actual (subjective) expectation of privacy and, second, that the expectation be one that society is prepared to recognize as "reasonable." Thus a man's home is . . . a place where he expects privacy. . . . On the other hand, conversations in the open would not be protected against being overheard, for the expectation of privacy under the circumstances would be unreasonable.[55]

The Supreme Court found Charles Katz had a reasonable expectation of privacy in the phone booths. He believed his calls were private because he went into the phone booth and closed the door. The court also found that we, as a society, would consider that belief to be reasonable. The court therefore overruled the Olmstead decision, and intercepting telephone calls became a search under the Fourth Amendment, which meant officers must obtain a search warrant before conducting such an interception.

The Katz case was the first of two decisions the Supreme Court has issued on the applicability of the Fourth Amendment to telephone technology. The other decision came in 1979.[56]

On March 5, 1976, Baltimore resident Patricia McDonough was robbed. She gave the police a description of the robber and a 1975 Monte Carlo automobile she saw near the scene of the crime. Patricia began to receive "threatening and obscene" calls from a man who said he was the robber. At one point, he called and asked her to go out to her front porch. When she did, she saw the Monte Carlo driving slowly by her home. A few days later, police saw a man matching her description of the robber driving a car that matched her description of the Monte Carlo. They used the license plate number to trace the car to Michael Lee Smith. The next day, officers had the telephone company install "a pen register at its central offices to record the numbers dialed from the telephone" at Smith's home. The officers did not get a search warrant authorizing installation of the pen register; they simply asked the phone company to install it, and the phone company complied.

The pen register did not—could not—capture the contents of the calls Smith made. All it could do was to record the numbers he dialed from his home phone.

The day after the pen register was installed, Smith called Patricia, and the pen register recorded him dialing her number. Police used that and other evidence to get a warrant to search Smith's home, where they found evidence implicating him in the robbery. After he was indicted for robbery, Smith moved to suppress the evidence recorded by the pen register on the grounds that using it to discover the phone numbers he dialed from home was a search under the Fourth Amendment. Similar to Katz, Smith lost at the lower court level; the trial court and the Maryland Court of Appeals both held that using the pen register was not a Fourth Amendment search.

Smith appealed to the Supreme Court, which agreed to hear the case. Unlike Katz, he lost. The court applied the standard Justice Harlan articulated in the Katz ruling and found Smith did not have a reasonable expectation of privacy in the numbers he dialed from his home phone. The court found, first, that Smith could not have believed the numbers he was dialing were private because he knew he was "giving" them to the phone company: "All telephone users realize that they must 'convey' phone numbers to the telephone company, since it is through telephone company switching equipment that their calls are completed."[57]

The court also held that even if Smith subjectively believed the numbers he dialed were private, this was not a belief society accepts as objectively reasonable: "This Court consistently has held that a person has no legitimate expectation of privacy in information he voluntarily turns over to third parties."[58] In making that statement, the court cited a case decided a few years earlier, in which it held that bank customers have no Fourth Amendment expectation of privacy in information they share with their bank:

[C[hecks are not confidential communications but negotiable instruments to be used in commercial transactions. . . . [F]inancial statements and deposit slips, contain only information voluntarily conveyed to the banks and exposed to their employees in the ordinary course of business. . . .

The depositor takes the risk, in revealing his affairs to another, that the information will be conveyed by that person to the Government.[59]

The Katz and Smith decisions mean that the applicability of the Fourth Amendment to our use of telephones is governed by a dichotomy: If the government engages in conduct analogous to what it did in the Katz case (i.e., intercept the contents of phone calls as we make them), that will be a Fourth Amendment search under the Katz ruling. If the government uses the modern equivalent of pen registers and trap and trace devices (which capture the phone numbers of people who call a particular phone[60]) to record the phone numbers we call and the phone numbers of the people who call us, that is not a search under the Smith decision.

Many, myself included, believe the Supreme Court got it right in the Katz case but got it very wrong in the Smith case. Justice Marshall wrote a dissent in the Smith case in which he, similar to Justice Brandeis in the Olmstead case, pointed out the flaw in the majority's reasoning. Justice Marshall took issue with the majority's holding that Smith, similar to a bank depositor, assumed the risk the phone company would reveal the information he shared with it to the government. He noted that "[i]mplicit in the concept of assumption of risk is some notion of choice."[61] He then pointed out that "unless a person is prepared to forego use of what for many has become a personal or professional necessity, he cannot help but accept the risk of surveillance. . . . It is idle to speak of 'assuming' risks in contexts where, as a practical matter, individuals have no realistic alternative."[62] Similar to Justice Brandeis and unlike his colleagues, Justice Marshall understood that communications technology had already become an intricate component of everyday life.

Unfortunately, the Supreme Court has never revisited—and therefore never reversed—its decision in the Smith case. The Katz and Smith dichotomy has become increasingly difficult to apply as technology has advanced far beyond what it was when the Smith decision was made. Some of the difficulties involve advanced telephone technology. However, as we will see in the next section, most of them—the most problematic of them—involve evolved communications technologies such as e-mail.

FOURTH AMENDMENT: COMPUTER TECHNOLOGY

Computer technology raises a number of Fourth Amendment issues, but none is more intimately entwined with personal privacy than the applicability of the Fourth Amendment to online communications: e-mail and other messages, the comments and information we post on Web sites, and data generated by our online transactions. In the following sections, we examine the Fourth Amendment issues each type of communication presents.E-mail

Because the same issues arise for e-mail, texts, and instant messages and because e-mail has been the primary focus of Fourth Amendment litigation, we will concentrate on it. In deciding the extent to which e-mail is "private" and therefore protected by the Fourth Amendment, courts must decide which of the Supreme Court cases we previously examined govern e-mail:

Is it a phone call (the Katz case), a letter (the Jackson case), or the equivalent of giving financial information to a bank or phone numbers to the phone company (the Smith case)?

In making that decision, courts must deal with the fact that similar to a letter or a phone call, e-mails involve two types of information: the contents of the message and the data that are used to transmit the message from the sender to the recipient. The former is known as "content data" and the latter as "traffic data."[63] We will begin by analyzing the extent to which the Fourth Amendment applies to content data and then consider traffic data.

If we analogize e-mail to a sealed letter, the content data are the substance of the communication—the digital equivalent of what is written on a letter inside an envelope. The traffic data are the addressing information used to send it—the digital equivalent of the names and addresses written on the outside of the envelope. If that analogy is correct, then under the Supreme Court decision in the Jackson case, the Fourth Amendment protects the contents of an e-mail but not the traffic data used to send it. This would mean that law enforcement officers could not access the contents of an e-mail in the process of being sent unless they first obtain a search warrant. (In a moment, we will get to e-mails that have arrived and are being stored in someone's e-mail account.)

I suspect most Americans assume this analogy is correct and their e-mails are immune from law enforcement inspection unless and until officers get a warrant that lets them read one or more e-mails. There is, however, a problem with the analogy. In the Jackson ruling, the Supreme Court emphasized that the Fourth Amendment applies to sealed letters because the sender took steps to prevent postal employees from reading them. This premise is consistent with the Katz ruling. Under the Katz ruling, the Fourth Amendment protects the contents of sealed letters because by sealing the envelope, the sender makes an effort to keep the contents of the letter private and therefore does not assume the risk that it will be read by postal employees. The Jackson court also held that the Fourth Amendment does not protect items that are not sealed—newspapers and postcards—because the sender has assumed the risk that others will read them as they travel through the mail.

That brings us back to e-mails. To be analogous to a letter, an e-mail must be sealed, that is, the sender must do something to prevent its being read as it travels to its intended recipient. The only way to seal an e-mail is to encrypt it, but almost no one (outside the military and intelligence communities) encrypts e-mails for two reasons. One reason is that encrypting e-mail tends to be a complex, cumbersome process; the other reason is that most people—certainly most Americans—assume e-mail is already private, so there is no need to encrypt. Most Americans, in other words, assume an e-mail is the equivalent of a sealed letter; it will not be read by anyone except its intended recipient.

That, though, is not true. ISPs can, and do, scan the contents of at least some of the e-mails sent via their systems.[64] The same is true of noncommercial providers such as universities.[65] E-mail providers screen e-mails in an effort to prevent their systems from being used for illegal purposes, but they are not the only ones who can read e-mails as the messages travel through a system. The employees of an ISP or other provider can read unencrypted e-mails in the same way that a postal employee can read a postcard.[66] Because of that, some, including the U.S. Department of Justice, claim the Fourth Amendment does not protect unencrypted e-mail. In a recent case, the Justice Department argued that e-mail "resembles less a sealed letter than a postcard amenable to warrantless inspection, because 'its contents are plainly visible to the [ISP], who can access it via its servers at any time.' "[67]

I suspect most of us do not agree with this position, but it is difficult to distinguish unencrypted e-mail from a postcard. We have not, as the court in the Jackson case put it, sealed the message to keep it from prying eyes. Therefore, we have, as the court in the Katz case would say, assumed the risk that employees of our ISP will read our e-mail. Unless and until the Supreme Court takes up this issue and holds that unencrypted e-mail is somehow more private than a postcard, it is prudent to assume that unencrypted e-mail is outside the protection of the Fourth Amendment.[68] If that is true, it means that if an ISP scans e-mail and finds evidence of a crime, it can turn the e-mail over to law enforcement officers without the officers having to get a search warrant.[69] It might also mean officers could ask an ISP to scan someone's e-mail and report what it finds, without getting a search warrant.[70]

There is another way to argue that the contents of e-mail—even unencrypted e-mail—are protected under the Fourth Amendment. It analogizes e-mails to phone calls instead of letters (or postcards). In 1968, Congress adopted a statutory scheme to implement the Supreme Court decision in the Katz case. Known as Title III (because it was the third title of a larger, more comprehensive bill), this legislative scheme requires officers to obtain a warrant before intercepting telephone calls and to otherwise comply with the requirements of the Fourth Amendment. In 1986, Congress expanded Title III so that its provisions also apply to the interception of e-mail; Congress wanted to ensure that this new medium of communication was also protected from arbitrary eavesdropping.[71]

Under Title III, law enforcement officers use the same procedure to eavesdrop on telephone calls and to intercept the contents of e-mails that are in the process of being transmitted from a sender to a recipient.[72] Because Title III is a statute rather than a Supreme Court decision, it does not extend Fourth Amendment protection to the contents of e-mail.[73] It does, however, support an argument for analogizing e-mails to phone calls: Similar to ISPs, phone companies can, and do, listen in on calls.[74] Notwithstanding that, the court in the Katz case held that we have a Fourth Amendment expectation of privacy in our phone calls.[75] If the communication service provider's ability to intercept the content of communications does not defeat a Fourth Amendment expectation of privacy in phone calls, then it should not defeat such an expectation with regard to the content of unencrypted e-mails. So far, no court has ruled on this issue, although a federal court of appeals noted in passing that it found the argument "convincing."[76] The issue has presumably not arisen because state and federal law enforcement officers assume they must comply with the requirements of Title III in order to obtain any e-mails (encrypted or unencrypted) lawfully.

A related issue has come up, most notably in the federal court of appeals case I noted earlier: whether the Fourth Amendment protects the contents of e-mails once they arrive at their destination and are stored on the ISP servers. This issue does not arise for telephone calls because the only way the government can acquire the contents of a phone call is to capture the conversation as it occurs. The creation and transmission of the content occur simultaneously, and the content exists only momentarily.[77] E-mails, on the other hand, are stored on an ISP server for some period of time after they arrive and until we read them. After we read e-mails, many of us keep them in a file in our e-mail account. This means that the government has an additional way to obtain the content of e-mails: Law enforcement officers can ask an ISP to copy the archived e-mails and give the copies to the officers. If the archived e-mails are protected by the Fourth Amendment under the Katz or Jackson cases, then the officers must get a search warrant to obtain copies of the e-mails. If the e-mails are not protected by the Fourth Amendment, then officers can simply ask for the copies and the ISP can, if so inclined, create them and turn them over to the officers.

This was the issue in the case I noted earlier: In 2005, federal agents were investigating Steven Warshak for "mail and wire fraud, money laundering and related federal offenses."[78] As part of the investigation, the agents obtained copies of e-mails Warshak had archived in his Yahoo! e-mail account. The agents did not use a search warrant. Instead, they relied on a procedure in another statutory scheme—the Stored Communications Act (SCA)—to obtain the e-mails. Under the SCA, officers can obtain the contents of stored e-mails by getting a judge to order an ISP to copy the e-mails and give the copies to the officers.[79] Unlike a magistrate issuing a search warrant, the judge who issues such an order does not have to find there is probable cause to believe the e-mails are evidence of a crime.[80] The SCA procedure therefore does not comply with the requirements of the Fourth Amendment and is unconstitutional if the Fourth Amendment protects the privacy of e-mails that are stored on an ISP server.

As I noted earlier, stored e-mails are not analogous to the phone call at issue in the Katz case; they consist of text and are acquired after the message has been received. Although they are, to some extent, analogous to the mail at issue in the Jackson case, we use the mail only to transmit letters; we do not store read letters with the U.S. Postal Service. That leaves the Smith decision. The Supreme Court has not addressed this issue, but the Department of Justice and others believe stored e-mail comes under the Smith holding, that is, data we share with a third-party loses its Fourth Amendment protection. The SCA is based on this proposition. The assumption is that the SCA gives some protection to stored e-mails, which would otherwise be available to law enforcement on demand. Under the Smith ruling, by leaving e-mails stored on our ISP servers, we assume the risk that the ISP will give copies of those e-mails to law enforcement officers, even without a search warrant.

Steven Warshak challenged this view; he sued the Department of Justice for violating his rights by obtaining his stored e-mails without a warrant. Warshak relied on the argument outlined previously, that is, because the ability of the phone company to listen in on phone calls does not deprive calls of Fourth Amendment protection, the ability of an ISP to read stored e-mails should not deprive them of Fourth Amendment protection. A federal district court agreed with him, and so did a three-judge panel of the U.S. Court of Appeals for the Sixth Circuit. For a few months, the Fourth Amendment protected the contents of all e-mails. The Department of Justice was not pleased with this ruling because it meant officers and agents had to get a search warrant to obtain stored e-mails. So the Justice Department appealed the decision of the three-judge panel to the entire Court of Appeals for the Sixth Circuit in what is called an *en banc* procedure, and that court blinked.

The *en banc* court ducked the issue by using a technical rule to hold that the case was not "ripe" for review by the courts.[81] The *en banc* court said the lower courts should not have entertained Warshak's claims because there was no live controversy. Warshak had already been indicted, and there was no indication the government would seek further copies of his e-mails from Yahoo! The *en banc* court therefore vacated the opinions of the lower courts, which means they ceased to have any legal effect. One of the judges dissented, pointing out the fallacy in the majority's reasoning and noting the importance of the issue that would be left undecided:[82]

If I were to tell James Otis and John Adams that a citizen's private correspondence is now . . . subject to ex parte and unannounced searches by the government without a warrant supported by probable cause, what would they say? Probably nothing, they would be left speechless.

If the *en banc* Warshak court had agreed with the lower courts, the issue would almost certainly have gone to the Supreme Court because the Department of Justice would have asked the Supreme Court to reverse the lower courts. By holding there was no controversy, the *en banc* court prevented that and put an end to this attempt to apply the Fourth Amendment to the content of stored e-mails. As a result, we remain, where we were before Warshak sued. The assumption is that stored e-mails are governed by the Smith holding and therefore are not protected by the Fourth Amendment.

The information used to transmit e-mail—the "to" and "from" fields in an e-mail plus the data an e-mail generate as it moves through a series of mail servers to its final destination[83]—is clearly not protected by the Fourth Amendment. E-mail traffic data are logically indistinguishable from the numbers we dial to place phone calls. In both instances, we surrender Fourth Amendment privacy by sharing that information with a third party.

Web Postings

Under the Katz ruling, the Fourth Amendment does not protect any content we post on a publicly accessible Web site. As the court said in the Katz decision, what we knowingly expose to public view is not private. Because anyone can access the site and see what we posted, law enforcement officers can do the same without obtaining a search warrant. Officers can, and do, use postings on MySpace and other Web sites in investigating criminal activity.[84]

What if the site is password-protected? That was the issue in *United States v. D'Andrea*,[85] a federal prosecution for sexually abusing a child. On December 2, 2004, an anonymous woman called a child abuse hotline and said the eight-year-old daughter of Kendra D'Andrea "was being sexually abused by her mother and the mother's live-in boyfriend." She said they had posted photographs of the abuse on a password-protected Web site and provided the log-in name and password needed to access the site. A child abuse investigator used the information to log into the site, where he found photos of a child being sexually abused. He downloaded the images and called the police, who used the images and the information from the caller to get a warrant to search D'Andrea's apartment. When they executed the search warrant, they found information that further incriminated D'Andrea and her boyfriend.

After being charged with sexually abusing a child, D'Andrea moved to suppress the images the investigator downloaded from the password-protected site. She said the investigator violated the Fourth Amendment by accessing the site and downloading the images without first getting a search warrant. D'Andrea claimed the site was protected by the Fourth Amendment because only those who knew the log-in name and password could access it. She argued that by using a password and log-in name, she ensured the privacy of the Web site, just as Charles Katz ensured the privacy of his phone calls by using a phone booth. In ruling on this issue, the federal district court noted that the leading expert on Fourth Amendment law believes "that a person who avails herself of a website's password protection should be able to claim a reasonable expectation of privacy in the site's contents."[86]

Although the judge found this view persuasive, he concluded that he did not have to decide this issue because the investigator did not break into the site (i.e., did not bypass the measures D'Andrea used to secure it). He used the login information the anonymous caller provided to access the site. Because she was not a law enforcement officer (she was a former girlfriend of D'Andrea's boyfriend), the Fourth Amendment did not apply to her. Similar to any private citizen, she was free to share information with the police. By sharing the login information with this person, D'Andrea assumed the risk she would give it to the police. As the Supreme Court said in *United States v. Jacobsen*,[87] "when an individual reveals private information to another, he assumes the risk that his confidant will reveal that information to the authorities, and if that occurs the Fourth Amendment does not prohibit governmental use of that information." Although D'Andrea almost certainly created a Fourth Amendment expectation of privacy in the site by password-protecting it, she lost that right by giving the log-in information to someone who gave it to the police.

Like others, I believe that password-protecting a Web site creates a reasonable expectation of privacy in the contents of that site and therefore requires law enforcement to obtain a search warrant to access the contents of the site without the owner's permission. Password-protecting a site should trigger full Fourth Amendment protection. If the owner of the site shares login information for the site with someone, he assumes the risk that this person will betray him by sharing that information with law enforcement. This means the only way that someone can sustain Fourth Amendment protection for a password-protected site is by not sharing login information for the site with anyone else.

Transactions

When we surf the Web, shop online, or engage in any other type of online activity, we leave a record of where we have been and what we have done. We may be alone in a private, locked room while we do any or all of these things and therefore assume that what we are doing is private, but that is not true. We are more visible online than we are in the real, physical world.

If law enforcement wants to track our activities in the real world, it will have to assign officers to monitor our movements in public and to interview witnesses who can describe what we were doing in private places. Law enforcement officers can install and use certain technologies such as GPS tracking devices to keep track of where we go in our vehicles, but beyond that, they will have to use officers to monitor our movements. Because that is a time-consuming and resource-intensive process, law enforcement can track only a few of us at any one time.

Monitoring what we do online is much easier. Technology keeps track of every site we visit and every action we take on each site. It also keeps a record of that activity, which will be stored with our ISP and/or with the operators of the sites we visit. This information can be very useful for law enforcement officer. For example, federal agents investigating the possibility that a suspect is planning a terrorist bombing could use the records of his Internet activity to find out if he is trying to buy explosives or researching how to build a bomb. If he is using the Internet, there will be records showing what sites he visited and what he did on those sites.

Is that information protected by the Fourth Amendment? If it is, then the agents will have to obtain a search warrant to gain access to it. To obtain a search warrant, they must convince a magistrate they have probable cause to believe this person is planning a terrorist bombing. That is not an impossible task, but it means the agents will not be able to obtain the online records early in their investigation; they will have to wait until they develop the necessary probable cause from other sources. If the Fourth Amendment does not protect the information, the agents can obtain it without getting a search warrant; they could simply ask the suspect's ISP and the Web sites to provide it. If the ISP and/or Web sites refuse, the agents can use a subpoena

—a judicial order that commands the recipient to take certain action or be held in contempt[88]—to require the ISP and/or Web sites to comply. Unlike a search warrant, a subpoena issues without a showing of probable cause to believe evidence of a crime is in a particular place.[89]

A few courts have considered whether the Fourth Amendment protects the data we generate when we shop or do anything else in the public areas of cyberspace. In *United States v. Forrester*,[90] for example, federal agents installed a "mirror port"—the twenty-first century equivalent of a pen register—on Louis Alba's account with an ISP. The agents suspected Alba and Forrester were involved in manufacturing Ecstasy, a controlled substance.

They used the mirror port to monitor "the IP addresses of the websites that Alba visited." An Internet Protocol (IP) address is "a numerical identification . . . that is assigned to" Web sites and other "devices in a computer network."[91] Google has many different IP addresses, one of which is, or was, 216.239.51.99.[92] To access Google or any other site, we do not use the numerical IP address; instead, we use a domain name, a pattern of text that our computer translates as a request to access an IP address and implements.[93] In the Forrester case, the federal agents used the mirror port installed on Alba's account with his ISP to track the Web sites Alba visited, in the same way officers in the Smith case used a pen register to capture the numbers Smith dialed from his home phone.

In the Forrester case, the evidence the mirror port compiled was used to indict Alba for violating federal drug laws and to convict him on those charges. He appealed his conviction, arguing that the use of the mirror port violated the Fourth Amendment. The U.S. Court of Appeals for the Ninth Circuit disagreed:

[T[he surveillance techniques the government employed here are constitutionally indistinguishable from the use of a pen register that the Court approved in *Smith*. . . . Internet users, like the telephone users in Smith, rely on third-party equipment to engage in communication. *Smith* based its holding that telephone users have no expectation of privacy in the numbers they dial on the users' imputed knowledge that their calls are completed through telephone company switching equipment. . . . Internet users have no expectation of privacy in the . . . IP addresses of the websites they visit because they should know this information is provided to and used by Internet service providers for the specific purpose of directing the routing of information. Like telephone numbers, which provide instructions to the "switching equipment that processed those numbers," . . . IP addresses are not merely passively conveyed through third party equipment, but rather are voluntarily turned over in order to direct the third party's servers.[94]

As long as the Smith decision is a valid precedent, courts cannot reach any other conclusion.

Unless and until the Supreme Court revisits this issue and overrules the Smith decision, the data we generate when we are online are outside the Fourth Amendment. In other words, the data are not private. That has certain consequences, one of which is that law enforcement officers can track our online activity in real time or retroactively without getting a search warrant. This use of online data is simply an extension of traditional investigative methods. As such, it usually focuses on one individual or only on one individual at a time.

The Smith decision not only supports this traditional investigative methodology, it creates the possibility of a new investigative methodology: data mining. Data mining consists of compiling massive amounts of information in databases and then analyzing it to identify patterns that are not ascertainable otherwise.[95] Because the Smith ruling puts the information we share with third-parties outside the scope of the Fourth Amendment, it creates the possibility that law enforcement can compile this information in databases and use sophisticated programs to analyze it and identify patterns officers can use to commence and conduct investigations. Not surprisingly, law enforcement is interested in this possibility. Some data mining efforts, such as the unfortunately named MATRIX project,[96] have been implemented, but most have not been successful, due in part to concerns about privacy.

That does not mean such efforts will not succeed in the future. As long as the Smith decision stands, there is no constitutional impediment to a process the drafters of the Bill of Rights would certainly have found objectionable. As long as the Smith decision survives, Fourth Amendment privacy and the use of modern communications technologies are irreconcilable. I cannot use any communication technology without sharing information with a third-party, which leaves the information unprotected by the Fourth Amendment. I believe Justice Marshall was correct when he argued in his dissent with the Smith ruling that the result in that case creates a technological Hobson's choice: If I use technology, I lose privacy; to have privacy, I must give up technology. I suspect most, if not all, of us would agree with Justice Marshall that this is a choice we should not have to make.

There is a way we can invoke Fourth Amendment protection for our online activities. As we have seen, the Fourth Amendment presumably protects encrypted e-mails because we have, in effect, sealed the envelope. Encryption can also be used to protect other online activities and to secure hard drives and other data storage devices,[97] thereby making it difficult or even impossible for law enforcement to access the data they contain. As we will see in the next section, law enforcement can try to compel us to give up the key needed to access encrypted data or devices, but the Fifth Amendment may give us the ability to resist such efforts.

FIFTH AMENDMENT

Similar to the Fourth Amendment, the Fifth Amendment is part of the Bill of Rights—the first 10 amendments to the Constitution. It contains several clauses, each of which establishes a distinct right. For example, one clause creates the prohibition against double jeopardy (i.e., against trying someone twice for the same crime).

Our concern is with the clause that says "[n]o person . . . shall be compelled in any criminal case to be a witness against himself." Similar to the Fourth Amendment, this clause has its roots in English law and history. In the sixteenth and seventeenth century, two powerful English courts—the Court of High Commission and the Court of Star Chamber—used a procedure called the oath ex officio to bring people into court and force them to answer questions that could implicate them in crimes "of which they were neither formally accused nor suspected."[98] If someone refused to take the oath ex officio or, having taken it, refused to answer questions, he or she would be punished. For example, the Court of Star Chamber ordered John Lilburne to be "whipt through the streets, from the prison of the Fleet unto the pillory" for refusing to comply.[99] In 1641, Parliament outlawed the use of the oath ex officio, prompted by complaints from citizens who said no one should be forced to testify against himself or herself. The theory was that people had a right not to be compelled to betray themselves—that the government should collect its own evidence instead of forcibly extracting what it needed from a suspect. English colonists brought that notion to what would become the United States, and it was eventually incorporated into the Fifth Amendment.

The Fifth Amendment clause with which we are concerned is known as the privilege against self-incrimination because it operates in the same way as an evidentiary privilege (i.e., it gives someone the privilege of refusing to testify). In that regard, it is similar to the marital privilege (i.e., one spouse cannot be forced to testify against the other) or the attorney-client privilege. The Fifth Amendment is not, as the Supreme Court has explained, a privilege that bars the government from asking someone questions; it simply gives the person the ability to refuse to answer those questions.[100] The Fifth Amendment gives us an option that was not available to those summoned before the Court of Star Chamber: Their only options were to answer truthfully (implicating themselves in a crime), lie (committing perjury and condemning their souls to eternal damnation), or refuse to answer and be punished. The Fifth Amendment gives us a fourth option: refuse to answer and suffer no consequences for doing so.

However, the privilege is available only in certain circumstances. To be able to invoke the Fifth Amendment privilege, a person must be compelled to give testimony that incriminates him (implicates him in a crime).[101] If someone is willing to testify voluntarily, there is no need for compulsion, and the Fifth Amendment does not apply. It usually comes into play when the government wants someone to testify at a trial or a grand jury proceeding, but that person refuses. The government can use a subpoena—a trial subpoena or a grand jury subpoena—to force the person to appear. If someone who was served with a subpoena shows up at the trial or grand jury proceeding and refuses to answer questions, he will be held in contempt and incarcerated until he agrees to testify . . . unless he can invoke the Fifth Amendment privilege.

The subpoena satisfies the first requirement because it compels the person to testify (absent a claim of the privilege). The second requirement limits the application of the privilege to testimony (i.e., to communicating facts or opinions). The Supreme Court has held that the Fifth Amendment does not apply to physical evidence, which means we can invoke the privilege and refuse to answer questions posed by a prosecutor, but we cannot invoke it to refuse to let the government take samples of our blood or hair. If the prosecutor is using the subpoena to get the witness to answer questions, then the person will be able to invoke the Fifth Amendment privilege if answering the questions will incriminate him or her (i.e., will implicate him in criminal activity). The Fifth Amendment is not a privilege to refuse to speak; it is a privilege to refuse to be a witness against yourself (i.e., to give testimony that can be used to prosecute you for a crime). That brings us to Sebastien Boucher.

On December 27, 2006, Sebastien Boucher and his father crossed the Canadian border into the United States at Derby Line, Vermont.[102] Like everyone entering the United States, they were subjected to an initial inspection of their passports; however, unlike most who enter the United States, the Bouchers were selected for secondary inspection. If the federal agent who conducts the initial inspection thinks the traveler is carrying contraband, he will refer the person for a secondary inspection, which involves searching the person's luggage.

As Officer Pike conducted the secondary inspection, he saw a laptop in the car, booted it up, and looked through the files it contained. Pike found

40,000 image files, "some of which appeared to be pornographic based on the names of the files." He asked Sebastien if there was child pornography on the laptop; Sebastien said he was not sure. Sebastien said he downloaded pornography and sometimes his downloads included child pornography; Sebastien said he deleted those images when he found them.

At that point, Pike called Agent Curtis for assistance because he had experience with locating digital child pornography. Curtis asked Sebastien to show him where the downloaded files were. Sebastien was given access to the laptop and "navigated to a part of the hard drive designated as drive Z." Curtis began looking through the Z drive and saw what he believed was child pornography. After searching further, Curtis arrested Boucher, shut down the laptop, and seized it as evidence. Two days later, another officer took custody of the laptop and began conducting a forensic examination of it. When he tried to access the Z drive, he could not because it was encrypted "through the use of the software Pretty Good Privacy . . . which requires a password." Curtis and a Secret Service agent tried repeatedly to access the Z drive but could not. According to the Secret Service agent, the only way to access the drive without having the password "is to use an automated system which repeatedly guesses passwords." The agent noted that "the process to unlock drive Z could take years based on efforts to unlock similarly encrypted files in another case."

Because it was clear that the only way to access the Z drive was with the password and that Boucher would not voluntarily provide the password, the government resorted to a subpoena. A federal grand jury served Sebastien with a subpoena that ordered him to enter the password into the laptop or be held in contempt. Boucher took the Fifth Amendment, claiming that providing the password would be compelled testimony that incriminated him. The Department of Justice argued that the password was physical evidence, not testimony, and so claimed Sebastien was not entitled to take the Fifth Amendment as the basis for refusing to enter the password.

In responding to this argument, Sebastien relied on the Supreme Court case of *Fisher v. United States*.[103] In that case, the court held that while someone cannot claim the Fifth Amendment privilege as the basis for refusing to provide physical evidence such as hair samples because physical evidence is not testimony, someone subpoenaed by a grand jury can invoke the Fifth Amendment if the act of producing the evidence would itself be testimonial. The court in the Fisher case said the act of producing evidence is a testimony within the Fifth Amendment if it concedes that the evidence exists, that the subpoenaed person has it, and that the evidence produced is what the grand jury asked for (i.e., producing it authenticates it). The court in the Fisher case also said that the act of producing evidence will not be testimonial if all of these are a "foregone conclusion" (i.e., if the government already knows the person has the evidence).

When I teach the Fisher case, I use this example to illustrate when the act of producing evidence will be testimonial and when it will not: If a grand jury issues a subpoena to a murder suspect that demands she "produce to the grand jury the gun you used to kill Martin Balco," she can take the Fifth Amendment and refuse to comply. By handing over the gun, she is implicitly saying that it exists, that she has it, and that this is the gun she used to kill Balco. On the other hand, if the grand jury knows the suspect has the gun that was used to kill Balco (e.g. they have videotape of her buying it or one of her friends saw it and heard her say, "This what I used to kill Balco"), then handing it over does not tell the government anything it does not already know. If the act does not communicate anything, it is not testimonial, and she cannot take the Fifth Amendment.

In the Boucher case, the federal magistrate judge who was assigned to decide the issue held that giving up the password was a testimonial and incriminating act:

Compelling Boucher to enter the password forces him to produce evidence that could . . . incriminate him. . . .

Entering a password into the computer implicitly communicates facts. By entering the password Boucher would be disclosing . . . that he knows the password and has control over . . . drive Z. The procedure is equivalent to asking Boucher, "Do you know the password to the laptop?"[104]

The judge therefore quashed the grand jury subpoena (i.e., withdrew it). Because it could not compel Sebastien to provide the password, the only way the government could get it was to give him immunity from prosecution, but it was not willing to do that. Giving him immunity would defeat the purpose because it would mean that none of the files on the laptop could be used to prosecute Sebastien for child pornography or any other crime.

The Department of Justice instead chose to appeal the magistrate judge's decision to the federal district judge who presides over the U.S. District Court for the District of Vermont.[105] It also decided to change tactics somewhat. In its appeal to the district judge, the Justice Department said it was not asking Sebastien to provide "the password for the encrypted hard drive, but . . . to produce the contents of his encrypted hard drive in an unencrypted format by opening the drive before the grand jury."[106] The Department of Justice also argued that Sebastien could not take the Fifth

Amendment as to the contents of the laptop because they were a foregone conclusion under the Fisher ruling.

The Department of Justice won. The magistrate judge had decided the foregone conclusion principle did not apply in this case "because the government has not viewed most of the files on the Z drive, and therefore does not know whether most of the[m] . . . contain incriminating material." The district court judge disagreed; he found that for the foregone conclusion principle to apply, the government does not have to be "aware of the incriminatory *contents* of the files"; all it needs to know is that they exist in a particular location. The judge pointed out that the government knew this because Agent Curtis had looked through parts of the Z drive and had seen files, some of which appeared to be child pornography. The district court judge also held that Sebastien producing an unencrypted version of the hard drive would not authenticate it or the files on it because "he has already admitted to possession of the computer, and provided the Government with access to the Z drive." The judge therefore reversed the magistrate judge's ruling quashing the subpoena, reinstated the subpoena, and ordered Sebastien to provide an unencrypted version of the hard drive. I assume the decision is being appealed to the U.S. Court of Appeals for the Second Circuit. If it is, it could take years for that court to decide the case. If it is not, then Sebastien either decided to produce an unencrypted version of his hard drive, or he is sitting in jail for contempt.

The Boucher case is not about e-mail or real-time Web surfing, but it does deal with our ability to protect digital information from the government. In other words, it deals with the same privacy concerns that prompted the adoption of the Fourth Amendment. If we can use encryption to secure data, e-mail, and other online activity, we can alleviate the effects of the Smith and Jackson rulings. But encryption is effective only if we cannot be forced to give our encryption keys to the government. Under the federal magistrate judge's ruling, we can use encryption to put digital data permanently beyond the government's reach. Under the district court judge's ruling, we can use encryption to protect our data from private citizens but not from the government.

FINAL THOUGHTS

In this chapter, we have dealt with only a few of the many privacy issues that result from our use of computer technology. However, the issues we addressed are representative of the questions that arise in this context. The dominant theme in this area of the law is that we have to make a choice:

Do we want to be able to assume privacy, or are we satisfied with having to invoke privacy?

If I can assume privacy, then I will not need to encrypt my e-mail or take other measures to ensure that the government cannot gain access to what I have created or what I have done online. I can simply assume that the government cannot obtain that information without obtaining a search warrant. Making it easier for us to enjoy privacy will in no way erode the government's ability to obtain information, as long as it complies with the Fourth Amendment. Creating a system in which we can assume privacy brings more information within the scope of the Fourth Amendment, which simply means that the government has to comply with the requirements of the Fourth Amendment to obtain that information.

If we were going to shift from an environment in which we must invoke privacy to one in which we can assume privacy, we would have to decide what standards we would use to distinguish between what is, and is not, constitutionally private. More precisely, we would have to decide what standards we would use to decide what aspects of our online activities are, and are not, private. The standards we have in place for real-world searches and seizures are, for the most part, satisfactory because they are grounded in activity that has changed very little, if at all, in the last 400 years.

The problem we would face in fashioning standards to expand online privacy is the one I noted earlier: portable privacy. Privacy has historically been spatial privacy; enclaves (homes, businesses, locked boxes, sealed letters) were private because they were spatially isolated. We still live parts of our lives in spatially isolated enclaves, but even in those enclaves, we are linked with the external world. Modern communications technology has created a twenty-first-century version of the Olmstead issue.

In the Olmstead case, the Prohibition agents were able to hear what Olmstead was saying inside his home by tapping into wires outside his home and listening to his phone calls. In so doing, they did not violate the spatial privacy of his home by crossing his threshold without a warrant, but they achieved the same thing by using technology. Under the Katz case, law enforcement officers cannot obtain the contents of a phone call without getting a search warrant, but they can obtain a great deal of other information. As we have seen, they can find out who I am calling and who is calling me; who is e-mailing me and who I am e-mailing; and the information I post in publicly accessible areas of the Internet (and, if someone betrays me, the information I post on password-protected sites). They also can track what I do when I am online, the Web sites I visit, how long I stay on a site, what I do there, what I buy at online stores, and so forth. In addition to all of that, under the Smith decision, the officers can obtain my financial records, my utility records, my mortgage or leasing information, information about my insurance policies, and a host of other data, all without obtaining a search warrant. If I have an alarm system in my home, they can gain access to records that will let them know when I leave and when I return (assuming I arm it when I leave and disarm it when I return).

We have come close to realizing the prediction Justice Brandeis made 80 years ago: "Ways may . . . be developed by which the government, without removing papers from secret drawers, can reproduce them in court, and by which it will be enabled to expose . . . the most intimate occurrences of the home."[107] Because technology will become more sophisticated and more pervasive, its corrosive effect on privacy will only accelerate unless the Supreme Court revisits the Smith case and some of its other decisions and develops an interpretation of the Fourth Amendment that goes beyond spatial privacy.

New Ways to Fight Cybercrime

INTRODUCTION

Cybercrime—similar to all crime—involves a battle between good and evil, between the forces of order and the forces of disorder. Cybercrime, though, is something new. As we have seen, a very small part of cybercrime consists of committing entirely new offenses—crimes we have never seen in the past. Most cybercrime consists of committing traditional offenses by new means. All cybercrime is new crime, however, because it presents law enforcement with challenges it has never confronted, and the nature of these challenges makes it difficult for law enforcement to overcome them.

As a result, cybercriminals are flourishing, and that is not a state of affairs the governments of the world can tolerate for long. As we have seen, one consequence of cybercrime is that the citizens of Country A can prey on the citizens of Country B (and C and D and so on) with little risk of being identified, apprehended, and sanctioned for their crimes. That makes cybercrime an attractive endeavor for those who are so inclined, which means the number of cybercriminals is increasing, as is the number of victims.

This creates an untenable situation for the countries whose citizens are being victimized. As we saw in Chapter 10, countries must maintain internal order to survive and prosper. Until recently, they could keep order by discouraging their citizens from preying on each other. Now countries not only have to deal with domestic criminals, they also have to respond to criminals who operate in cyberspace. As we saw in Chapter 10, countries eventually developed a system—a law enforcement model—to keep domestic criminals under control. As we also saw, that model is not particularly effective against cybercriminals, at least not the ones who operate from abroad.

It seems, then, that if countries are going to improve their ability to discourage and thereby control cybercrime, they will have to (1) modify the current law enforcement model so it can deal effectively with transnational cybercrime and/or (2) develop new approaches for dealing with cybercrime. In the following sections, we will review proposals for modifying the law enforcement model and for implementing new approaches.

MODIFYING THE CURRENT MODEL

As we saw in Chapter 10, the law enforcement model is based on this premise: Officers react to a crime by conducting an investigation that focuses on the physical scene of the crime. As a result of this investigation, they identify the perpetrator, who is arrested, convicted, and punished for what he did. The fact that he was caught and punished both discourages him from committing future crimes and discourages others from following his example. More precisely, the fact that the perpetrator was caught and punished discourages enough others from committing crimes that the country is able to maintain the level of internal order necessary for it to survive.

As we also saw in Chapter 10, this model assumes real-world crime, which is why it is not particularly effective against cybercrime. As currently configured, the law enforcement model cannot create a credible threat of apprehension and punishment for cybercriminals. Logically, then, one solution is to modify the model to improve its effectiveness against cybercriminals. The following sections review proposals for doing this.

Convention on Cybercrime

In Chapter 10, we traced the process that led to the drafting of the treaty known as the Convention on Cybercrime. We now need to review what the Convention does and why.

Those who drafted the Convention believed gaps and conflicts in national laws impede law enforcement's ability to respond to cybercrime. Therefore, the Convention is intended to remedy this by ensuring that countries outlaw the various cybercrimes and give law enforcement the authority it needs to investigate cybercrimes. The Convention is implicitly predicated on the assumption that all countries will eventually ratify it, which would mean every country would have comprehensive, consistent cybercrime laws.

To be a party to the Convention and be bound by its provisions, a country must sign the Convention and formally ratify it.[1] The Convention was opened for signature on November 23, 2001. As I write this, almost eight years later, it has been signed by 46 countries and ratified by 20.[2] Most of the countries that have signed it are European countries that are entitled to sign because they are part of the Council of Europe.[3] Four non-European countries—Canada, Japan, South Africa, and the United States—were allowed to sign because they were involved in drafting the Convention.[4] Of the four, only the United States has also ratified it, which means the United States is the only one of the four that is bound by it. Other non-European countries are being invited to sign and ratify the Convention, but none has done so at this writing. Because there are 195 countries, the Convention on Cybercrime so far is having little impact on improving law enforcement's effectiveness against cybercrime.

Some think this is a transient state of affairs; they believe the scope and pace of ratification will increase as countries become more aware of the threat cybercrime poses. Others, including the U.S. Department of Justice and the United Nations, are engaged in efforts they believe will make it easier for countries to ratify the Convention. These efforts focus on the complexity of the Convention: It contains 48 Articles, at least 33 of which require parties to adopt legislation to implement its provisions.[5] This is not a difficult task for countries such as the United States, which already have cybercrime law. It can be a very difficult task for countries that have no experience with cybercrime law and may have other, more pressing priorities. In an effort to address this problem, the U.S. Department of Justice conducts training sessions in how to draft cybercrime legislation, and the United Nations commissioned a set of model laws countries can use as a guide in implementing the Convention.[6]

These efforts, however, are designed to make it easier for countries that *want* to sign and ratify the Convention to do so. They do not address the possibility that some (many?) countries may *not* want to become parties to the Convention. In 2008, Russia refused to sign it. The justification then-Russian Federation President Vladimir Putin gave for Russia's refusal to sign the treaty was that one of the Articles of the Convention threatened Russian sovereignty.[7] Some suspected the decision was really prompted by the country's notorious lack of enthusiasm for prosecuting Russian cybercriminals who attack targets outside Russia.[8]

That brings us to havens. High-seas pirates historically used a haven—a city that served as their base of operations—to avoid being prosecuted and hanged. A haven city either could not prosecute pirates because it had no law against piracy or would not prosecute them because they brought in revenue. In the seventeenth century, the Jamaican city of Port Royal was a famous pirate haven.[9] The old pirate havens were eventually destroyed, but a new kind of haven emerged three centuries later: bank secrecy havens. In the 1980s, some countries adopted laws that made it a crime for local bank employees to reveal information about a customer's account. These stringent bank secrecy laws attracted deposits from customers who wanted to shelter funds from law enforcement, internal revenue services, former spouses, and so forth. Similar to pirate havens, bank secrecy havens profited (at least to some extent) from illegal activities. Although these countries did not directly aid and abet the commission of crimes, their secrecy laws often prevented law enforcement officers from gathering evidence of criminal activity.[10] By the beginning of the twenty-first century, a combination of U.S. legislation and international effort had reduced the impact of bank secrecy havens on law enforcement efforts.[11]

Russia's attitude toward cybercrime—prosecute cybercriminals who strike domestic targets, and ignore the ones who attack foreign targets—raises the specter of cybercrime havens. How would a cybercrime haven work? If it emulated bank secrecy havens, then its law would either legalize cybercrime as such (which seems unlikely) or legalize some aspect of that activity. If it emulated the pirate havens, then it would either not have laws criminalizing cybercrime or would simply decline to enforce those laws.

At the moment, Russia seems to fall into the latter category, that is, it seems to be functioning as an ad hoc cybercrime haven. The same could be said of other countries around the world, for varying reasons. As I noted earlier, cybercrime will not be a priority in countries that are dealing with basic needs, such as stability and feeding their people. Other countries may ignore cybercrime because their citizens are not being victimized. Why should Country A care if Country B's citizens commit cybercrimes against citizens of Country C? In an ideal world, Country A would care, but we live in a world that is far from ideal. As a practical matter, if a country's citizens are not being victimized, it may not see cybercrime as a problem, especially if it perceives the cybercriminals as attacking people in "rich" countries such as the United States. Some residents of poorer countries may see this kind of cybercrime as a wealth-sharing process, an online Robin Hood activity.

My point is that although the Convention on Cybercrime goal of ensuring that as many countries as possible have adequate, consistent cybercrime laws is admirable, the approach it represents is exceedingly unlikely to transform the law enforcement model into an effective means of combating cybercrime.

The Convention may play a part in this process, but it cannot be our only solution.

Law Enforcement Strike-Back

Instead of focusing on law, two other proposals assume the best way to improve our ability to react to cybercrime and thereby deter cybercriminals is to sanction the use of "strike-back" techniques.[12] Strike-back techniques bypass traditional legal processes such as arrest, trial, and punishment in favor of direct, punitive action against the attacker.[13] The primary difference between the two proposals is the status of the person who is authorized to strike back against an attacker: One authorizes law enforcement strike-back techniques; the other allows the victim of a cybercrime to strike back at an attacker. We will examine law enforcement strike-back in this section and civilian strike-back in the next section.

A few years ago, Joel Reidenberg, a Fordham University law professor, argued that nation-states should allow law enforcement officers to use "electronic sanctions" to react to cybercrime.[14] Electronic sanctions include hacking, launching DDoS attacks, and disseminating viruses and other types of malware. According to Professor Reidenberg, a DDoS attack could become "an online death penalty" that prevented a cybercriminal from accessing the Internet, and officers could use "hacking techniques to 'seize' or paralyze rule-violating web pages."

What he proposes is an official version of an approach that has been discussed for some time: the civilian self-help or strike-back techniques we will examine in the next section. His proposal is not an advisable strategy for improving law enforcement's ability to react to cybercrime for two reasons. One reason is that it suffers from the problems outlined in the following text. The other reason is that it adds the official imprimatur of the state to what Professor Reidenberg concedes are illegal acts.[15] Law enforcement strike-back means the law enforcement officers of Country A are committing crimes against citizens of Country B. Even if this approach were to incrementally improve law enforcement's effectiveness against some cybercriminals, it would create new problems and new risks.

What would happen if the government of Country B demanded Country A turn over the officers who had launched a DDoS attack against its citizens to be prosecuted for their crime? If both countries had criminalized DDoS attacks and if an extradition treaty encompassing cybercrime was in effect between the two countries,[16] then Country A would be legally obligated to turn over the officers, unless it could come up with some excuse for refusing to do so. If Country A made a practice of having its officers launch strike-back attacks against citizens of Country B (and Country C and Country D) and then refused to extradite the officers for prosecution, it would have become a haven for a particular type of cybercrime—state-sponsored cybercrime. If we were to go down this path, it would not only destroy any hope of international cooperation in dealing with cybercrime, it could also create the possibility that one of the targeted states (e.g., Country B) would eventually respond with military force.

Civilian Strike-Back

As noted in the preceding section, the notion of authorizing civilian use of strike-back techniques antedates Professor Reidenberg's proposal for official strike-back.[17] The premise is that if we permit civilian victims to react when they become the targets of cybercrime, their efforts will supplement the reactive capabilities of law enforcement officers and improve the overall effectiveness of the law enforcement model. This strategy may seem appealing, but it is flawed in at least two respects.

First, strike-back raises difficult legal questions. The proponents of civilian strike-back usually claim it is a form of self-defense, but that justification would seldom apply in this context. Self-defense refers to our right to use force to protect ourselves from being killed or injured by an attacker; however, we are entitled to use force only if we have no other alternative and if we use only the amount of force that is necessary to protect ourselves.[18] Assume a man with a knife is chasing me down the street. If I can escape by running into a police station, I cannot use the gun in my purse to kill him and claim self-defense. The principle of self-defense will seldom, if ever, apply to civilian strike-back because it requires that the person who retaliates is responding to a threat of death or bodily injury. Because cybercrimes so far pose little, if any, risk of bodily injury, self-defense cannot serve as a blanket justification for allowing civilian strike-back.

Another justification that might apply is defense of property. We have the right to use only the amount of force that is necessary to protect our property from "unlawful entry" or from being damaged or stolen.[19] As with self-defense, we cannot use force unless we have no other alternative. Defense of property could conceivably justify the use of civilian strike-back techniques, but to qualify for the defense, the cybercrime victim would have to show he used digital force because that was his only option. What other options might he have? He might be able to shut down his system to frustrate the attack, but shutting down the system could bring its own risks.[20] He could contact law enforcement, and that option will defeat his ability to claim self-defense unless he can show that taking the time to contact law enforcement would have been futile (i.e., that by striking back, he mitigated what would otherwise have been massive damage to the computer system and/or to the clients it served).[21] The application of the defense in this context raises these and other difficult issues, but the defense of property could conceivably justify the use of civilian strike-back techniques. (It would not justify law enforcement strike-back because the officers implementing the strike-back would not be the victims of a cybercrime.)

Ultimately, civilian strike-back founders on the practical risks involved in authorizing victim self-help. The primary concern here is error in the need to use force, error in the amount of force that is used, and/or error in selecting the target against whom force is used.[22] If we define civilian strike-back as a legitimate response to cybercrime, we run the risk of encouraging people to launch retaliatory cyberattacks when those attacks are neither necessary nor justifiable. If the cybercrime has been committed, the defense of property principle cannot justify striking back. Defense of property justifies the use of force only to prevent or interrupt a crime. Striking back after the cybercrime is completed is revenge, not the defensive use of force. Because striking back necessarily involves committing a cybercrime, the civilian victim could be prosecuted for violating the law.

That brings us to the related issue of using too much force in a retaliatory strike. People often find it difficult to calibrate the level of force that can appropriately be used to defend property in the real world,[23] where the dynamics of crime and defense tend to be less ambiguous than in the online world. To decide how much force to use in a retaliatory strike, the victim of an ongoing cyberattack will have to assess the amount of harm the attack will inflict if it succeeds and then identify a retaliatory technique that is severe enough to stop the attack but will not inflict "too much" retaliatory harm. Imagine that a small retail business is hit with a DDoS attack. Because the company earns most of its revenue from online sales, it is losing money and will continue to do so until the DDoS attack stops.[24] Assume that Fred, the company computer security officer, has access to a logic bomb, a program that can be installed remotely on a computer and that, once triggered, will erase or corrupt all data on the hard drive. Also assume that (1) Fred has identified the computer that is launching the DDoS attack and (2) can use his home computer to install the logic bomb on the attacking computer and then trigger it, which will shut down the computer and stop the DDoS attack. Would this be a justifiable use of digital force under the defense of property principle? Is destroying the data in a computer a justifiable way of ending a DDoS attack? Or is it too much force? Should the company respond in kind by launching its own DDoS attack on the attacking computer?

Finally, as we saw in Chapter 8, cybercriminals often route their attacks through a series of intermediate computers to cover their tracks. This creates the possibility that a civilian bent on striking back against an attacker may not be able to trace the attack to the perpetrator's computer and so may "retaliate" against the wrong computer system.[25] The "retaliation" could shut down a computer system used by a hospital, a government agency, or a telecommunications company and injure not only the legitimate system that was attacked erroneously, but also those who relied on the system for vital services.[26] In this scenario, the civilian victim truly becomes a cybercriminal in his own right.

More Officers

This seems an obvious solution: increase the number of officers who can react to cybercrimes. As we saw in Chapter 10, cybercrime undermines the effectiveness of the reactive strategy, in part, by increasing the number of crimes to which officers must respond. It is an increment of new crime that is added to the real-world crime with which they must still deal. It seems, then, that increasing the number of officers who can react should offset this effect and restore the efficacy of the reactive strategy.

There are two problems with this theory. One problem is that most countries already find it difficult to allocate the resources needed to support existing law enforcement agencies. Therefore, it is highly improbable that they could summon the resources needed to recruit, train, and equip enough officers to make the reactive strategy an effective way of dealing with cybercrime. The other problem is that because cybercrime is and will continue to be increasingly automated, there is no guarantee that increasing the number of officers will improve the efficacy with which law enforcement agencies react to cybercrime. Policing in cyberspace is not as straightforward as sending officers to the physical place where a crime occurred so they can track down the perpetrator and apprehend him before he can offend again. As we have seen, cybercrime shatters the crime scene into shards, most of which will be scattered throughout cyberspace. Identifying cybercriminals is unusually difficult because of their ability to assume anonymity or a false online identity. While officers are seeking a cybercriminal, that cybercriminal can use automated systems to commit hundreds or even thousands of other crimes,[27] to which the officers will also have to react.

Instead of relying primarily on human officers, we could automate the reactive strategy. This would involve using automated agents to react to cybercrimes. It could also involve using them to patrol cyberspace in an effort to interrupt cybercrime and apprehend criminals, just as state troopers patrol interstate highways and apprehend speeders. Although automated cyberpolicing is a logical alternative, its adoption and implementation would be fraught with technical and legal difficulties[28] that make it an unrealistic option for the foreseeable future.

NEW APPROACHES

No one is calling for us to abandon the law enforcement model as way to control cybercrime. Instead, because it appears difficult to markedly improve the ability of the model to deal with cybercrime, some suggest that we develop a two-pronged approach to cybercrime by adding prevention to reaction.

The idea is that to the extent we can prevent cybercrimes from being committed, we reduce the number of cybercrimes to which law enforcement officers must react. We also reduce the amount of damage cybercrime inflicts each year and, in so doing, may begin to create disincentives for taking up a career in cybercrime.

That all sounds reasonable, but then we come to the difficult issue: How do we implement prevention as a cybercrime control strategy? Most cybercrime targets civilian victims, so civilians are the obvious focus of a cybercrime prevention strategy. In a sense, what a civilian cybercrime prevention strategy seeks to do is restore at least a measure of the protection our borders have always provided. As we have seen, until recently, crime was a purely domestic matter. A bank in Waco, Texas, had to worry about being robbed by someone who was in Waco but not about Russian hackers. The U.S. borders meant that the universe of crime about which we had to be concerned came from local criminals. Because our law enforcement agencies dealt effectively with this domestic crime, we could assume that we were reasonably secure from crime. We might install alarm systems and take other precautions to protect ourselves, but as we saw in Chapter 10, it was not up to us to get involved in the fight against crime. For the last century and a half, combating crime has been the exclusive province of professionalized police forces.

As we have seen, those forces are losing their battle against cybercrime. As was shown in Chapter 10, before police officers assumed responsibility for controlling crime by reacting to completed crimes, crime control was the responsibility of civilians. Bringing civilians back into the crime control process could be a way to support law enforcement officers in their battle with cybercrime. We could deputize civilians and have them work with the officers who investigate cybercrimes. However, that strategy is inadvisable for at least two reasons. One reason is that the civilians would have to be given some level of law enforcement training to ensure that they stayed within the law as they investigated violations of the law. Therefore, the approach would consume resources that could more effectively be utilized by professional law enforcement officers and thereby reduce its overall efficacy.

The other reason this is an inadvisable strategy is that similar efforts have been disastrous. Ninety-two years ago, concern about German sabotage led to the creation of the American Protective League.[29] The League was a volunteer organization that was intended to help catch saboteurs. It was created because federal and state law enforcement officers did not have the resources to combat what some thought was a serious threat of sabotage.[30] Thus, a group of businessmen organized the league. By June 1917, the league had nearly 100,000 members and branches in 600 towns; by 1918, the league had nearly 250,000 members.[31] But what began as a way to support law enforcement descended into lawlessness. League members wiretapped phones, "impersonated federal officers, opened mail, broke into and searched offices, ransacked the homes of 'suspects,' and made illegal arrests."[32] The league was disbanded when World War I ended.

As far as I know, no one is suggesting we create an American Cyber-Protective League to supplement law enforcement efforts against cybercrime. I mention the league because it illustrates the difficulty of integrating even well-intentioned civilians into a professional law enforcement effort. I cannot say it would be impossible to use civilians to support and enhance law enforcement efforts to react to cybercrimes. There is a large pool of civilians who have expertise in computer security and computer forensics, and it might be possible to integrate them into the law enforcement effort in a way that avoids the problems that arose with the American Protective League. Even if this were possible, I suspect it would not be particularly productive because it would presumably require that law enforcement officers carefully supervise what the civilians did. Otherwise, the effort could descend into league-style vigilantism.

Because it seems inadvisable to incorporate civilians into the process of reacting to cybercrime, we are left with using civilians to prevent cybercrimes from being committed. As I noted earlier, this not only reduces the amount of cybercrime to which police must react, it also reduces the damage cybercrime inflicts. Conceptually, this approach is the mirror image of the premise that "the best defense is a good offense"; here, a good defense is actually an offensive strategy. By preventing cybercriminals from committing crimes, we interrupt and disrupt their criminal endeavors. We prevent them from using online attacks to undermine order in our country.

Using civilians to prevent cybercrimes does not raise the resource and control issues that attend any effort to incorporate civilians into the process of reacting to crime, or cybercrime, because it is an essentially passive endeavor. It is the online analog of asking citizens to lock their car doors and be skeptical of telemarketers. Encouraging people to do their best to avoid becoming victims of cybercrime requires more effort and more computer expertise than these and other crime-prevention efforts. However, it does not depend on diverting scarce law enforcement resources, and it raises little, if any, risk of American Protective League-style vigilantism.

The most challenging aspect of implementing a civilian cybercrime prevention strategy is figuring out how to get people to participate. Logically, there are two ways to do this: We can require people to prevent cybercrime, or we can encourage people to voluntarily prevent cybercrime.

As I have explained elsewhere, I think any effort that requires people to prevent cybercrime is doomed to failure. Doing that presumably would mean we would adopt laws that mandate cybercrime prevention. Some have analogized cybercrime prevention laws to the laws that require us to wear seat belts. They point out that after seat-belt laws went into effect, the use of seat belts increased markedly, and the number of deaths and injuries from traffic accidents declined dramatically. However, I do not think that seat-belt laws are analogous to cybercrime prevention laws. Seat belts are already installed in our vehicles and are easy to use. Cybercrime prevention tools may come pre-installed on our computers (or not), but they are not as simple to use as a seat belt, and they must be updated and even replaced as technology evolves.

There is another difference between seat-belt laws and cybercrime prevention laws. We use seat belts in public; we drive on public streets where it is easy for police officers to determine if we are wearing our seat belts. If we are not wearing our seat belts, the officers can pull us over and give us a ticket. Giving me a ticket for not wearing a seat belt will probably encourage me to wear one in the future and may encourage others to follow my example. We tend to use computers in private—in our homes and our offices. A police officer has no way of knowing if I am using cybercrime prevention tools at home. What I do, or fail to do, at home is not visible to someone outside (unless they use surveillance techniques, which would no doubt violate the Fourth Amendment). We could create an agency to monitor compliance with cybercrime prevention law, but that seems counterproductive. Instead of using those resources to investigate citizens, law enforcement could use them to pursue cybercriminals. If cybercrime prevention laws apply to businesses as well as individuals (which is reasonable, given the extent to which cybercriminals target businesses), then our employers could monitor the extent to which we are using the tools they provide to prevent the commission of cybercrimes targeting the company (and ourselves).

Overall, I think mandating cybercrime prevention is a bad idea. We would have to set standards that defined the base level of prevention efforts required of individuals and businesses. We would have to enforce those standards, and we would have to come up with some way of sanctioning those who failed to abide by them. It seems that all of this simply diverts us from the real task at hand: combating cybercrime.

The alternative is to encourage people to prevent cybercrime. How would we do this? It would obviously involve encouraging people to prevent cybercrime by educating them about the risks it creates for the victims and for the entire country. In some respects, these efforts would be analogous to the campaigns countries mounted to convince citizens to participate in civil defense blackouts during World War II.[33] The efforts would also have to include educating people about tools they could use to prevent cybercrime, as well as how to use the tools and how to keep those tools updated. It might be necessary to provide tools for free or at reduced cost to some citizens.

How effective are such efforts likely to be? No doubt, they would encourage some individuals to take steps to prevent cybercrime, and their influence might become more pronounced if the efforts were sustained over time. The goal of such efforts is really to change our culture from one in which we assume law enforcement officers will protect us in cyberspace to one in which we realize we bear the primary responsibility for protecting ourselves from cybercriminals. One way to enhance the success of these efforts would be to concentrate on business and corporate computer users, both because they are likely targets of cybercriminals and because they could become an example for individuals.

Encouraging cybercrime prevention is not a particularly exciting strategy, but it would probably help to make cybercriminals' lives more difficult. It is not a tactic that can defeat or even control cybercrime on its own, but it could increase the effectiveness of law enforcement efforts to combat cybercrime.

SUM

Ironically, the "bad guys" often see the advantage of new technology before the "good guys" do. As we saw in Chapter 9, bank robbers had cars before the police did. In the nineteenth-century, criminals used encrypted telegrams to orchestrate robberies and frauds.[34] In the late twentieth century, they began to realize how computers could be used to commit crimes. The police then must play catch-up, which has become much more difficult than it used to be. As we saw in Chapter 9, it took a few years for police to convince citizens that they needed automobiles if they were to compete effectively with the Bonnie and Clydes of the world. When telegrams gave way to telephones, as we saw in Chapter 10, police also learned how to exploit that technology to their advantage.

These and the other technologies that were criminal tools before they became implements of law enforcement differ in two notable respects from computer technology. They were basically stable technologies. An automobile from the 1930s bears little resemblance to a modern vehicle, but both perform the same function of moving people and things from place to place. Although criminals could use some of the technologies such as the automobile and telephone to transcend spatial limitations, their use in this regard was limited. Bonnie and Clyde could rob a bank in Oklahoma and flee to Texas but not to France or Russia.

The stability of the technologies meant that once law enforcement had caught up with the criminal uses of a technology, they had effectively nullified the advantages that technology conferred. The primary difference between the high-speed chases conducted by police in the 1930s and the ones they conduct today is how fast the vehicles travel; the dynamic is the same. The fact that some of the technologies could be used to evade spatial limitations meant law enforcement had to expand its sphere of influence. As we saw in Chapter 9, U.S. law enforcement dealt with criminals using vehicles to flee across state borders by federalizing many crimes. Also, as we saw in Chapter 11, law enforcement dealt with criminals using telephones to orchestrate crimes by developing surveillance technology and federal law authorizing the use of that technology.

Computer technology is a far more complex and much less stable phenomenon than the technologies that preceded it. The basic principles of computer technology are stable, but the manifestations of those principles are constantly evolving in functionality. This means that to compete with cybercriminals, law enforcement officers cannot simply acquire and master the technology of the moment. Cybercriminals have the luxury of being able to innovate. They can acquire (or develop) new technology and experiment with it until they learn how best to exploit it to their advantage. Law enforcement is left to play catch-up, over and over again. The difficulty of keeping up with what cybercriminals are doing is exacerbated by the obscurity of the environment in which they operate. As we have seen, it is a complex, time-consuming, and sometimes problematic task for law enforcement officers to track down a cybercriminal, especially if he or she is in another country.

As I noted in Chapter 10, the problems law enforcement confronts in dealing with cybercrime would be significantly reduced if we implemented a global policing system to react to this type of crime. As I also noted in Chapter 10, that will not happen, at least not anytime in the foreseeable future. Therefore, we must come up with other ways to maintain law and order in cyberspace. The alternatives outlined in this chapter are the only ones proposed so far, and as we have seen, most are unworkable or inadvisable.

I think part of the problem is that we are still approaching cybercrime as if it is simply a variant of crime—a kind of twenty-first-century Bonnie-and-Clyde phenomenon. I do not think that is the way to approach cybercrime because, as we have seen, crime is territorially grounded and cybercrime is not. We must approach cybercrime as what it is: a nonphysical, nonterritorial phenomenon. We need to devise some way—other than implementing global cybercrime police—to prevent cybercriminals from exploiting national boundaries to their advantage and our disadvantage.

Notes

CHAPTER 1. TWENTY-FIRST CENTURY *TWILIGHT ZONE*: STALKING A TOWN

1. For information on the episode, *see* "The Monsters Are Due on Maple Street," Wikipedia, http://en.wikipedia.org/wiki/The_Monsters_Are_Due_on _Maple_Street. The entire episode is available, in three installments, on YouTube, http://www.youtube.com/.

2. The account that follows is drawn from these sources: Michele Kurtz, "The 'Stalker' Who Stayed at Home: A Town Terrorized over the Internet," *Boston Globe*, September 2, 2001, A1; Michele Kurtz, "'Cyberspace Terrorist' Gets Jail: Townsend School Was His Target," *Boston Globe*, June 6, 2001, B1; Jessica Heslam, "Missouri Man Pleads Innocent to Terrorizing Students Online," *Boston Herald*, August 15, 2000, 2; Bill Graham, "Charges Filed in Threat, Porn Case," *Kansas City Star*, October 26, 1999, A1.

3. The police's identification of Hunold as their perpetrator is also attributable to a mistake he made back home in Missouri. According to an account in the *Kansas City Star*, Hunold used a computer in a community college computer lab to access the Hawthorne Brooke Middle School chat room. On one occasion, he used the lab computer while sitting next to a student who knew him. Finished, Hunold left the room but left a disk labeled "Columbine" in the lab computer. The other student retrieved it, inserted it in the computer he was using, and began looking at the files. When he saw violent images and threats against Hawthorne Brooke Middle School, he contacted the FBI in Kansas City and gave the disk to them. Bill Graham, "Disk Tied to Threat," *Kansas City Star*, October 27, 1999, B1.

4. Christian Hunold, was prosecuted in two states and plea-bargained in both. In Missouri, he pled guilty to three felony counts: two counts of disseminating child pornography and one count of harassment. A Missouri judge sentenced him to 15 years in prison—five years on each count, the terms to be served consecutively. The judge reserved the right to release Hunold on probation if he served 120 days with good behavior, which he did. The Missouri judge then put Hunold on probation, subject to conditions that included Hunold not using computers, the Internet, or e-mail.

In Massachusetts, Hunold was charged with two counts of disseminating matter harmful to minors, two counts of attempting to do so, and one count each of assault, threatening to commit a crime, disturbing the peace, and disturbing a school. In June 2001, he pled guilty and was sentenced to a year in a Massachusetts prison and five years of probation following his release from prison. Similar to the Missouri judge, the judge who sentenced Hunold in Massachusetts required that Hunold not use the Internet while he was on probation. Hunold apparently served his time in Massachusetts and was released. He presumably returned to Missouri and lives a quiet, law-abiding life.

CHAPTER 2. FROM MAINFRAMES TO METAVERSE: THE ORIGINS AND EVOLUTION OF CYBERCRIME

1. *See* Susan W. Brenner, "Is There Such a Thing as 'Virtual Crime'?" *California Criminal Law Review* 4 (2001): 1, http://www.boalt.org/CCLR/v4/v4 brenner.htm.

2. *See* Ulrich Sieber, *Legal Aspects of Computer-Related Crime in the Information Society* (Brussels, Belgium: European Commission, 1998), 19; Donn Parker, *Crime by Computer* (New York: Charles Scribner's Sons, 1976), x–xi.

3. For an excellent history of modern computing, *see* Martin Campbell-Kelly and William Aspray, *Computer: A History of the Information Machine* (New York: Basic Books, 1996). The summary of the history of mainframes in the text is drawn in large part from this book.

4. *See* Campbell-Kelly and Aspray, *Computer: A History of the Information Machine, supra*, 100–121.

5. *See* Campbell-Kelly and Aspray, *Computer: A History of the Information Machine, supra*, 125–30.

6. *See* Campbell-Kelly and Aspray, *Computer: A History of the Information Machine, supra*, 131.

7. There was computer crime in the 1950s. However, as we will see later in the text, it was much more limited in scope because the mainframes were stand-alone, non-networked computers. That limited the amount and type of harm they could inflict.

8. *See* Steven Levy, *Hackers: Heroes of the Computer Revolution* (New York: Doubleday, 1984), 19.

9. Levy, *Hackers: Heroes of the Computer Revolution, supra,* 18–25. The description of an IBM mainframe in this paragraph is drawn from this source.

10. *See* "Mainframe Computer," Wikipedia, http://en.wikipedia.org/wiki/Mainframe_computer ("Users gained access through specialized terminals").

11. *See* Mark D. Rasch, *The Internet and Business: A Lawyer's Guide to the Emerging Legal Issues,* Chapter 11 § II (Fairvax, VA: Computer Law Association, 1996), http://www.swiss.ai.mit.edu/6805/articles/computer-crime/rasch-criminal-law.html.

12. For an account of some computer sabotage cases from this era, *see* Gerald McKnight, *Computer Crime* (New York: Walker and Company, 1973), 97–112. For a case in which the employees of a company's computer department successfully extorted higher salaries by subtly threatening to erode the computer's performance, *see id.,* 114–18.

13. The account of this crime is taken from Parker, *Crime by Computer, supra,* 71–77. Val Smith is the alias Parker uses for this computer criminal.

14. *See id.*

15. In 1976, *Forbes* reported that because companies were concerned about bad publicity, they reported only one of five computer embezzlement incidents. *See* "Keypunch 'Operators'," *Forbes,* September 15, 1976, 9. For cases similar to Smith's, *see* McKnight, *Computer Crime, supra,* 28–32.

16. *See* David Pauly et al., "Crime in the Suites: On the Rise," *Newsweek,* December 3, 1979, 114. *See also* Allan J. Mayer, "The Computer Bandits," *Newsweek,* August 9, 1976, 58.

17. Larry Kramer, "Action Urged to Curb Crime by Computer," *Washington Post,* June 22, 1978, D11. In the mid-1970s, Senator Ribicoff lobbied for a bill that would make computer crimes of varying types federal offenses.

18. For a detailed description of the case, *see* Parker, *Crime by Computer, supra,* 118–74.

19. *See* "New American Way of Life," *U.S. News & World Report,* May 31, 1976, 29.

20. *See id.*

21. *See United States v. Lambert,* 446 F Supp. 890 (D. Conn. 1978).

22. *See,* e.g., "'The Nagging Feeling' of Undetected Fraud," *U.S. News & World Report,* December 19, 1977, 42.

23. *See,* e.g., Bernard D. Nossiter, "Scotland Yard Deprograms Great Computer Tape Heist," *Washington Post,* January 14, 1977, A15.

24. "Phreaking," Wikipedia, http://en.wikipedia.org/wiki/Phreaking.

25. *See* "Phreaking," Wikipedia, *supra. See also* Gary D. Robson, "The Origins of Phreaking," April 2004, http://www.robson.org/gary/writing/phreaking.html.

26. *See* Robson, "Origins of Phreaking," *supra.* The description of phreaking in the text is taken from this source and from the Wikipedia entry previously cited. The Bell Telephone System, which was *the* phone system at the time, made the phreakers' task easier by publishing the frequencies it used to rout calls. The articles appeared in

1955 and 1950. *See* "Blue Box (Phreaking)," Wikipedia, http://en.wikipedia.org/wiki/Blue_box.

27. *See* Tom Barbalet, "Who Is John Draper?" 1995, http://www.barbalet.net/crunch/.

28. *See* "Blue Box (Phreaking)," Wikipedia, *supra*. Blue boxes were followed by red boxes and black boxes, each adding new functions. *See* Robson, "Origins of Phreaking," *supra*.

29. *See*, e.g., "Theft of Services," Wikipedia, http://en.wikipedia.org/wiki/Theft_of_services. Theft of services consists of stealing services, such as cable TV service, electric service, or, in the case of the phone phreaks, telephone service. It is based on the recognition that using services without paying for them is a type of stealing, even though the thief does not take anything tangible.

30. Ron Rosenbaum, "Secrets of the Little Blue Box," *Esquire*, October 1971, 116.

31. *See* Paul Mungo and Bryan Glough, *Approaching Zero: The Extraordinary Underworld of Hackers, Phreakers, Virus Writers and Keyboard Criminals*, http://www.windowsecurity.com/whitepapers/Approaching_Zero__The_Extraordinary_Underworld_of_Hackers_Phreakers_etc.html.

32. *See id.*

33. *See* Elizabeth McCracken, "Dial-Tone Phreak," *New York Times*, December 30, 2007.

34. *See* "RIP—Joybubbles, Honorary Geekdad," *Wired*, August 18, 2007, http://www.democraticwarrior.com/forum/showthread.php?p=155216.

35. *See* Chris Rhoads, "The Twilight Years of Cap'n Crunch," *Wall Street Journal*, January 13, 2007, 1.

36. *See* "Phreaking," Wikipedia, *supra*.

37. *See* Levy, *Hackers: Heroes of the Computer Revolution*, *supra*. The account of the MIT hackers in the text is taken from this source.

38. FAQ, MIT Hack Gallery, http://hacks.mit.edu/Hacks/misc/faq.html. *See also* Levy, *Hackers: Heroes of the Computer Revolution*, *supra*.

39. *See* Mary Thornton, " 'Hackers' Ignore Consequents of Their High-Tech Joy Rides," *Washington Post*, 1984, A1.

40. *See id.*

41. *See id.* The Cookie Monster hack program is available here: "Cookie Monster" program from MIT Multics, http://ftp.stratus.com/vos/multics/pg/cookie.pl1. The Sesame Street Cookie Monster had not been created in 1970 when this program was written; the program was based on a cartoon bear that appeared in a cereal commercial. *See id.*

42. *See* Levy, *Hackers: Heroes of the Computer Revolution*, *supra*, 26–36.

43. *See* "History of Free and Open Source Software," Wikipedia, http://en.wikipedia.org/wiki/History_of_free_software.

44. The definitive history of the ARPANET is the book by Katie Hafner and Matthew Lyon, *Where Wizards Stay Up Late: The Origins of the Internet* (New York: Touchstone, 1996).

45. *See*, e.g., Eric S. Raymond, *A Brief History of Hackerdom*, 2000, http://oreilly.com/catalog/opensources/book/raymond.html.

46. When the ARPANET was designed, no one thought there would ever be a need for more than 256 linked computers. *See* Vinton Cerf, "The Birth of the ARPANET," http://www.netvalley.com/archives/mirrors/cerf-how-inet.txt.

47. *See* "History of Personal Computers," Wikipedia, http://en.wikipedia.org/wiki/History_of_personal_computers.

48. Joseph B. Treaster, "Hundreds of Youths Trading Data on Computer Break-ins," *New York Times*, September 5, 1983, 1.

49. The account of the 414s is taken from two sources: Barton Gellman, "Young Computer Bandits Byte Off More than They Could Chew," *Washington Post*, August 30, 1983, A2; and "The 414s," Wikipedia, http://en.wikipedia.org/wiki/The_414s.

50. *See* John Gallant, "Film Provided Model for NASA Security Breach, Teen Says," *Computerworld*, August 27, 1984, 18.

51. *See* Hafner and Lyon, *Where Wizards Stay Up Late*, *supra*, 164–92.

52. Hess eventually was apprehended and prosecuted for espionage by German authorities. He was convicted and given a prison sentence of a year and eight months, but the sentence was suspended, and he was put on probation. *See id.*, 224–49. He currently works in computer security and has not been in trouble since then.

53. *See* Michael Weinstein, "Electronic Funds Transfer Review: A Look at Security," *American Banker*, April 2, 1984, 11. The film accurately depicted a hacking technique that came to be known as wardialing because the screenwriters consulted a number of hackers, including Captain Crunch (who claimed responsibility for wardialing). *See* Scott Brown, "War Games: A Look Back at the Film That Turned Geeks and Phreaks into Stars," *Wired*, July 21, 2008.

54. *See* Brown, "War Games," *supra*.

55. *See* Tom Shea, "The FBI Goes after Hackers," *InfoWorld*, March 26, 1984, 38. The FBI was, as several noted, "embarrassingly slow" to understand the hacker threat.

56. *See id.* Hackers stole phone services because, as I already noted, they used telephone lines to communicate with each other via bulletin boards and to hack computer systems. *See supra* note29. The hacker who was cited in the text said he became an informant for two reasons. One reason was to stop what he believed had become dangerous intrusions into essential computer systems; the other was for the intellectual challenge of "hacking the hackers." *See id.*

57. *See id. See also* Thornton, " 'Hackers' Ignore Consequents of Their High-Tech Joy Rides," *supra* (an "epidemic" of hacking among the nation's teenagers).

58. *See* "Hacker (Computer Security)," Wikipedia, http://en.wikipedia.org/ wiki/Hacker_(computer_security). *See also* "Black Hat," The Jargon File—Glossary, http://www.catb.org/jargon/html/B/black-hat.html. There are also "grey hat" hackers, which are hackers known for "ambiguous ethics and/or borderline legality." "Hacker (Computer Security)," Wikipedia, *supra*.

59. "Black Hat," The Jargon File—Glossary, *supra*.

60. *See* William Gibson, *Neuromancer* (New York: Ace Books, 1995 reissue edition), 51.

61. The name of the group came from comic books. In Superman comics, The Legion of Doom was a group of super-villains led by Lex Luthor. *See* Bruce Sterling, *The Hacker Crackdown* (New York: Bantam Books, 1992), 87–88.

62. *See* "Legion of Doom (Hacking)," Wikipedia, http://en.wikipedia.org/wiki/ Legion_of_Doom_(hacking).

63. *See* Michele Slatalla and Joshua Quittner, *Masters of Deception* (New York: HarperCollins, 1995), 63–67.

64. "Masters of Deception," Wikipedia, http://en.wikipedia.org/wiki/ Masters_of_Deception.

65. *See* Slatalla and Quittner, *Masters of Deception*, *supra*, 134–49.

66. *See id*, 200–206. The indictment is available here: *Computer Underground Digest*, July 17, 1992, http://www.textfiles.com/magazines/CUD/cud0431.txt.

67. *See* Slatalla and Quittner, *Masters of Deception*, *supra*, 206–19.

68. *See* Douglas Thomas, *Hacker Culture* (Minneapolis: University of Minnesota Press, 2002), 81.

69. The account of Kevin Poulsen's career as a hacker is taken from these sources: Jonathan Littman, *The Watchman: The Twisted Life and Crimes of Serial Hacker Kevin Poulsen* (Boston: Little, Brown & Co., 1997); and Jonathan Littman, "The Last Hacker," *Los Angeles Times Magazine*, September 12, 1993, 18. *See* "Phreaking," Wikipedia, *supra* (listing Poulsen as a famous phone phreak). *See also* Littman, *Watchman*, *supra*, 11–24.

70. *See* Littman, *Watchman*, *supra*, 24–35.

71. *See* Littman, *Watchman*, *supra*, 8–45.

72. *See* Littman, *Watchman*, *supra*, 42–60.

73. Poulsen had rented the unit under an alias. *See United States v. Poulsen*, 41 F.3d 1330, 1331 (9th Cir. 1994).

74. *See* Littman, *Watchman*, *supra*, 100–180.

75. For a detailed account of the scheme, *see* Littman, *Watchman*, *supra*, 3–7, 214–19.

76. *See* Janet Gilmore, "Former Van Nuys Man Pleads Guilty to Computer Fraud," *Daily News (Los Angeles)*, June 15, 1994, N6.

77. *See* "Unsolved Mysteries," Wikipedia, http://en.wikipedia.org/wiki/ Unsolved_Mysteries.

78. *See* Littman, *Watchman*, *supra*, 240–42.

79. *See* Littman, *Watchman*, *supra*, 244–45.

80. *See* Littman, *Watchman*, *supra*, 245–47. *See also* Benjamin Wittes, "Is Law Enforcement Ready for Cybercrime?" *Legal Times*, October 10, 1994, 1.

81. *See* Littman, *Watchman*, *supra*, 265–71.

82. *See* "Hacker Gets 51 Months in Radio Contest Scam," *Los Angeles Times*, April 11, 1995, 2 ($36,925 to radio station KIIS, $20,000 to KPWR, and $1,000 to KRTH).

83. Leslie Berger, "Computer Hacker Who Jumped Bail Gets 41 Months," *Los Angeles Times*, November 28, 1995, 5 (article about the sentencing of "Agent Steal").

84. Leslie Berger, "Spying Charge against Hacker Is Dropped," *Los Angeles Times*, November 10, 1995, 1. He would probably have spent more time in prison, but federal prosecutors dropped the espionage charges that had been brought against him earlier. *See* Littman, *Watchman*, *supra*, 279. They apparently dropped the charges because of the sentence he received on the other charges and because of the amount of time that had passed since his alleged espionage activity. Some speculate that the decision was also influenced by concern that the charge was no longer viable.

Poulsen became a journalist, first for the computer security company Security Focus and later for *Wired* magazine. He has been a senior editor at *Wired* since 2005. *See* "Kevin Poulsen," Wikipedia, http://en.wikipedia.org/wiki/Kevin _Poulsen.

85. *See* Littman, *Watchman*, *supra*.

86. *See*, e.g., Mark Guidera, "Hackers Targeting Credit Cards," *(Albany) Times Union*, August 14, 1994, A8; Stevan Rosenlind, "Criminals Lurk in Alleys of Cyberspace," *Baltimore Sun*, April 1, 1994, 6C.

87. *See*, e.g., Brian Akre, "Cybercrime Epidemic at Major Corporations," *Times-Picayune*, October 25, 1995, C1; Ellen Messmer, "Firms Face Business Pitfalls on the 'Net'," *Network World*, October 16, 1995, 35.

88. *See* "Reno Urges Cybercrime Crackdown in Americas," *Deseret News*, November 26, 1998, A03.

89. *See* "Malware," Wikipedia, http://en.wikipedia.org/wiki/Malware. The general description of malware is taken from this entry.

90. Malware includes viruses, worms, Trojan horse programs, rootkits, spyware, adware, botnet programs, keystroke loggers, and dialers. *See* "Malware," Wikipedia, *supra*.

91. *See* "Computer Virus," Wikipedia, http://en.wikipedia.org/wiki/Computer _virus. The general description of computer viruses is taken from this entry.

92. *See* "Malware," Wikipedia, *supra*.

93. *See* Robert Lemos, "The Computer Virus—No Cures to Be Found," *ZD Net*, November 25, 2003, http://news.zdnet.com/2100-1009_22-5111442.html. Pervading Animal was not the first virus. That seems to have been "the Creeper," which infected ARPANET computers in the early 1970s. It caused an infected machine to display the message "I'M THE CREEPER: CATCH ME IF YOU CAN." *See* "History of Malware: 1970s," *Viruslist.com*, http://www.viruslist.com/ en/viruses/encyclopedia?chapter=153310937.

94. *See* Lemos, "Computer Virus," *supra*.

95. *See* "Computer Viruses Hit One Million," *BBC News*, April 10, 2008, http://news.bbc.co.uk/2/hi/technology/7340315.stm (1,122,311).

96. The description of computer worms is taken from "Computer Worm," Wikipedia, http://en.wikipedia.org/wiki/Computer_worm.

97. John Brunner, *The Shockwave Rider* (New York: Ballantine Books, 1975).

98. *See* Andy Sudduth, *The What, Why, and How of the 1988 Internet Worm: History of Worm Like Programs*, 1988, http://snowplow.org/tom/worm/worm.html. The history of worms prior to the appearance of the Morris worm comes from this source.

99. The account of the Morris worm is primarily drawn from *United States v. Morris*, 927 F.2d 504 (2d Cir. 1991).

100. *See* Sudduth, *What, Why, and How of the 1988 Internet Worm*, *supra*.

101. Most of the infected computers were in the United States because in 1988, most of the computers linked to the Internet were in the United States. *See* "History of the Internet," Wikipedia, http://en.wikipedia.org/wiki/History_of_the_Internet.

102. A subsequent investigation by Cornell University criticized Morris for "his minimal efforts to limit the damage of the worm." Frances Dinkelspiel, "Hacker's Actions Selfish," *Syracuse Post-Standard*, April 1, 1989, A1. The investigators found that instead of wasting time with his friend from Harvard, Morris should have gone to the Dean of the Computer Science Department for help in stopping the worm.

103. *See* Matthew Spina, "The Worm Had Venom," *Syracuse Post-Standard*, February 12, 1989, A1.

104. *See* Lauren DiDio, "Virus Victims Are Stoic in Face of Multinet Attack," *Network World*, November 14, 1988, 6.

105. Michael Alexander, "Morris Felony Charge Expected by End of July," *Computerworld*, July 17, 1989, 4.

106. *See* "Designer of Computer 'Virus' Indicted," *Tulsa World*, July 27, 1989, A5.

107. *See* John Markoff, "Computer Intruder Is Found Guilty," *New York Times*, January 23, 1990, A21.

108. *See* John Markoff, "Computer Intruder Is Put on Probation and Fined $10,000," *New York Times*, May 5, 1990, 11.

109. *See* "Robert Tappan Morris," Wikipedia, http://en.wikipedia.org/wiki/Robert_Tappan_Morris.

110. The account of Mitnick's career is taken from these sources: Thomas C. Green, "Chapter One: Kevin Mitnick's Story," *Register*, January 13, 2003, http://www.theregister.co.uk/2003/01/13/chapter_one_kevin_mitnicks_story/; Hafner and Lyon, *Where Wizards Stay Up Late*, *supra*, 13–137; Richard Power, *Tangled Web* (Indianapolis, IN: Que, 2000), 57–59.

111. *See* Elinor Mills Abreu, "Ex-hacker Hawks Laptops, Hypes Book," *Chicago Tribune*, October 7, 2002, 2.

112. This description of Shimomura's investigation is taken in part from Joe Flower, "Catching Kevin and His Friends," *New Scientist*, September 2, 1995, 22.

113. "Ben MacIntyre," *Times (UK)*, July 5, 1994, 14.

114. "Drop the Phone: Busting a Computer Whiz," *Time*, January 9, 1989, 49.

115. John Markoff, "Cyberspace's Most Wanted," *New York Times*, July 4, 1994, 11.

116. Ibid.

117. Gregory T. Huang, "The Talented Mr. Mitnick," *Technology Review*, March 1, 2005, 21.

118. Ibid.

119. The 1995 movie *Hackers* also features a villainous hacker ("Plague"). *See* "Hackers," Wikipedia, http://en.wikipedia.org/wiki/Hackers_(film).

120. The account of this attack is primarily taken from two sources: Jonathan Ungoed-Thomas, "The Schoolboy Spy," *Sunday Times (UK)*, March 29, 1998, 1; and Chris Williams, "Air Force in Dogfight with Hackers," *San Antonio Express-News*, August 11, 1996, 01A.

121. Ungoed-Thomas, "Schoolboy Spy," *supra*.

122. *See* Paul Campbell, Ben Calvert, and Steven Boswell, *Security+ In Depth 216* (Boston, MA: Thomson Course Technology, 2003).

123. *See* Ungoed-Thomas, "Schoolboy Spy," *supra*. *See also* Kathryn Lister, "The Boy Who Hacked into the Pentagon's Computer," *The Sun (UK)*, April 10, 1998, 6.

124. *See* "Password Cracking," Wikipedia, http://en.wikipedia.org/wiki/Password_cracking.

125. *See United States v. Salgado*, U.S. District Court for the Northern District of California (Case #3.97-30257 OEW), http://jya.com/smak.htm.

126. *See* "Packet Sniffer," Wikipedia, http://en.wikipedia.org/wiki/Packet_sniffer.

127. *See* Criminal Complaint, *United States v. Salgado, supra*.

128. *See* Jon Swartz, "Hacker Suspect Faces 15 Years," *San Francisco Chronicle*, May 24, 1997, D1.

129. *See United States v. Salgado*, Indictment, U.S. District Court for the Northern District of California (Case # CR97—00197 VRW), http://jya.com/smak.htm.

130. *See* Power, *Tangled Web, supra*, 90.

131. *See* "Willie Sutton," Wikipedia, http://en.wikipedia.org/wiki/Willie_Sutton.

132. The account of this scheme is taken from two sources: Sharon Gaudin, "Interview with a Convicted Hacker," *Information Week*, September 26, 2007; and Ken Belson and Tom Zeller Jr., "Hacker Said to Resell Internet Phone Service," *New York Times*, June 7, 2006.

133. Moore pled guilty to federal computer fraud and was sentenced to two years in prison; Penal fled the country. Gaudin, "Interview with a Convicted Hacker," *supra*.

134. *See* Thea Alberto, "7 International Cyber Thieves Nabbed in RP," Inquirer.net, March 12, 2007, http://newsinfo.inquirer.net/breakingnews/infotech/view_article.php?article_id=54389.

135. The account of the hack comes from Eileen Sullivan, "FEMA Phones Hacked," *Washington Post*, August 20, 2008.

136. *See* "Computer virus," Wikipedia, http://en.wikipedia.org/wiki/Computer_virus; "Macro Virus (Computing)," Wikipedia, http://en.wikipedia.org/wiki/Macro_virus_(computing). The description of macro viruses is taken from these sources.

137. Linda Musthaler, "Dispelling the Myths about Viruses Is a First Step to Keeping Your Net Healthy," *Network World*, May 13, 1996, 42.

138. Ibid.

139. *See* Stephen Manes, "'Innocent' Files Can Carry a Virus," *New York Times*, September 12, 1995, C8. The phrase was in a Concept macro that was never activated. *See* Deborah Gage, "Viruses Abound," *Computer Reseller News*, May 13, 1996.

140. For a chronology of malware, *see* "Timetable of Notable Computer Viruses and Worms," Wikipedia, http://en.wikipedia.org/wiki/Notable_computer_viruses_and_worms.

141. This account of the original Melissa virus is taken from two sources: U.S. Attorney for the District of New Jersey, Press Release, "Creator of Melissa Virus Sentenced to 20 Months in Federal Prison," May 1, 2002; and Craig Menefee, "NAI Warms of Fastest Virus Spread Ever," *Newsbytes*, March 29, 1999. There were other versions. *See* "Melissa (Computer Worm)," Wikipedia, http://en.wikipedia.org/wiki/Melissa_virus.

142. *See* Miguel Helft, "Mutant E-Mail Viruses Battled," *San Jose Mercury News*, March 30, 1999, 1A.

143. *See* Daniel Sforza, "N.J. Creator of Melissa Virus Pleads Guilty," *The Record (N.J.)*, December 10, 1999.

144. Rutrell Yasin, "The Internet Decade," *Internet Week*, December 20, 1999. "Internet time" refers to the "accelerated pace of business and life brought about by" networked computers. Some say "a year of Internet time equals seven years of calendar time," but the term is really used illustratively, such as the phrase "a New York minute." *See* Internet Time Group, "What Is Internet Time?" http://abu9.blogspot.com/2004/11/time.html.

145. This account of the investigation is taken from Dean Takahashi and Dean Starkman, "How the Melissa Case Was Cracked," *Globe & Mail (Toronto)*, April 6, 1999, B5.

146. *See* "Programmer Pleads Guilty," *Los Angeles Times*, December 10, 1999, 3. Smith originally faced up to 40 years in prison on the state and federal charges. *See* Hiawatha Bray, "N.J. Man Charged in Computer Virus Case," *Boston Globe*, April 3, 1999, A1.

147. *See Pearson v. Moore*, 767 So.2d 1235, 1236 n. 2 (Florida Court of Appeals 2000) ("A coterminous sentence [is] a sentence that runs concurrently with another and terminates simultaneously").

148. Sforza, "N.J. Creator of Melissa Virus Pleads Guilty," *supra*, 1. The account of the sentencing hearing is taken from this source.

149. The quotations for both prosecutors are taken from the Sforza article "N.J. Creator of Melissa Virus Pleads Guilty," *supra*.

150. *See* "Creator of Melissa Virus Gets 20 Months in Jail," *New York Times*, May 2, 2002, 8.

151. For what Smith did, see "David L. Smith (virus writer), Encyclopedia," AllExperts.com, http://en.allexperts.com/e/d/da/david_l._smith_%28virus_writer %29.htm.

152. *See* Robert Lemos, "Melissa's Long Gone, but Lessons Remain," *CNET*, March 29, 2005, http://news.cnet.com/Melissas-long-gone,-but-lessons-remain/2100-7349_3-5643900.html. The state court judge originally sentenced Smith to serve five years in prison but later reduced the sentence so it would end at the same time as Smith's federal sentence. *See* Karen Sudol, " 'Melissa' Creator to Be Freed," *Asbury Park Press*, November 15, 2003, 1.

153. *See* "ILOVEYOU," Wikipedia, http://en.wikipedia.org/wiki/ILOVEYOU.

154. *See*, e.g., Jack Rejtman, " 'Love' Bug Paralyzes E-Mail Networks," *Miami Herald*, May 5, 2000, 1A.

155. *See* "ILOVEYOU," Wikipedia, *supra*.

156. *See* James Niccolai, "Love Bug Hits 'Tens of Millions' Worldwide," *Network World*, May 5, 2000.

157. *See* Curt Suplee, "Anatomy of a 'Love Bug,' " *Washington Post*, May 21, 2000, A01.

158. Clarence Page, " 'Love Bug:' Vengeful Email Virus Acts Like a True Love," *Seattle Post-Intelligencer*, May 12, 2000, A23.

159. *See* Tom McCann, "The Virus War," *Chicago Tribune*, August 21, 2000, C1.

160. The account of the Love Bug investigation is taken from these sources: " 'Love Bug' Virus Case Dropped in Philippines," *Washington Post*, August 22, 2000; Dick Kelsey, " 'Love Bug' Suspect Charged in Philippines," *Newsbytes*, June 29, 2000; Rajiv Chandrasekaran, "Virus May Have Been Act of 'Youthful Exuberance'," *Washington Post*, May 12, 2000, A34; Rajiv Chandrasekaran, "Philippines Shifts Focus of Internet Virus Probe," *Washington Post*, May 10, 2000, A01.

161. *See* Marc D. Goodman and Susan W. Brenner, "The Emerging Consensus on Criminal Conduct in Cyberspace," *UCLA Journal of Law & Technology* 3, 2002.

162. *See* Uli Schmetzer, " 'Love Bug' Virus the One That Got Away, Hackers Say," *Chicago Tribune*, February 1, 2001, N5.

163. *See* Byron Acohido, "Air Force Seeks Better Security from Microsoft," *USA Today*, March 11, 2002, 03B.

164. *See* "Warhol Worm," Wikipedia, http://en.wikipedia.org/wiki/Flash_worm. Flash worms are also known as Warhol worms because, similar to the celebrities Warhol posited, they have 15 minutes of fame.

165. *See* "Warhol worm," Wikipedia, *supra*.

166. *See* "Taking Steps to Secure Your Process Control System," *Control Engineering*, November 1, 2007, 1; Breanne Wagner, "Electronic Jihad," *National Defense*, July 1, 2007, 34.

167. *See* Tim Lemke, "Worm Slows Local, Worldwide Computers," *Washington Times*, May 4, 2004, C08.

168. *See* "Ransomware (Malware)," Wikipedia, http://en.wikipedia.org/wiki/Ransomware_(malware). Ransomware is a type of malware that encrypts data on the victim's computer system and demands a ransom for restoring the data to the original, unencrypted form.

169. The summary of malware trends is taken primarily from Sophos Security Threat Report 2008, http://www.sophos.com/pressoffice/news/articles/2008/01/security-report.html.

170. *See* "Computer Viruses Make It to Orbit," *BBC News*, August 27, 2008.

171. Devin Powell, "Space Station Computer Virus Raises Security Concerns," *New Scientist—Space*, August 29, 2008.

172. "Experts Map Out Future Malware Creation Hotspots," *F-Secure*, January 17, 2008, http://www.f-secure.com/f-secure/pressroom/news/fsnews_20080117_1_eng.html.

173. *See* Sarah Arnott, "How Cyber Crime Went Professional," *Independent*, August 13, 2008, http://www.independent.co.uk/news/business/analysis-and-features/how-cyber-crime-went-professional-892882.html. *See also* Finjan Malicious Code Research Center, Web Security Trends Report: Q2 2008.

174. *See* Byron Acohido, "Meet A–Z: The Computer Hacker behind a Cybercrime Wave," *USA Today*, August 5, 2008, http://www.usatoday.com/tech/news/computersecurity/2008-08-04-hacker-cybercrime-zeus-identity-theft_N.htm.

CHAPTER 3. THREE CATEGORIES OF CYBERCRIME

1. *See*, e.g., *The Electronic Frontier: The Challenge of Unlawful Conduct Involving the Use of the Internet: A Report of the President's Working Group on Unlawful Conduct on the Internet* § II(A), March 2000.

2. *See*, e.g., Scott Charney, "Computer Crime," *Federal Bar News & Journal* 41 (August 1994): 489.

3. *Colo. Rev. Stat. Ann.* § 18-4-504.

4. Law defines "real property" as land and anything "growing on, attached to, or erected on it" except for things that "can be severed without injury to the land." "Property," *Black's Law Dictionary*, 8th ed. (St. Paul, MN: Thomson West, 2004), 723. It defines "personal property" as "[a]ny movable or intangible thing that is subject to ownership" and does not constitute real property. *Id.*

5. A few states have taken that approach, as this Washington law illustrates: "A person is guilty of computer trespass . . . if the person, without authorization, intentionally gains access to a computer system." *Wash. Rev. Code Ann.* § 9A.52.120.

6. *Tenn. Code Ann.* § 39-14-408(a).

7. *See*, e.g., "Operating System," Wikipedia, http://en.wikipedia.org/wiki/Operating_system (a computer's operating system is the software that coordinates its application software and hardware so the computer can function). Microsoft Windows, Linux, and Mac OS are the more common operating systems in use today.

8. *Night Watch* is one of Rembrandt's most famous paintings. *See*, e.g., "Night Watch (Painting)," Wikipedia, http://en.wikipedia.org/wiki/Night_Watch _(painting).

9. The same is true in the first version of my laptop "vandalism" scenario, in which the virus deletes data on my laptop. If I have—as I should have—made a backup copy of the data, I can easily restore it and return to what law calls the status quo ante (i.e., the state of affairs that existed before the virus infected my laptop). This illustrates another aspect of digital property: It tends to be fungible. In law, fungible items are items that are "interchangeable with other property of the same kind." "Fungible," *Black's Law Dictionary*, 8th ed. (St. Paul, MN: Thomson West, 2004), 381. Corn is fungible, and data can be fungible; Rembrandt's *Night Watch* is not fungible.

10. *See* Nicholas Ianelli and Aaron Hackworth, "Botnets as a Vehicle for Online Crime," *CERT Coordination Center*, December 1, 2005, http://www.cert.org/archive/pdf/Botnets.pdf. For a good overview of DDoS attacks and botnets, *see* Mac-Afee North America Criminology Report, *Organized Crime and the Internet 2007*, http://www.mcafee.com/us/local_content/misc/na_criminology_report_07.pdf.

11. *See*, e.g., Brian Krebs, "Bringing Botnets out of the Shadows," *Washington Post*, March 21, 2006, http://www.washingtonpost.com/wp-dyn/content/article/2006/03/21/AR2006032100279.html.

12. This example is taken from Susan W. Brenner, "Is There Such a Thing as 'Virtual Crime'?" *California Criminal Law Review* 4 (June 2001): 1.

13. *People v. Davis*, 19 Cal. 4th 301, 305, 965 P.2d 1165, 1166 (California Supreme Court 1998).

14. The account of the Levin case is primarily taken from "How to Catch a Hacker," *USA Today*, September 19, 1997, 12A; and David Gow and Richard Norton-Taylor, "Surfing Superhighwaymen," *Guardian*, December 7, 1996, 28.

15. *See* "Vladimir Levin," Wikipedia, http://en.wikipedia.org/wiki/Vladimir _Levin; Gow and Norton-Taylor, *Surfing Superhighwaymen, supra*; "The Tale of the Russian Hacker," *Attrition.org*, 1996, http://attrition.org/~jericho/works/security/pwn-50-15.html.

16. *See* Gow and Norton-Taylor, *Surfing Superhighwaymen, supra*.

17. *Colo. Rev. Stat. Ann.* § 18-4-301(a).

18. The account of the McGuire case is taken from these sources: "Melanie McGuire Sentenced to Life in Prison for Murdering, Dismembering Her Husband

in 2004," *U.S. State News*, 2007 WLNR 13887167, July 19, 2007; Harriet Ryan, "On Nurse's Computer, an Internet How-to for Murder," *Court TV*, March 21, 2007; http://www.courttv.com/trials/mcguire/031307_ctv.html.

19. *See*, e.g., Becky Gillette, "MSU at Forefront of Cybercrime Training for Law Enforcement," *Mississippi Business Journal* 30 (May 26, 2008): A29 (drug dealers use computers, e-mail, and spreadsheets).

CHAPTER 4. TARGET CYBERCRIMES: HACKING, MALWARE, AND DISTRIBUTED DENIAL OF SERVICE ATTACKS

1. *Fla. Stat. Ann.* § 810.02(1)(a). *See also Uniform Laws Annotated, Model Penal Code* § 221.1(1).

2. *State v. Chatelain*, 220 Or. App. 487, 493, 188 P.3d 325, 328 (Oregon Court of Appeals 2008).

3. "Trespass," *Black's Law Dictionary*, 8th ed. (St. Paul, MN: Thomson West, 2004), 689.

4. 18 *U.S. Code* § 1030(a)(5).

5. *Ark. Code Ann.* § 5-41-203(b).

6. *Computer Misuse Act 1990, United Kingdom Statute 1990*, Chapter 18 § 1.

7. *See*, e.g., *Penal Code of France*, Article 323-1; *Penal Code of Italy*, Article 615 ter; *Singapore, Computer Misuse Act*, Chapter 50A.

8. The account of McKinnon's life and hacking is taken primarily from these sources: Clark Boyd, "Profile: Gary McKinnon," *BBC News*, July 30, 2008, http://news.bbc.co.uk/2/hi/technology/4715612.stm; Jamie Doward, "The Briton Facing 60 Years in Prison after Hacking into Pentagon," *Guardian*, July 27, 2008, http://www.guardian.co.uk/world/2008/jul/27/internationalcrime.hacking.

9. Doward, "Briton Facing 60 Years in Prison," *supra*.

10. "Gary McKinnon," Wikipedia, http://en.wikipedia.org/wiki/Gary _McKinnon.

11. "Gary McKinnon," Wikipedia, *supra*.

12. Boyd, "Profile: Gary McKinnon," *supra*.

13. *See* Doward, "Briton Facing 60 Years in Prison," *supra*. *See also* The Disclosure Project, http://www.disclosureproject.org/.

14. *See* Boyd, "Profile: Gary McKinnon," *supra*.

15. *See* Doward, "Briton Facing 60 Years in Prison," *supra*.

16. *See* Boyd, "Profile: Gary McKinnon," *supra*.

17. "Brit Accused of Hacking Pentagon," *Wired*, November 11, 2002, http://www.wired.com/politics/law/news/2002/11/56332.

18. *See* U.S. Department of Justice, *British National Charged with Hacking*, November 18, 2002, http://www.usdoj.gov/criminal/cybercrime/mckinnonIndict2 .htm.

19. Tim Luckhurst, "Is This the Most Dangerous Hacker on Earth, or a Net Nerd Who Struck Unlucky?" *Independent*, June 12, 2005, 18.

20. We will examine extradition in Chapter 10.

21. *See* Kevin Poulsen, "U.K. Hacker Gary McKinnon Plays the Asperger's Card," *Wired*, August 28, 2008, http://blog.wired.com/27bstroke6/2008/08/uk-hacker-gary.html.

22. Free Gary McKinnon, http://freegary.org.uk/.

23. Poulsen, "U.K. Hacker Gary McKinnon Plays the Asperger's Card," *supra*.

24. Poulsen, "U.K. Hacker Gary McKinnon Plays the Asperger's Card," *supra*.

25. Poulsen, "U.K. Hacker Gary McKinnon Plays the Asperger's Card," *supra*. The House of Lords opinion cited previously describes the plea offer.

26. *See* Chapter 2.

27. *See*, e.g., John Leyden, "McKinnon a 'Scapegoat for Pentagon Insecurity'," *Register*, September 3, 2008, http://www.theregister.co.uk/2008/09/03/mckinnon_bevan_interview_analysis/; Francis Gibb, "Gary McKinnon, British Hacker, Loses Appeal over US Extradition," *Times*, July 31, 2008, http://www.timesonline.co.uk/tol/news/uk/crime/article4428270.ece; Owen Bowcott, "Pentagon's Pursuit of 'Scapegoat' Hacker Hides Real Threat from the Web," *Guardian*, June 11, 2005, http://www.guardian.co.uk/technology/2005/jun/11/hacking.internetcrime.

28. *See*, e.g., Leyden, "McKinnon a 'Scapegoat for Pentagon Insecurity'," *supra*.

29. 18 *U.S. Code* § 1030(e)(8) defines "damage" as "any impairment to the integrity or availability of data, a program, a system, or information."

30. *Colo. Rev. Stat. Ann.* § 18-5.5-102(1)(a).

31. *Colo. Rev. Stat. Ann.* § 18-5.5-101(6.7).

32. *See* 18 *U.S. Code* § 1030(e)(6).

33. 18 *U.S. Code* § 1030(a)(2)(c).

34. *See Computer Misuse Act 1990, United Kingdom Statute 1990*, Chapter 18 § 1; *Singapore Computer Misuse Act*, pt. II, § 3 (1998), http://agcvldb4.agc.gov.sg/; *Japan Unauthorized Computer Access Law* (Law No. 128 of 1999), Article 3.

35. 2002 WL 31127751 (Ohio Court of Appeals—First District, 2002). The account of this case in the text comes from the facts given in this opinion.

36. As the Court of Appeals noted, "access to law enforcement databases is restricted." *State v. Moning*, *supra*.

37. The account of Yontz's activity is taken from two sources: Grant Gross, "Former Gov't Worker Pleads Guilty to Viewing Passport Files," *Infoworld*, September 22, 2008, http://www.infoworld.com/news/feeds/08/09/22/Former-govt-worker-pleads-guilty-to-viewing-passport-files.html; Eric Lichtblau, "Ex-Employee Pleads Guilty to Viewing Passport Files," *New York Times*, September 22, 2008, http://www.nytimes.com/2008/09/23/washington/23passport.html.

38. 850 A.2d 1290 (Superior Court of Pennsylvania 2004). The description of the facts in the case is taken from this opinion and from this story: "Ex-Officers Convicted of Sending Anthrax Joke," *Charleston Gazette & Daily Mail*, October 19, 2002, 9A.

39. *See* "Mobile Data Terminal," Wikipedia, http://en.wikipedia.org/wiki/Mobile_data_terminal.

40. 243 Ga. App. 268, 531 S.E.2d 187 (Georgia Court of Appeals 2000). The description of the facts in the case is taken from this opinion.

41. *Fugarino v. Sates*, 243 Ga. App. at 268–69, 531 S.E.2d at 188.

42. Ibid.

43. *See Georgia Code* § 16-9-93(b).

44. Ibid.

45. *See* "Mens Rea," Wikipedia, http://en.wikipedia.org/wiki/Mens_rea.

46. For the standard of proof required under each of the four mental states, see *Model Penal Code* § 2.02 (Philadelphia, PA: American Law Institute, 1962).

47. *Fugarino v. Sates*, 243 Ga. App. at 270, 531 S.E.2d at 189.

48. *See* Orin S. Kerr, "Cybercrime's Scope: Interpreting 'Access' and 'Authorization' in Computer Misuse Statutes," *New York University Law Review* 78 (2003): 1596.

49. Erik Larkin, "Web 2.0 Sites a Thriving Marketplace for Malware," *PC World*, June 2, 2008, http://www.pcworld.com/article/146117/web_20_sites_a _thriving_marketplace_for_malware.html.

50. *See* John Leyden, "Mexico and Africa to Become Malware Hotspots," *Register*, January 18, 2008, http://www.theregister.co.uk/2008/01/18/future_cybercrime _hotspots/.

51. *See* Maksym Schipka, "The Online Shadow Economy," *Message Labs Whitepaper*, 2007, http://www.fstc.org/docs/articles/messaglabs_online_shadow _economy.pdf.

52. The description of the malware economy is taken primarily from Schipka, "Online Shadow Economy," *supra*.

53. Sue, "Majority of Malware Attacks Go Undetected," *SC Magazine*, August 12, 2008, http://www.securecomputing.net.au/News/119338,majority-of-malware-attacks-go-undetected.aspx.

54. *See* Sue, "Majority of Malware Attacks Go Undetected," *supra*.

55. *See* Larkin, "Web 2.0 Sites a Thriving Marketplace for Malware," *supra*.

56. 18 *U.S. Code* § 1030(a)(5)(A).

57. *See Senate Report No. 101-544, The Computer Abuse Amendments Act of 1990* (October 19, 1990), 101st Cong., 2d Sess. 1990, 1990 WL 201793.

58. *California Penal Code* § 502(c)(8).

59. *See California Penal Code* § 502(b)(10).

60. *See*, e.g., *Georgia Code* § 16-9-153(a)(1)(A) (crime to transmit a "computer virus"); *17-A Maine Revised Statutes* § 433(1)(C) (crime to "knowingly introduce" a "computer virus" into "any computer resource").

61. *See*, e.g., *Georgia Code* § 16-9-151 (5) (defining "computer virus" as a "program or other set of instructions that is designed to degrade the performance of or disable a computer or computer network and . . . to replicate itself").

62. At the end of 2008, I searched Westlaw, a comprehensive set of legal databases, for decisions concerning state malware prosecutions and found none.

63. *See* Susan W. Brenner and Joseph J. Schwerha IV, "Transnational Evidence Gathering and Local Prosecution of International Cybercrime," *John Marshall Journal of Computer and Information Law* 20 (2002): 347.

64. *See* Robert Vamosi, "Make the Punishment Fit the Cybercrime," *CNET Reviews*, September 10, 2003, http://reviews.cnet.com/4520-3513_7-5073597-1.html.

65. The description of the facts in the Parson case is taken from these sources: *United States v. Jeffrey Lee Parson*, Criminal Complaint, Case # 03-457M, U.S. District Court for the Western District of Washington, August 28, 2003; Judgment: *United States v. Jeffrey Lee Parson*, Case # CR03-0379P, U.S. District Court for the Western District of Washington, August 11, 2004; "Teen Arrested for Internet Attack," CBC News (August 29, 2003), http://www.cbc.ca/world/story/2003/08/29/blaster_arrest030829.html; "Cyberprints, Police Work Led to Arrest of Suspected Virus Author," *USA Today*, August 30, 2003, http://www.usatoday.com/tech/news/computersecurity/2003-08-30-how-hacker-caught_x.htm.

66. 18 *U.S. Code* § 1030(a)(5)(A).

67. About the Bureau of Prisons, Federal Bureau of Prisons, http://www.bop.gov/about/index.jsp. *See also United States v. Dion L.*, 19 F. Supp. 2d 1224, 1227 (D.N.M. 1998).

68. The description of the facts and charges in this case is taken from these sources: U.S. Attorney for the Western District of Washington, Press Release, "Juvenile Arrested for Releasing Variant of Blaster Computer Worm That Attacked Microsoft," September 26, 2003, http://www.usdoj.gov/criminal/cybercrime/juvenileArrest.htm; U.S. Attorney for the Western District of Washington, Press Release, "Juvenile Sentenced for Releasing Worm That Attacked Microsoft Web Site," February 11, 2005, http://www.usdoj.gov/criminal/cybercrime/juvenileSent.htm.

69. Stipulation of Parties Concerning Restitution Owed to Microsoft Corporation, *United States v. Jeffrey Lee Parson*, Case # CR03-0379P, U.S. District Court for the Western District of Washington, March 29, 2005. Microsoft eventually waived restitution in return for Parson doing more hours of community service.

70. Robert Vamosi, "Make the Punishment Fit the Cybercrime," *supra*. Microsoft software engineers worked with law enforcement officers, analyzing the Blaster code and using an infected computer to determine how the worm functioned. *See* Todd Bishop and Paul Shukovsky, "Blaster Worm Trail Leads to Arrest," *Seattle Post-Intelligencer*, August 30, 2003, http://seattlepi.nwsource.com/business/137369_blaster30.html.

71. *See*, e.g., Susan W. Brenner, "Toward a Criminal Law for Cyberspace: Product Liability and Other Issues," *University of Pittsburgh Journal of Technology Law and Policy* 5 (2005): 2.

72. John McMullan and Aunshul Rege, "Cyberextortion at Online Gambling Sites: Criminal Organization and Legal Challenges," *Gaming Law Review* 11 (2007): 648, 652.

73. McMullan and Rege, *Cyberextortion at Online Gambling Sites, supra.*

74. McMullan and Rege, *Cyberextortion at Online Gambling Sites, supra.*

75. Christopher Nickson, "Gaming Co. Hit by Major DDoS Attack," *Digital Trends*, March 10, 2008, http://news.digitaltrends.com/news-article/15992/gaming-co-hit-by-major-ddos-attack.

76. The description of the Gala Coral attack is taken from these sources: Nick Heath, "UK Gambling Company Warns of DDoS-Attack Risk," *ZDNet.co.uk*, March 7, 2008, http://news.zdnet.co.uk/security/0,1000000189,39364638,00.htm; Nickson, "Gaming Co. Hit by Major DDoS Attack," *supra.*

77. Heath, "UK Gambling Company Warns of DDoS-Attack Risk," *supra.*

78. "Russian Business Network," Wikipedia, http://en.wikipedia.org/wiki/Russian_Business_Network. Some speculate that the Russian Business Network (RBN) might have been responsible for the Estonian DDoS attacks. *See id.*

79. Gregg Kelzer, "Russian Hosting Network Running a Protection Racket, Researcher Says," *Computer World*, February 19, 2008, —http://www.computerworld.com/s/article/9063418/Russian_hosting_network_running_a_protection_racket_researcher_says.

80. *See, e.g., United States v. Carneglia*, 47 Fed. Appx. 27, 29–31 (2d Cir. 2002).

81. *See, e.g.,* Richard Adhikari, "Report Warns of More Cybercrime," *Internetnews.com*, December 9, 2008, http://www.internetnews.com/bus-news/article.php/3789956/Report+Warns+of+More+Cybercrime.htm; "Schneier on the Criminal Threat," *Know It All*, November 4, 2008, http://blogs.cioinsight.com/knowitall/content001/bruce_schneier/schneier_on_the_criminal_threat.html.

82. "Man Pleads Guilty to Infecting Thousands of Computers Using Worm Program Then Launching Them in Denial of Service Attacks," *U.S. Federal News*, December 28, 2005, 2005 WLNR 22108280.

83. *See, e.g., Georgia Code* § 16-9-153(a)(1); *Ohio Rev. Code* § 2909.01; 18 *Pennsylvania Cons. Stat.* § 7612; *South Carolina Code* ß 16-16-10(k).

84. *United Kingdom, Computer Misuse Act 1990*, Chapter 18 § 3.

85. The description of the facts and charges in the case is taken from these sources: U.S. Attorney for the Southern District of California, Press Release, "Two Men Charged with Conspiring to Launch Cyberattacks against Websites of Two U.S. Companies," October 2, 2008; Kevin Poulsen, "Feds Bust DDoS 'Mafia'," *Register*, August 27, 2004, http://www.theregister.co.uk/2004/08/27/ddos_mafia_busted/.

86. Matt Viser, "Sudbury Man Hunted by FBI for Cybercrime," *Boston Globe*, December 12, 2004, http://www.boston.com/news/local/articles/2004/12/12/sudbury_man_hunted_by_fbi_for_cybercrime/.

87. Poulsen, "Feds Bust DDoS 'Mafia'," *supra.*

CHAPTER 5. TOOL CYBERCRIMES: FRAUD, HARASSMENT . . . MURDER?

1. *See* Chapters 2 and 3.

2. *See* Chapter 3.

3. The account of this hack is taken from "Two Cryptologic Casinos Hacked," *Casinomeister*, September 20, 2001, http://www.casinomeister.com/news/september.html. Video slots are video slot machines, which function the same way as traditional slot machines.

4. Cryptologic, which owned the casinos, was out only $600,000; the remaining $1.3 million was covered by an insurance policy. *See* "Two Cryptologic Casinos Hacked," *supra*.

5. *Iowa Code* § 714.1(1).

6. *See*, e.g., Federal Criminal Jury Instructions of the U.S. Court of Appeals for the Seventh Circuit 500[2] (Chicago, IL: Seventh Circuit, 1999).

7. 18 *U.S. Code* § 1030(e)(8).

8. 173 Or. App. 301, 21 P.3d 1128 (Oregon Court of Appeals 2001). The description of the facts in this case is taken entirely from the court's opinion.

9. 173 Or. App. 303–4, 21 P.3d at 1129–30 (Oregon Court of Appeals 2001).

10. Ibid.

11. Ibid.

12. Ibid. (quoting *Ore. Rev. Stat.* § 164.015(2)(c)).

13. *Ore. Rev. Stat.* § 164.015.

14. 173 Or. App. at 311–16, 21 P.3d at 1135–37 (Oregon Court of Appeals 2001).

15. Ibid.

16. William Blackstone, *Commentaries on the Laws of England—Volume IV* (Chicago: University of Chicago Press, 1979), 230–32.

17. 11 *Delaware Code* § 857(3). *See also North Dakota Century Code* § 12.1-23-10(2)(3).

18. *See* "Wireless Freeloader Charged Because He Never Bought Coffee," *TechwebNews*, June 22, 2006, 2006 WLNR 10939330.

19. There are similar cases *See* Andrew Wellner, "Using Free Wireless at Library Described as Theft," *Anchorage Daily News*, February 24, 2007, http://www.mail-archive.com/infowarrior@attrition.org/msg01609.html; Alexandra Topping, "Man Using Laptop on Garden Wall Charged with Wireless Theft," *Guardian*, August 23, 2007, http://www.guardian.co.uk/uk/2007/aug/23/ukcrime.news.

20. The activity is also known as wireless (or wi-fi) piggybacking and leeching. *See* "Leech (Computing)," Wikipedia, http://en.wikipedia.org/wiki/Leech_(computing).

21. 50 *American Jurisprudence 2d, Larceny* § 66 (St. Paul, MN: Thomson West, 2008).

22. *See Commonwealth v. Rivers*, 31 Mass. App.Ct. 669, 671, 583 N.E.2d 867, 869 (Massachusetts Court of Appeals 1991).

23. *See Model Penal Code* § 223.7 (Philadelphia, PA: American Law Institute, 1962).

24. *See Model Penal Code* § 223.7(1), *supra*.

25. *See Model Penal Code* § 223.7(2), *supra*.

26. *See* Wayne R. LaFave, *Substantive Criminal Law* § 19.4 (St. Paul, MN: Thomson West, 2008).

27. *See*, e.g., *Commonwealth v. Gerulis*, 420 Pa. Super. 266, 287–88, 616 A.2d 686, 695–96 (Pennsylvania Superior Court 1992).

28. Some states have addressed the services issue by adopting computer theft of services laws. *See*, e.g., *N.H. Rev. Stat.* § 638:17(II).

29. Tim Ferguson, "Wi-fi Piggybacking Is OK, Say Silicon.com Readers," *Silicon.com*, November 19, 2007, http://networks.silicon.com/mobile/0,39024665,39169199,00.htm (quoting e-mail from reader).

30. *See*, e.g., "Leech (Computing)," Wikipedia, *supra*.

31. *See* Wayne R. LaFave, *Substantive Criminal Law*, § 20.4 (St. Paul, MN: Thomson West, 2008).

32. *See* Rollin M. Perkins and Ronald N. Boyce, *Criminal Law*, 3rd ed. (Mineola, NY: Foundation Press, 1982), 351.

33. *Alabama Code* § 13A-8-13.

34. *Wyo. Stat.* § 6-2-402.

35. *See*, e.g., *Kans. Stat.* § 21-3428; 21 *Okla. Stat.* § 1488; *Wyo. Stat.* § 6-2-402.

36. The description of the facts in the Tereshchuk case is taken from these sources: U.S. Department of Justice (2004), "Press Release—Wi-Fi Hacker Pleads Guilty to Attempted $17,000,000 Extortion," http://www.usdoj.gov/criminal/cybercrime/tereshchukPlea.htm; Robyn Lamb, "Maryland Man Pleads Guilty to Extortion," *Baltimore Daily Record*, June 29, 2004.

37. The revisions to § 1030(a)(7) were made by the *Identity Theft Enforcement and Restitution Act of 2008*, Pub. L. 110–326, Title II, §§ 203–8, 122 Stat. 3561 (2008).

38. *See*, e.g., *Rendelman v. State*, 175 Md. App. 422, 435–36, 927 A.2d 468, 476 (Maryland Court of Appeals 2007).

39. *See* Chapter 4 (DDoS attacks).

40. *See*, e.g., Dan Mangan, "Guilt in Extort Scheme," *New York Post*, May 28, 2003, 2003 WLNR 15019466.

41. The facts in this case are taken from the following sources: Brad Hicks, "Sungkook Kim Indicted on Multiple Charges," *Times-Tribune*, December 22, 2008, http://www.thetimestribune.com/local/local_story_357092739.html; Bill Estep, "Indictment: Cumberlands Student Tried to Blackmail Woman with Sex Video," *Lexington Herald-Leader*, December 19, 2008, 2008 WLNR 24340196.

42. *See* note 43, *supra*. *See also South Carolina Code* § 16-17-640.

43. *See* Wayne R. LaFave, *S ubstantive Criminal Law* § 20.4(a) (St. Paul, MN: Thomson West, 2008).

44. *Kans. Stat.* § 21-3428. *See also* 21 *Okla. Stat.* § 1488; *R.I. General Laws* § 11-42-2.

45. He was not prosecuted for blackmail under Kentucky law because, for some reason, Kentucky repealed its blackmail statute several years ago and replaced it with a pure extortion statute. *See Ky. Stat.* § 435.270 (blackmail statute—

repealed); *Ky. Stat.* § 514.080 (extortion statute criminalizing use of threats to obtain "property").

46. *See* "Man Charged with Extorting Nude Photo of Teen," *MSNBC*, August 22, 2006, http://www.msnbc.msn.com/id/14465796/.

47. *See* "Mom Allegedly Threatens to Post Nude Pictures of Daughter's Ex-Boyfriend," *Fox News*, October 8, 2008, http://www.foxnews.com/story/0,2933,434842,00.html.

48. *See* "Internet Fraud," Wikipedia, http://en.wikipedia.org/wiki/Internet _fraud (identity theft; purchase scams; money transfers fraud; dating scams; click fraud; international modem dialing; Internet marketing and retail fraud; Internet marketing and SEO fraud; phishing; e-mail spoofing; pharming; and stock market manipulation schemes).

49. *See* Chapter 2.

50. *See*, e.g., "Advance-Fee Fraud," Wikipedia, http://en.wikipedia.org/wiki/ Advance_fee_fraud. *See also* "The 'Nigerian Scam': Costly Compassion," *Federal Trade Commission*, http://www.ftc.gov/bcp/edu/pubs/consumer/alerts/alt117.shtm. This type of fraud began in Nigeria but has spread to other countries as well. Nigeria, though, is still a hub of this type of fraud.

51. "Advance-Fee Fraud," Wikipedia, *supra*.

52. "Spanish Prisoner," Wikipedia, http://en.wikipedia.org/wiki/Spanish _Prisoner.

53. "Advance-Fee Fraud," Wikipedia, *supra*.

54. "Nigeria Scams 'Cost UK Billions'," *BBC News*, November 20, 2006, http://news.bbc.co.uk/2/hi/business/6163700.stm.

55. Office of the Attorney General, Former Alcona County Treasurer Charged with Embezzling Public Monies, January 17, 2007, http://www.michigan.gov/ag/0,1607,7-164-34739_34811-160250–,00.html. Katona pled guilty and was sentenced to 914 years in prison for embezzling approximately 25 percent of the county's total budget. Office of the Attorney General, "Former Alcona County Treasurer Sentenced to 9–14 Years in Nigerian Scam Case," June 12, 2007, http://mi.gov/ag/0,1607,7-164-34739-170122–,00.html.

56. *See* Anna Song, "Woman Out $400K to 'Nigerian Scam' Con Artists," *KATU.com*, November 13, 2008, http://www.katu.com/news/34292654.html.

57. *See* "Oregon Woman Loses $400,000 to Nigerian E-Mail Scam," *Fox News*, November 17, 2008, http://www.foxnews.com/story/0,2933,453125,00.html?s Page=fnc/scitech/cybersecurity.

58. "Nigeria Scams 'Cost UK Billions'," *supra*.

59. *See*, e.g., Internet Crime Complaint Center, "Reported Dollar Loss from Internet Crime Reaches All Time High," April 3, 2008, http://www.ic3.gov/media/2008/080403.aspx.

60. *United States v. Godin*, 534 F.3d 51 (U.S. Court of Appeals for the First Circuit 2008). The facts described in the text come from this opinion.

61. *United States v. Godin*, *supra*.

62. Ibid.

63. Ibid.

64. Ibid.

65. *See Flores-Figueroa v. United States*, 129 S.Ct. 1886 (U.S. Supreme Court 2009).

66. *State v. Baron*, 2008 WL 2201778 (Wisconsin Court of Appeals).

67. Ibid.

68. *See* Susan W. Brenner, "Fantasy Crime: The Role of Criminal Law in Virtual Worlds," *Vanderbilt Journal of Entertainment and Technology Law* 11 (2008): 1. The description of how criminal law has come to encompass some "soft" harms is taken from this article.

69. For more on these issues, *see* Susan W. Brenner, "Toward a Criminal Law for Cyberspace: Distributed Security," *Boston University Journal of Science and Technology Law* 10 (2004): 1.

70. *See* Kathleen G. McAnaney, Laura A. Curliss, and C. Elizabeth Abeyta-Price, "From Imprudence to Crime: Anti-Stalking Law," *Notre Dame Law Review* 68 (1993): 819, 863 (quoting 27 George 2, Chapter 15 [1754]). The description of how threat law evolved is taken from this source.

71. *See State v. Robbins*, 253 N.C. 47, 116 S.#.2d 192 (Supreme Court of North Carolina 1960).

72. *See*, e.g., Robert Kurman Kelner, Note, "*United States v. Jake Baker*: Revisiting Threats and the First Amendment," *Virginia Law Review* 84 (1998): 287, 311–12.

73. G. Robert Blakey and Brian J. Murray, "Threats, Free Speech, and the Jurisprudence of the Federal Criminal Law," *B.Y.U. L. Rev.* (2002): 829, 1061–62.

74. 104 F.3d 1492 (1997). The description of the facts in the case is taken from this opinion.

75. The use of interstate commerce gives the federal government jurisdiction to prosecute what would otherwise be a state crime. As to what constitutes interstate commerce, Baker's use of the Internet qualifies as interstate commerce. *See*, e.g., *United States v. Sutcliffe*, 505 F.3d 944, 953 (U.S. Court of Appeals for the Ninth Circuit 2007).

76. 458 F.3d 1208 (U.S. Court of Appeals for the Eleventh Circuit 2006).

77. *See*, e.g., James, *Web Site Sued for Posting Cops' Personal Data*. This Web site is no longer online.

78. *See*, e.g., James, *Web Site Sued for Posting Cops' Personal Data, supra*.

79. *See*, e.g., James, *Web Site Sued for Posting Cops' Personal Data, supra*.

80. *See*, e.g., James, *Web Site Sued for Posting Cops' Personal Data, supra*.

81. *See*, e.g., James, *Web Site Sued for Posting Cops' Personal Data, supra*.

82. *Sheehan v. Gregoire*, 272 F.Supp.2d 1135 (U.S. District Court—Western District of Washington 2003).

83. *Virginia v. Black*, 538 U.S. 343, 359 (U.S. Supreme Court 2003).

84. *Sheehan v. Gregoire*, 272 F.Supp.2d 1135, *supra*.

85. Ibid.

86. *See*, e.g., *The Swedish Personal Data Protection Act 1998, Information Policy,* 2008, http://i-policy.typepad.com/informationpolicy/2008/10/the-sweden-personal-data-protection-act-1998.html (describing a case in which a woman who included information about fellow church volunteers on her own Web site was held to have violated the act).

87. *Darnell v. State*, 72 Tex. Crim. 271, 161 S.W. 971, 971 (Texas Court of Criminal Appeals 1913).

88. *See id. See also* Andrea J. Robinson, Note, "A Remedial Approach to Harassment," *Virginia Law Review* 70 (1984): 507.

89. *See* Robinson, Note, "Remedial Approach to Harassment," *supra.*

90. *See id.*

91. *See* Robert A. Guy, Jr., "The Nature and Constitutionality of Stalking Laws," *Vanderbilt Law Review* 46 (1993): 991. *See also* E. A. Torriero, "The Strange Ways of Slaying Suspect," *San Jose Mercury News*, July 21, 1989, 1989 WLNR 814458.

92. *See* Guy, "Nature and Constitutionality of Stalking Laws," *supra.*

93. *See* Joseph C. Merschman, "The Dark Site of the Web: Cyberstalking and the Need for Contemporary Legislation," *Harvard Women's Law Journal* 24 (2001): 255, 266.

94. *See* Guy, "Nature and Constitutionality of Stalking Laws," *supra.*

95. *See* Guy, "Nature and Constitutionality of Stalking Laws," *supra.*

96. Nick Zimmerman, Comment, "Attempted Stalking: An Attempt-to-Almost-Attempt-to-Act," *Northern Illinois University Law Review* 20 (2000): 219.

97. *See* Guy, " Nature and Constitutionality of Stalking Laws," *supra.* We considered this view of threat crimes earlier in this chapter.

98. Naomi Harlin Goodno, "Cyberstalking, a New Crime: Evaluating the Effectiveness of Current State and Federal Laws," *Missouri Law Review* 72 (2007): 125.

99. *Vernon's Ann. Mo. Stat.* § 565.225.

100. *Mich. Comp. Laws Ann.* § 750.411h(1)(b). Similar to the Missouri statute, the Michigan statute criminalizes stalking, which it defines as "a willful course of conduct involving repeated or continuing harassment of another individual that would cause a reasonable person to feel terrorized, frightened, . . . harassed, or molested and . . . causes the victim to feel terrorized, frightened, . . . harassed, or molested." *Mich. Comp. Laws Ann.* § 750.411h(1)(d). *See also Mich. Comp. Laws Ann.* § 750.411h(2) (stalking is a crime). It defines "harassment" as "conduct directed toward a victim that includes, but is not limited to, repeated or continuing unconsented contact that would cause a reasonable individual to suffer emotional distress and that actually causes the victim to suffer emotional distress." *Mich. Comp. Laws Ann.* § 750.411h(1)(c).

101. *See*, e.g., *Colo. Rev. Stat.* § 18-9-111(b)(III); *D.C. St.* § 22-404(b); *Fl. Stat. Ann.* § 784.048; *Idaho Code* § 18-7906(1)(a); *La. Stat. Ann.* § 14:40.2(A); *Montana Code* § 45-5-220(1); 21 *Okla. Stat. Ann.* § 1173; 18 *Pa. Cons. Stat. Ann.* § 2709.1

(a); *Tennessee Code Ann.* § 39-17-315; *Utah Code Ann.* § 76-5-106.5(2); *West Virginia Code* § 61-2-9a; *Wis. Stat. Ann.* § 940.32; *Wy. Stat. Ann.* § 6-2-506(a).

102. *See Snowden v. State*, 677 A.2d 33, 38 (Del. 1996). *See also People v. Furey*, 2 Misc. 3d 1011(A), 784 N.Y.S.2d 922, 2004 WL 869586 *2 (N.Y. City Crim. Ct. 2004).

103. 11 *Delaware Code* § 1311(a)(1). *See also Mass. Gen. Laws Ann.* 265 § 43A (a); *N.M. Stat. Ann.* § 30-3A-2(A).

104. *State v. Cline*, 2008 WL 1759091 (Ohio Court of Appeals for the Second District 2008).

105. *State v. Parmelee*, 108 Wash. App. 702, 32 P.3d 1029 (Court of Appeals of Washington 2001). The facts described in the text come from this opinion.

106. *See Model Penal Code* § 2.06(2)(a) (Philadelphia, PA: American Law Institute, 1962).

107. Davan Maharaj, "Chilling Cyber-Stalking Case Illustrates New Breed of Crime," *Los Angeles Times*, January 23, 1999. 1999 WLNR 6626941.

108. For the facts in the case, *see* Corinne Rose, "Wabash Sisters Cyber-stalked," *Indiana's NewsCenter*, August 13, 2008, http://www.indianasnewscenter.com/news/26932289.html.

109. *See* Comment by Anonymous on Weird Cyberstalking Case, CYB3RCRIM3, August 14, 2008, http://cyb3rcrim3.blogspot.com/2008/08/weird-cyberstalking-case.html (post from one of the victims).

110. "Stalking," Wikipedia, http://en.wikipedia.org/wiki/Stalking.

111. Rose, "Wabash Sisters Cyber-stalked," *supra*.

112. Rose, "Wabash Sisters Cyber-stalked," *supra*.

113. Rose, "Wabash Sisters Cyber-stalked," *supra*.

114. *See* Comment by Anonymous on Weird Cyberstalking Case, *supra*.

115. E-mail from Mr. X's sister to Susan Brenner (October 7, 2008) (on file with Susan Brenner).

116. Mr. X was actually charged with felony stalking, but because felony stalking is simply an aggravated version of harassment, he cannot be charged or convicted if he did not engage in harassment.

117. E-mail from Mr. X's sister to Susan Brenner (October 7, 2008) (on file with Susan Brenner).

118. *See* Comment by Anonymous on Weird Cyberstalking Case, *supra*.

119. E-mail from Mr. X's sister to Susan Brenner (October 7, 2008) (on file with Susan Brenner).

120. *See* Comment by Anonymous on Weird Cyberstalking Case, *supra*.

121. *See* Susan W. Brenner, "Is There Such a Thing as 'Virtual Crime'?" *California Criminal Law Review* 4 (2001): 1, http://boalt.org/CCLR/v4/v4brenner.htm.

122. *See* Brenner, "Is There Such a Thing as 'Virtual Crime'?" *supra*.

123. When we think of assault, we are really thinking of the distinct crime of battery. Battery is defined as "the unlawful application of force to another person." Wayne R. LaFave, *Substantive Criminal Law* § 16.2 (St Paul, MN: Thomson West,

2008). Battery therefore consists of striking or otherwise inflicting physical injury on another person. The term "assault" is sometimes used to describe such activity, but battery is the preferred term. *See id.* Assault essentially consists of either attempting to commit battery but failing, or of putting someone in fear of being battered. *See* Wayne R. LaFave, *Substantive Criminal Law* § 16.3 (St. Paul, MN: Thomson West, 2008).

124. *See* Susan Brenner, "Undue Influence in the Criminal Law: A Proposed Analysis of the Criminal Offense of 'Causing Suicide'," *Albany Law Review* 47 (1982): 62.

125. *Continuation of Discussion of Model Penal Code*, 36 *American Law Institute Proceedings* 137 (1959).

126. *Model Penal Code* § 210.5 (Philadelphia, PA: American Law Institute, 1962).

127. The description of the facts in the Megan Meier case is taken from these sources: "Mom: MySpace Hoax Led to Daughter's Suicide," *Fox News*, November 16, 2007, http://www.foxnews.com/story/0,2933,312018,00.html; Steve Pokin, "Pokin Around: A Real Person, a Real Death," *St. Charles Journal*, November 10, 2007, http://stcharlesjournal.stltoday.com/articles/2007/11/10/news/sj2tn20071110-1111stc_pokin_1.ii1.txt.

128. *See Model Penal Code* §§ 210.1–210.4 (Philadelphia, PA: American Law Institute, 1962). Law also criminalizes recklessly or negligently causing someone's death. The discussion in the text focuses exclusively on murder for two reasons. One reason is that it is the most serious homicide crime and, indeed, most serious crime included in civilian penal codes. The other reason is that the heightened intent required for murder can make it easier to prove than reckless or negligent homicide, even when the conduct occurred in the real world. Murder, therefore, is the most appropriate vehicle for analyzing online homicide.

129. *See* Brenner, "Is There Such a Thing as 'Virtual Crime'?" *supra.*

130. The description of the case is taken from these sources: "Nurse-hacker Alters Hospital Prescriptions," *Computer Audit Update*, February 1, 1994, 1994 WLNR 3804526; "'Hacker' Nurse Risked Boy's Life," *Guardian*, December 21, 1993.

131. *See* FX et al., *Stealing the Network: How to Own a Continent* (Rockland, MA: Syngress Publishing, 2004), 53, 66.

132. *See* Dean Takahashi, "Defcon: Excuse Me While I Turn Off Your Pacemaker," *Venture Beat*, August 8, 2008, http://venturebeat.com/2008/08/08/defcon-excuse-me-while-I-turn-off-your-pacemaker/.

133. *See* Roger Highfield, "Hacking Fears over Wireless Pacemakers," *Telegraph*, March 14, 2008, http://www.telegraph.co.uk/scienceandtechnology/science/science-news/3336025/Hacking-fears-over-wireless-pacemakers.html. Chris Soghoian, "Security Researchers to Unveil Pacemaker, Medical Implant Hacks," *CNET News*, March 3, 2008, http://news.cnet.com/8301-13739_3-9883822-46.html.

CHAPTER 6. CYBER-*CSI*: COMPUTER CRIME SCENE

1. For DDoS attacks, see Chapters 3 and 4. The account of the Port of Houston attack and subsequent prosecution is taken from these sources: Alison Purdy, "Hacker Cleared of Causing Biggest US Systems Crash," *Birmingham Post*, October 18, 2003, 5, 2003 WLNR 10260204; "Teenager Cleared of US Internet Attack," *Times (UK)*, October 18, 2003, 7, 2003 WLNR 4987635; "Teen Hacker Cleared by Jury," *Sophos*, October 17, 2003, http://www.sophos.com/pressoffice/news/articles/2003/10/va_caffrey.html; "Cyber Attack on US Shipping Exploited Known Security Hole," *Computer Weekly*, October 13, 2003, http://www.computerweekly.com/Articles/2003/10/13/197876/cyber-attack-on-us-shipping-exploited-known-security-hole-teenager.htm. Steve Bird, "Lovelorn Hacker Sabotaged Network of U.S. Port," *Times (UK)*, October 7, 2003, 9, 2003 WLNR 16299445.

2. Bird, "Lovelorn Hacker Sabotaged Network of U.S. Port," *supra*.

3. A log file is a record "automatically created and maintained by a server of activity performed by it." "Server Log," Wikipedia, http://en.wikipedia.org/wiki/Server_log. Like every computer system, the Port of Houston system servers logged the traffic on the system, including the traffic involved in the DDoS attack.

4. *See*, e.g., "IP Address," Wikipedia, http://en.wikipedia.org/wiki/IP_address; "What Is an IP Address?" *howstuffworks.com*, http://computer.howstuffworks.com/question549.htm.

5. *See* Andy McCue, " 'Revenge' Hack Downed US Port Systems," *ZDNet UK*, October 7, 2003, http://news.zdnet.co.uk/security/0,1000000189,39116978,00.htm?r=3.

6. *See* Purdy, "Hacker Cleared of Causing Biggest US Systems Crash," *supra*.

7. *See* Chapter 4 (McKinnon case).

8. John Chapman, "The Nerdy Brit Who Paralysed a U.S. City," *Express (U.K.)*, October 7, 2003, 24, 2003 WLNR 8350946.

9. *See* "Internet Relay Chat," Wikipedia, http://en.wikipedia.org/wiki/IRC (Internet relay chat (IRC) "is a form of real-time Internet text messaging" that is "mainly designed for group communication in discussion forums").

10. *See* McCue, " 'Revenge' Hack Downed US Port Systems," *supra*.

11. "Denial of Service Attack Meant for Chatroom User," *Computer Weekly*, October 13, 2003, http://www.computerweekly.com/Articles/2003/10/13/197877/denial-of-service-attack-meant-for-chatroom-user.htm, *See* Whois Source, http://whois.domaintools.com/.

12. *See*, e.g., John Leyden, "Caffrey Acquittal a Setback for Cybercrime Prosecutions," *Register*, October 17, 2003, http://www.theregister.co.uk/2003/10/17/caffrey_acquittal_a_setback/.

13. *See* "Trojan Horse (Computing)," Wikipedia, http://en.wikipedia.org/wiki/Trojan_horse_(computing).

14. *See* McCue, " 'Revenge' Hack Downed US Port Systems," *supra*.

15. Munir Kotadia, "Accused Port Hacker Says Log Files Were 'Edited'," *ZDNet.co.uk*, October 8, 2003, http://news.zdnet.co.uk/security/0,10000 00189,39116986,00.htm.

16. *See* McCue, "'Revenge' Hack Downed US Port Systems," *supra.*

17. *See* Purdy, "Hacker Cleared of Causing Biggest US Systems Crash," *supra.*

18. *See* Purdy, "Hacker Cleared of Causing Biggest US Systems Crash," *supra.*

19. Neil Barrett, "Scary Whodunit Will Have Sequels," *IT Week*, October 27, 2003, 2003 WLNR 4302075.

20. *See* Barrett, "Scary Whodunit Will Have Sequels," *supra.*

21. *See* Leyden, "Caffrey Acquittal a Setback for Cybercrime Prosecutions," *supra.*

22. *See* Leyden "Caffrey Acquittal a Setback for Cybercrime Prosecutions," *supra* (quoting Neil Barrett).

23. The United Kingdom and United States both require that to convict, the jury must find the prosecution proved every element of the offense beyond a reasonable doubt. *See*, e.g., *Mark Murdo Urquhart v. Her Majesty's Advocate*, [2009] HCJAC 18 (U.K. law); *Harris v. United States*, 536 U.S. 545 (2002) (U.S. law).

24. *See* Susan W. Brenner, Brian Carrier, and Jef Henninger, "The Trojan Horse Defense in Cybercrime Cases," *Santa Clara Computer & High Technology Law Journal* 21 (2004): 1, 9.

25. W. William Hodes, "Seeking the Truth versus Telling the Truth at the Boundaries of the Law: Misdirection, Lying, and 'Lying with an Explanation'," *South Texas Law Review* 44 (2002): 53, 59 n. 18.

26. *See* Brenner, Carrier, and Henninger, "Trojan Horse Defense in Cybercrime Cases," *supra*, 7–9.

27. Ibid.

28. *See* Wendy McElroy, "In Child Porn Case, Technology Entraps the Innocent," *Fox News*, January 16, 2007, http://www.foxnews.com/story/ 0,2933,244009,00.html.

29. A Massachusetts state employee used a version of the Trojan horse defense to persuade prosecutors not to charge him with possession of child pornography. *See* Laurel J. Sweet, "Probe Shows Kiddie Porn Rap Was Bogus," *Boston Herald*, June 16, 2008, 5, 2008 WLNR 11374039. The child pornography was on the state-issued laptop he issued, which was running "corrupted virus-protection software" and was otherwise open to invasion by malware and hackers. One factor the prosecutor cited in deciding not to charge the employee was that the child pornography was all found in the laptop's cache files, which meant the employee had not viewed it.

30. *See*, e.g., *State v. McKinney*, 699 N.W.2d 460 (S.D. 2005).

31. *See*, e.g., *State v. Tackett*, 2007 WL 4328084 (Ohio Court of Appeals 2007).

32. Ibid. *See also United States v. O'Keefe*, 461 F.3d 1338 (Court of Appeals for the Eleventh Circuit 2006).

33. *See*, e.g., *Wilson v. State*, 2008 WL 5501146 (Court of Appeals of Texas 2009) (a detective who testified that the defendant had child pornography on CDs

noted that no Trojan horse program " 'is capable of picking up a CD, placing it into a tray'," and installing child pornography on it). *See also Savage v. State*, 2008 WL 726229 (Court of Appeals of Texas 2008) (child pornography on external storage media as well as on a hard drive).

34. *See*, e.g., Micah Joel, "Safe and Insecure," *Salon.com*, at http://www .salon.com/tech/feature/2004/05/18/safe_and_insecure/ (May 18, 2004).

35. *See United States v. Miller*, 527 F.3d 54 (U.S. Court of Appeals for the Third Circuit 2008) (prosecution and defense experts agreed that child pornography or other material could be surreptitiously installed with a Trojan horse program).

36. John Schwartz, "Acquitted Man Says Virus Put Pornography on Computer," *New York Times*, August 11, 2003 (quoting, former head of Department of Justice Computer Crimes Unit).

37. *See*, e.g., "Trier of Fact," Wikipedia, http://en.wikipedia.org/wiki/Trier_of _fact#cite_ref-1.

38. *See*, e.g., *Aluisi v. Elliott Mfg. Co., Inc. Plan*, 2009 WL 565544 *6 (E.D. Cal. 2009).

39. *State v. Bell*, 145 Ohio Misc. 2d 55, 882 N.E. 2d 502 (Ohio Court of Common Pleas 2008).

40. *State v. Bell, supra.*

41. *State v. Bell, supra.*

42. *State v. Bell, supra.*

43. *State v. Bell, supra* (quoting *United States v. Tin Yat Chin*, 371 F.31, 38 [U.S. Court of Appeals for the Second Circuit 2004]).

44. *State v. Bell, supra.*

45. *United States v. Jackson*, 488 F. Supp. 2d 866 (U.S. District Court for the District of Nebraska 2007).

46. *U.S. v. Jackson, supra.*

47. *U.S. v. Jackson, supra.*

48. *U.S. v. Jackson, supra.*

49. "Chain of Custody," Wikipedia, http://en.wikipedia.org/wiki/Chain_of _custody.

50. *United States v. Wyss*, 2006 WL 1722288 (U.S. District Court for the Southern District of Mississippi 2006).

51. *U.S. v. Wyss, supra.*

52. *U.S. v. Wyss, supra.*

53. *U.S. v. Wyss, supra.*

54. *U.S. v. Wyss, supra.*

55. *U.S. v. Wyss, supra.*

56. *U.S. v. Wyss, supra.*

57. *U.S. v. Wyss, supra.*

58. *U.S. v. Wyss, supra.*

59. *State v. Colwell*, 715 N.W.2d 768 (Iowa Court of Appeals, 2006).

60. *Iowa Code Ann.* § 712.7.

61. *State v. Colwell, supra.*

62. *State v. Colwell, supra.*

63. *State v. Colwell, supra.*

64. *State v. Colwell, supra.*

65. *State v. Armstead*, 432 So.2d 837 (Louisiana Supreme Court 1983).

66. *Thomas v. State*, 2008 WL 4629572 (Florida Court of Appeals 2008).

67. *Thomas v. State, supra.*

68. *Thomas v. State, supra.*

69. "Business Records Exception," Wikipedia, http://en.wikipedia.org/wiki/Business_records_exception.

70. *Thomas v. State, supra.*

71. *Thomas v. State, supra.*

72. *Florida Statutes* § 90.805.

73. *Thomas v. State, supra.*

74. *Thomas v. State, supra.*

75. *Thomas v. State, supra.*

76. *Thomas v. State, supra.*

77. *See*, e.g., *Alaska Constitution Article I* § 22; *Montana Constitution Article 2* § 10.

78. *See* Ken Gormley, "One Hundred Years of Privacy," *Wisconsin Law Review* (1992): 1335, 1343 (by 1890 "there existed no coherent notion of privacy at all in American law").

79. *See McIntyre v. Ohio Elections Commission*, 514 U.S. 334 (1995); *NAACP v. State of Alabama ex rel. Patterson*, 357 U.S. 449, 462 (1958).

80. *See Katz v. United States*, 389 U.S. 347, 350 (1967).

81. *See Fisher v. United States*, 425 U.S. 391, 399 (1976).

82. Ibid.

CHAPTER 7. BEYOND *WAR GAMES*: WHO ARE THE CYBERCRIMINALS?

1. *See*, e.g., Fermin Leal et al., "Students, Parents Aghast at Tesboro High Cheating Allegations," *Orange County Register*, June 18, 2008, http://www.ocregister.com/ocregister/homepage/abox/article_2071946.php.

2. *See* "WarGames," Wikipedia, http://en.wikipedia.org/wiki/WarGames.

3. *See* James J. Flink, *America Adopts the Automobile, 1895–1910* (Cambridge, MA: MIT Press, 1970), 225–31.

4. *See*, e.g., "MS-DOS," Wikipedia, http://en.wikipedia.org/wiki/MS-DOS.

5. *See*, e.g., Dan Goodin, "Teen Hacker Confesses Three-Year Crime Spree," *Register*, November 19, 2008, http://www.theregister.co.uk/2008/11/19/dshocker_pleads_guilty/. The old hacker still surfaces on occasion, however. *See* "Student Charged in Palin E-Mail Hacking," *Washington Post*, October 8, 2008, 2008 WLNR 19147439 (student hacked former vice presidential candidate Sarah Palin's e-mail

account, changed the password to "popcorn," and posted the new password on a Web site).

6. *See* U.S. Secret Service, *Insider Threat Study: Illicit Cyber Activity in the Banking and Finance Sector*, August 2004; U.S. Secret Service, *Insider Threat Study: Computer System Sabotage in Critical Infrastructure Sectors*, May 2005. Both studies are available on the Secret Service Web site: http://www.ustreas.gov/usss/ntac_its.shtml.

7. U.S. Secret Service, *Computer System Sabotage in Critical Infrastructure Sectors, supra*, 3.

8. U.S. Secret Service, *Illicit Cyber Activity in the Banking and Finance Sector, supra*, 7.

9. U.S. Secret Service, *Illicit Cyber Activity in the Banking and Finance Sector, supra*, 10, 12.

10. Ibid.

11. U.S. Secret Service, *Illicit Cyber Activity in the Banking and Finance Sector, supra*, 14.

12. Ibid.

13. U.S. Secret Service, *Illicit Cyber Activity in the Banking and Finance Sector, supra*, 15.

14. U.S. Secret Service, *Illicit Cyber Activity in the Banking and Finance Sector, supra*, 21.

15. Eighty-two percent of the organizations in the study were "in private industry"; only 16 percent were government entities. The private organizations were involved in the following activities: banking and finance (8%), food (4%), information and telecommunications (63%), and public health (4%). The public entities were involved in continuity of government (16%), the defense industrial base (2%), and postal and shipping activities (2%). U.S. Secret Service, *Computer System Sabotage in Critical Infrastructure Sectors, supra*, 12.

16. U.S. Secret Service, *Computer System Sabotage in Critical Infrastructure Sectors, supra*, 11.

17. Ibid.

18. U.S. Secret Service, *Computer System Sabotage in Critical Infrastructure Sectors, supra*, 12.

19. Ibid.

20. U.S. Secret Service, *Computer System Sabotage in Critical Infrastructure Sectors, supra*, 14.

21. Ibid.

22. U.S. Secret Service, *Computer System Sabotage in Critical Infrastructure Sectors, supra*, 15.

23. U.S. Secret Service, *Computer System Sabotage in Critical Infrastructure Sectors, supra*, 20.

24. Ibid.

25. U.S. Secret Service, *Computer System Sabotage in Critical Infrastructure Sectors, supra*, 21.

26. U.S. Secret Service, *Computer System Sabotage in Critical Infrastructure Sectors, supra, 22.*

27. *See supra* note 15.

28. *See* Jerome Hall, *Theft, Law and Society* (Indianapolis, IN: Bobbs-Merrill, 1952), 304–6.

29. U.S. Secret Service, *Illicit Cyber Activity in the Banking and Finance Sector, supra*, 2.

30. A fraudster is "one who commits fraud." Dictionary.com, http://dictionary.reference.com/browse/fraudster.

31. The account of the Ukraine operation comes primarily from Ellen Messmer, "Ukrainian Cybercriminals Raked in $10K/day, Finjan Reports," *Network World*, March 23, 2009, http://www.networkworld.com/news/2009/032309-ukrainian-cybercriminals.html?hpg1=bn.

32. Messmer, "Ukrainian Cybercriminals Raked in $10K/day," *supra*. *See* Google Trends, http://www.google.com/trends.

33. *See* " 'Scareware' Scams Trick Searchers," *BBC News*, March 23, 2009, http://news.bbc.co.uk/2/hi/technology/7955358.stm.

34. Messmer, "Ukrainian Cybercriminals Raked in $10K/day," *supra*.

35. " 'Scareware' Scams Trick Searchers," *supra*.

36. For similar examples of online fraud, *see* Internet Crime Schemes, Internet Crime Complaint Center, http://www.ic3.gov/crimeschemes.aspx (Romanian auction fraud, third party receiver of funds, employment/business opportunities, and reshipping scams).

37. *See*, e.g., "Snake Oil," Wikipedia, http://en.wikipedia.org/wiki/Snake_oil.

38. We return to this issue in Chapter 8.

39. *See* Internet Fraud, Internet Fraud Watch, http://www.fraud.org/internet/intinfo.htm ("It's sometimes hard to tell the difference between reputable online sellers and criminals who use the Internet to rob people").

40. *See* Chapter 5.

41. *See* Lorraine Sheridan and Julian Book, "Stalker Typologies: Implications for Law Enforcement" in *Stalking and Psychosexual Obsession: Psychological Perspectives for Prevention, Policing, and Treatment*, ed. Julian Boon and Lorraine Sheridan (Chichester, England: Wiley, 2002), 63–81.

42. *See* Sheridan and Book, "Stalker Typologies," *supra*, 71–72.

43. The account of the Ligon case is taken from Vanessa Ho, "Cyberstalker Enters Guilty Plea," *Seattle Post-Intelligencer*, July 30, 2004, http://www.seattlepi.com/local/184213_cyberstalk30.html.

44. *See* Sheridan and Book, "Stalker Typologies," *supra*, 72–73.

45. *Litman v. George Mason University*, 131 F.Supp. 2d 795 (U.S. District Court for the Eastern District of Virginia, 2001).

46. *Litman v. George Mason University, supra*.

47. In *Swanson v. Livingston County*, 270 F.Supp. 2d 887 (U.S. District Court for the Eastern District of Michigan 2008), a woman brought a sexual harassment

suit against her employer based in part on an "infatuated co-worker" who persisted in sending her "romantic e-mails."

48. *See* Sheridan and Book, "Stalker Typologies," *supra*, 74–76.

49. *See* Sheridan and Book, "Stalker Typologies," *supra*, 74.

50. *See* Mark Reynolds, "Sick Cyberstalker Made Me Fear I'd Die, Says TV Girl," *Express*, March 17, 2009, 2009 WLNR 5044097. The account of the case in the text is taken from this source.

51. *See* Eva Jones, "Stalker Who Sent So Many Emails the Account Had to Be Closed," *Western Daily Press*, August 10, 2007, 2007 WLNR 15507667.

52. *See* Sheridan and Book, "Stalker Typologies," *supra*, 74–76.

53. *See* Sheridan and Book, "Stalker Typologies," *supra*, 76–77.

54. *See* Sheridan and Book, "Stalker Typologies," *supra*, 76.

55. *See* Sheridan and Book, "Stalker Typologies," *supra*, 74–76.

56. *See* Sheridan and Book, "Stalker Typologies," *supra*, 77.

57. Ibid.

58. The account of the Dellapenta case is taken from these sources: Nita Lelyveld, "Los Angeles Man Is Charged as Internet Poseur and Stalker," *Philadelphia Inquirer*, February 3, 1999, A3, 1999 WLNR 2504105; Greg Miller and Davan Maharaj, "Security Guard Charged in Cyber-Stalking Case," *Seattle Times*, January 22, 1999, A13, 1999 WLNR 1570714.

59. *See* Doug Simpson, "Feds Find Dangerous Cyberstalking Hard to Prevent," *CNN*, June 12, 2000, http://archives.cnn.com/2000/TECH/computing/06/12/cyberstalkers.idg/.

CHAPTER 8. CYBER-*LAW AND ORDER*: INVESTIGATING AND PROSECUTING CYBERCRIME

1. *United States v. Gorshkov*, 2001 WL 1024026 *1 (U.S. District Court for the Western District of Washington 2002).

2. U.S. Department of Justice, "Russian Computer Hacker Convicted by Jury," October 10, 2001, http://www.usdoj.gov/criminal/cybercrime/gorshkov convict.htm.

3. *See* Mike Brunker, "Judge OKs FBI Hack of Russian Computers," *ZDNet*, May 31, 2001, http://news.zdnet.com/2100-9595_22-115961.html.

4. *See* Brunker, "Judge OKs FBI Hack of Russian Computers," *supra*.

5. *See* Ariana Eunjung Cha, "A Tempting Offer for Russian Pair," *Washington Post*, May 19, 2003, http://www.washingtonpost.com/ac2/wp-dyn/A7774-2003May18?language=printer.

6. The account of the company president's negotiations with the Invita hackers is taken primarily from Eunjung Cha, "Tempting Offer for Russian Pair," *supra*.

7. *See* Eunjung Cha, "Tempting Offer for Russian Pair," *supra*.

8. *See* Eunjung Cha, "Tempting Offer for Russian Pair," *supra*. Federal authorities were afraid the hackers "had control of other computer networks that no one

knew about and . . . were attempting to create a 'credit card production system'" they "could tap at any time." "Tempting Offer for Russian Pair," *supra*.

9. *See* Eunjung Cha, "Tempting Offer for Russian Pair," *supra*.

10. *See* Eunjung Cha, "Tempting Offer for Russian Pair," *supra*. *See also* United States v. Wathne, 2008 WL 4355112 (U.S. District Court for the Northern District of California 2008).

11. *See* Eunjung Cha, "Tempting Offer for Russian Pair," *supra*.

12. *See* Eunjung Cha, "Tempting Offer for Russian Pair," *supra*.

13. Brendan I. Koerner, "From Russia with LØPHT," *Legal Affairs*, May–June 2002, http://www.legalaffairs.org/printerfriendly.msp?id=286.

14. *See* Eunjung Cha, "Tempting Offer for Russian Pair," *supra*.

15. *See* Koerner, "From Russia with LØPHT," *supra*.

16. *See* Koerner, "From Russia with LØPHT," *supra*. *See also* Communiqué—Meeting of Justice and Interior Ministers of the Eight, Annex, December 9–10, 1997, ("Investigation . . . of international high-tech crimes must be coordinated among all concerned States, regardless of where harm has occurred"). http://www.usdoj.gov/criminal/cybercrime/g82004/97Communique.pdf.

17. *United States v. Gorshkov, supra.*

18. *United States v. Gorshkov, supra.*

19. *United States v. Gorshkov, supra.*

20. *See The Criminal Code of the Russian Federation, Article 272, Russian Scam Investigator,* http://www.eecl.org/scam/criminalcode.shtml.

21. *United States v. Gorshkov, supra.*

22. U.S. Department of Justice, "Russian Hacker Sentenced to Prison," July 25, 2003, http://www.usdoj.gov/usao/nj/press/files/iv0725_r.htm.

23. *See* U.S. Department of Justice, "Russian Computer Hacker Sentenced to Three Years in Prison," October 4, 2002, http://www.usdoj.gov/criminal/cybercrime/gorshkovSent.htm.

24. *See* Mike Brunker, "FBI Agent Charged with Hacking," *MSNBC*, August 15, 2002, http://www.msnbc.msn.com/id/3078784/.

25. *See* Brunker, "FBI Agent Charged with Hacking," *supra*.

26. The account of the Rome Labs attacks is taken from these sources: Richard Power, *Tangled Web: Tales of Digital Crime from the Shadows of Cyberspace* (Indianapolis, IN: Que Books, 2000), 66–67; Jonathan Ungoed-Thomas, "The Schoolboy Spy," *Sunday Times*, March 29, 1998, 1, 1998 WLNR 5838030. U.S. Senate, Permanent Subcommittee on Investigations—Minority Staff Statement, Security in Cyberspace, Appendix B, June 5, 1996, http://www.fas.org/irp/congress/1996_hr/s960605b.htm.

27. U.S. Senate, Security in Cyberspace, *supra*.

28. Ungoed-Thomas, "Schoolboy Spy," *supra*.

29. Ungoed-Thomas, "Schoolboy Spy," *supra*.

30. Ungoed-Thomas, "Schoolboy Spy," *supra*.

31. Ungoed-Thomas, "Schoolboy Spy," *supra*.

32. Ungoed-Thomas, "Schoolboy Spy," *supra*.

33. U.S. Senate, Security in Cyberspace, *supra*.

34. Ungoed-Thomas, "Schoolboy Spy," *supra*.

35. Ungoed-Thomas, "Schoolboy Spy," *supra*.

36. Ungoed-Thomas, "Schoolboy Spy," *supra*.

37. U.S. Department of Justice, *Criminal Resource Manual 274*, http://www.usdoj.gov/usao/eousa/foia_reading_room/usam/title9/crm00274.htm.

38. 22 *Code of Federal Regulations* § 92.54. The description of the letter rogatory process is taken from Sections 274–282 of the U.S. Department of Justice *Criminal Resource Manual*.

39. U.S. Department of Justice, *Criminal Resource Manual 275*, http://www.usdoj.gov/usao/eousa/foia_reading_room/usam/title9/crm00275.htm#275.

40. *See* The Signe, 37 F. Supp. 819, 821 (U.S. District Court for the Eastern District of Louisiana 1941) (" 'we shall be pleased to do the same for you in a similar case' ").

41. *See* The Signe, *supra*, 37 F. Supp. at 820 (in a letter rogatory, one country asks another "to assist the administration of justice . . . such request being made, and . . . granted, by reason of the comity existing between nations in ordinary peaceful times").

42. U.S. Department of Justice, *Criminal Resource Manual 275*, http://www.usdoj.gov/usao/eousa/foia_reading_room/usam/title9/crm00275.htm#275.

43. *See*, e.g., Nicolai Seitz, "Transborder Search: A New Perspective in Law Enforcement," *Yale Journal of Law & Technology* 7 (2004–2005): 23.

44. U.S. Department of Justice, *Criminal Resource Manual 276*, http://www.usdoj.gov/usao/eousa/foia_reading_room/usam/title9/crm00276.htm.

45. *See* Mutual Legal Assistance (MLAT) and Other Agreements, U.S. Department of State, http://www.passportsusa.com/law/info/judicial/judicial_690.html (Antigua and Barbuda; Argentina; Australia; Austria; Bahamas; Barbados; Belize; Belgium; Brazil; Canada; Cyprus; Czech Republic; Dominica; Egypt; Estonia; France; Greece; Grenada; Hong Kong SAR; Hungary; India; Israel; Italy; Jamaica; Korea; Latvia; Liechtenstein; Lithuania; Luxembourg; Mexico; Morocco; Netherlands; Panama; Philippines; Poland; Romania; Russian Federation; Saint Kitts & Nevis; Saint Lucia; Saint Vincent and the Grenadines; South Africa; Spain; Switzerland; Thailand; Trinidad and Tobago; Turkey; United Kingdom; United Kingdom—Cayman Islands; United Kingdom—Anguilla; United Kingdom—British Virgin Islands; United Kingdom—Montserrat; United Kingdom—Turks and Caicos Islands; and Uruguay).

46. Geoffrey R. Watson, "Offenders Abroad: The Case for Nationality-Based Criminal Jurisdiction," *Yale Journal of International Law* 17 (1992): 41, 75.

47. U.S. Department of Justice, *Criminal Resource Manual 276*, http://www.usdoj.gov/usao/eousa/foia_reading_room/usam/title9/crm00276.htm.

48. Ibid.

49. Ibid.

50. Stefan D. Cassella, "Bulk Cash Smuggling and the Globalization of Crime," *Berkeley Journal of International law* 22 (2004): 98, 99 note 2.

51. *See*, e.g., Seitz, "Transborder Search," *supra.*

52. *See*, e.g., James J. Varellas, "The Constitutional Political Economy of Free Trade," *Santa Clara Law Review* 49 (2009): 717, 733.

53. U.S. Department of Justice, *Criminal Resource Manual 277*, http://www.usdoj.gov/usao/eousa/foia_reading_room/usam/title9/crm00277.htm.

54. Daseul Kim, " 'Perfectly Properly Triable' in the United States: Is Extradition a Real and Significant Threat to Foreign Antitrust Offenders?" *Northwestern Journal of International Law and Business* 28 (2008): 583, 599.

55. *See* Kim, " 'Perfectly Properly Triable" in the United States," *supra. See also* 18 *U.S. Code Ann.* § 3181 (list of countries with which the United States has a treaty).

56. Elise Keppler, "Preventing Human Rights Abuses by Regulating Arms Brokering," *Berkeley Journal of International Law* 19 (2001): 381, 402.

57. U.S. Department of Justice, *Criminal Resource Manual 602*, http://www.usdoj.gov/usao/eousa/foia_reading_room/usam/title9/crm00602.htm. Provisional arrest is used, as necessary, to ensure that the suspect does not flee the jurisdiction from which extradition is sought while the extradition process is pending. *See U.S. Attorney's Manual* § 9-15.230, http://www.usdoj.gov/usao/eousa/foia_reading _room/usam/title9/15mcrm.htm#9-15.230.

58. U.S. Department of Justice, *Criminal Resource Manual 603*, http://www.usdoj.gov/usao/eousa/foia_reading_room/usam/title9/crm00603.htm (location and citizenship of the fugitive; offense charged; case information about the prosecution; status of the case; facts of the offense; potential for going to trial; and whether there is time to prepare and submit the extradition request).

59. U.S. Department of Justice, *Criminal Resource Manual 603*, *supra.*

60. *See* U.S. Department of Justice, *Criminal Resource Manual* §§ 604–609.

61. *See*, e.g., Gabriella Blum, "Bilateralism, Multilateralism, and the Architecture of International Law," *Harvard International Law Journal* 49 (2008): 323, 260; Clint Williamson, "The Role of the United States in International Criminal Justice," *Penn State International Law Review* 25 (2007): 819, 823.

62. *See* Sarah E. Tilstra, "Prosecuting International Terrorists," *Pacific Rim Law and Policy Journal* 12 (2003): 835, 843–44.

63. *See Reese v. United States.* 76 U.S. 13, 21–22 (U.S. Supreme Court 1869).

64. *See United States v. Alvarez-Machain*, 504 U.S. 655 (U.S. Supreme Court 1992); *Ker v. Illinois*, 119 U.S. 436 (U.S. Supreme Court 1886).

65. *See United States v. Alvarez-Machain*, *supra*, 504 U.S. at 661–62. Needless to say, the United States' position on abducting suspects is not popular in other countries. *See*, e.g., Stephan Wilske and Teresa Schiller, "Jurisdiction over Persons Abducted in Violation of International Law in the Aftermath of *United States v. Alvarez-Machain*," *University of Chicago Law School Roundtable* 5 (1998): 205.

66. *U.S. Attorney's Manual* § 9-15.610, http://www.usdoj.gov/usao/eousa/foia _reading_room/usam/title9/15mcrm.htm#9-15.610.

67. Article 126 of the Russian criminal code makes abduction a crime, and Article 127 also criminalizes "illegal deprivation of liberty." The Criminal Code of the Russian Federation, http://www.russian-criminal-code.com/PartII/SectionVII/Chapter17.html.

CHAPTER 9. U.S. LAW ENFORCEMENT: AGENCIES AND CHALLENGES

1. "Federalism," Wikipedia, http://en.wikipedia.org/wiki/Federalism. *See also* Robert P. Sutton, *Federalism* (Westport, CT: Greenwood Press, 2002), 1–5.

2. *See Articles of Confederation—United States of America*, Article I ("The stile of this confederacy shall be 'The United States of America'"). *See*, e.g., "Articles of Confederation," Wikipedia, http://en.wikipedia.org/wiki/Articles_of _Confederation. Essentially, a confederation consists of a voluntary association of co-equal entities, whereas a federal system consists of a central authority that shares power with constituent entities.

3. "Articles of Confederation," Wikipedia, *supra*.

4. Articles of Confederation—United States of America, Article II.

5. Josh Chafetz, "Leaving the House: The Constitutional Status of Resignation from the House of Representatives," *Duke Law Journal* 58 (2008): 177, 204 n. 182.

6. Stuart Streichler, "Mad about Yoo, or, Why Worry about the Next Unconstitutional War?" *Journal of Law and Politics*, 24 (2008): 93, 110; Roy W. Breitenbach, *"Perpich v. United States Department of Defense*: Who Controls the Weekend Soldier?" *Saint John's Law Review* 64 (1989): 133, 133 n. 1.

7. *See*, e.g., Adam H. Kurland, "First Principles of American Federalism and the Nature of Federal Criminal Jurisdiction," *Emory Law Journal* 45 (1996): 1, 21–25.

8. Kurland, "First Principles of American Federalism," *supra*.

9. Kurland, "First Principles of American Federalism," *supra*.

10. Kurland, "First Principles of American Federalism," *supra*. There was a limited exception for "'piracies and felonies committed on the high seas'." *Id.* (quoting Articles of Confederation, Article IX).

11. Ken Gormly, "Exploring a European Union Constitution: Unexpected Lessons from the American Experience," *Rutgers Law Journal* 35 (2003): 69, 86.

12. Earl F. Martin, "America's Anti-Standing Army Tradition and the Separate Community Doctrine," *Mississippi Law Journal* 76 (2006): 135, 154.

13. Kurland, "First Principles of American Federalism," *supra* (quoting The Federalist No. 21, 138 [Alexander Hamilton]).

14. Kurland, "First Principles of American Federalism", *supra*.

15. Kurland, "First Principles of American Federalism," *supra*.

16. Kurland, "First Principles of American Federalism," *supra*.

17. *See* U.S. Constitution Article I § 8, clause 6 (counterfeiting); U.S. Constitution, Article I, § 8, clause 10 ("Piracies and Felonies on the high Seas, and

Offences against the Law of Nations"); U.S. Constitution Article III, § 3 clause 2 (treason). Crimes against the law of nations are essentially crimes that violate customary international law, i.e., the general principles of law nations apply to themselves. *See*, e.g., *Forlini v. United States*, 12 F.2d 631 (U.S. Court of Appeals for the Second Circuit 1926) (it was "an infraction of the law of nations to have foreign securities counterfeited in the United States without any attempt to make it an offense, and that it was incumbent upon this government to make it a criminal offense"); *United States v. Emmanuel*, 2007 WL 2002454 (U.S. District Court for the Southern District of Florida 2007) (*the Torture Act, 18 U.S. Code § 2340A*, was a valid exercise of the power to criminalize crimes against nations).

18. *See*, e.g., Kurland, "First Principles of American Federalism," *supra*.

19. *See*, e.g., Kurland, "First Principles of American Federalism," *supra. See also* U.S. Constitution Article I, § 8 clause 7. At the end of the nineteenth century, Congress adopted statutes designed to criminalize the use of the mails for the purpose of operating lotteries. *See*, e.g., Craig M. Bradley, "Racketeering and the Federalization of Crime," *American Criminal Law Review* 22 (1984): 213.

20. Lawrence M. Friedman, *Crime and Punishment in American History* (New York: Basic Books, 1993), 269.

21. Ibid., 261.

22. Article I § 8 of the U.S. Constitution gives Congress the power to "regulate commerce with foreign nations, and among the several states."

23. *Hoke v. United States*, 227 U.S. 308 (U.S. Supreme Court 1913) (quoting Act of June 25, 1910, Chapter 395, 36 Stat. 825).

24. *Act of Oct. 28*, 1919, Chapter 85, 41 Stat. 305.

25. *See*, e.g., Kathleen F. Brickey, "Criminal Mischief: The Federalization of American Criminal Law," *Hastings Law Journal* 46 (1995): 1135.

26. *See* Friedman, *Crime and Punishment in American History, supra*, 264–70.

27. Brickey, "Criminal Mischief," *supra*, 1143.

28. Friedman, *Crime and Punishment in American History, supra*.

29. *See*, e.g., Richard E. Myers II, "Responding to the Time-Based Failures of the Criminal Law through a Criminal Sunset Amendment," *Boston College Law Review* 49 (2008): 1327, 1344.

30. David Sklansky, "The Private Police," *U.C.L.A. Law Review* 46 (1999): 1165, 1211.

31. *See* James MacKay, *Allan Pinkerton: The First Private Eye* (Edison, NJ: Castle Books, 2007).

32. Sean J. Kealy, "The Posse Comitatus Act: Toward a Right to Civil Law Enforcement," *Yale Law and Policy Review* 21 (2003): 383, 429 n. 300.

33. *See* U.S. Secret Service: History, http://www.secretservice.gov/history.shtml.

34. *See* Federal Bureau of Investigation: Timeline of FBI History, http://www.fbi.gov/libref/historic/history/historicdates.htm.

35. *See* "Bureau of Alcohol, Tobacco, Firearms and Explosives," Wikipedia, http://en.wikipedia.org/wiki/Bureau_of_Alcohol,_Tobacco,_Firearms_and_Explosives. After tge 9/11 attacks, the name of the agencywas changed to encompass explosives.

36. *See* "Drug Enforcement Administration," Wikipedia, http://en.wikipedia.org/wiki/Drug_Enforcement_Administration.

37. *See* "U.S. Customs and Immigration Enforcement," Wikipedia, http://en.wikipedia.org/wiki/Immigration_and_Customs_Enforcement.

38. *See* "Federal Law Enforcement in the United States," Wikipedia, http://en.wikipedia.org/wiki/List_of_United_States_federal_law_enforcement_agencies.

39. Law Enforcement Statistics, U.S. Department of Justice— Bureau of Justice Statistics, http://www.ojp.gov/bjs/lawenf.htm; State and Local Law Enforcement Statistics, U.S. Department of Justice, Bureau of Justice Statistics, http://www.ojp.gov/bjs/sandlle.htm.

40. *See* "Law Enforcement in the United States," Wikipedia, http://en.wikipedia.org/wiki/Law_enforcement_in_the_United_States.

41. *See*, e.g., In re Walter, 2007 WL 4442650 (Superior Court of New Jersey—Appellate Division 2007).

42. *See*, e.g., 11 *Del. Code* § 8302(a).

43. Federal Law Enforcement Statistics, U.S. Department of Justice—Bureau of Justice Statistics, http://www.ojp.gov/bjs/fedle.htm. A full-time federal officer is someone who is "authorized to carry firearms and make arrests." *Id.* The remaining, roughly 60,000 officers were engaged in the following activities: police response and patrol (22,278); inspections (17,280); corrections (16,530); court operations (5,158); security/protection (4,524); and other (176).

44. Federal Law Enforcement Statistics, U.S. Department of Justice, *supra*.

45. *See* DEA Staffing & Budget, U.S. Drug Enforcement Administration, http://www.usdoj.gov/dea/agency/staffing.htm. U.S. Secret Service, Frequently Asked Questions, http://www.secretservice.gov/faq.shtml#faq8; "Bureau of Alcohol, Tobacco, Firearms and Explosives," Wikipedia, http://en.wikipedia.org/wiki/Bureau_of_Alcohol,_Tobacco,_Firearms_and_Explosives. The Secret Service also has 1,300 Uniformed Division officers who protect the White House and other federal facilities. *See* U.S. Secret Service, Frequently Asked Questions, *supra*.

46. Daniel C. Richman, "The Changing Boundaries between Federal and Local Law Enforcement," *Criminal Justice* 2 (2000): 81, 93.

47. *See* Richman, "Changing Boundaries between Federal and Local Law Enforcement," *supra*, 94.

48. In most U.S. states, counties are the "tier of organization immediately below the statewide tier and above . . . the municipal or . . . township tier." "County," Wikipedia, http://en.wikipedia.org/wiki/County#United_States. Louisiana calls these entities parishes instead of counties; in Alaska, they are known as boroughs.

49. *See* Steven W. Perry, "Prosecutors in State Courts, 2005," *Bureau of Justice Statistics Bulletin*, July 2006, 6, http://www.ojp.gov/bjs/abstract/psc05.htm.

50. *See* Perry, "Prosecutors in State Courts," *supra*.

51. *See* "Prosecutor," Wikipedia, http://en.wikipedia.org/wiki/Prosecution# United_States.

52. Prosecution Statistics, Bureau of Justice Statistics, http://www.ojp.usdoj .gov/bjs/pros.htm.

53. Prosecution Statistics, Bureau of Justice Statistics, *supra*. Half of the prosecutors' offices in the United States also "served a population of 36,500 or less." Perry, "Prosecutors in State Courts," *supra*.

54. *See*, e.g., Anita Alvarez, Cook County State's Attorney, http://www .statesattorney.org/ (Cook County, Illinois, prosecutor has a staff of more than 900 prosecutors).

55. American Bar Association—Criminal Justice Section, *The Federalization of Criminal Law, Preface* (Chicago, IL: American Bar Association, 1998).

56. Perry, "Prosecutors in State Courts," *supra*.

57. *See* "United States Federal Judicial District," Wikipedia, http://en .wikipedia.org/wiki/United_States_federal_judicial_district.

58. *See* "United States Attorney," Wikipedia, http://en.wikipedia.org/wiki/ United_States_Attorney.

59. *See* CHIP (Computer Hacking and Intellectual Property) Fact Sheet, U.S. Department of Justice, July 20, 2001, http://www.usdoj.gov/criminal/cybercrime/ chipfact.htm.

60. *See* U.S. Department of Justice, *U.S. Attorney's Manual* § 9-50.102, http:// www.usdoj.gov/usao/eousa/foia_reading_room/usam/title9/50mcrm.htm#9-50.102.

61. *See* U.S. Department of Justice—Computer Crime and Intellectual Property Section, *What Does CCIPS Do?*, http://ncsi-net.ncsi.iisc.ernet.in/cyberspace/ law/responsibility/cybercrime/www.usdoj.gov/criminal/cybercrime/ccips.htm.

62. U.S. Department of Justice, *U.S. Attorney's Manual* § 9-50.103, http://www .usdoj.gov/usao/eousa/foia_reading_room/usam/title9/50mcrm.htm#9-50.103.

63. *See*, e.g., "Prosecutor," Wikipedia, http://en.wikipedia.org/wiki/Prosecutor; "Municipal Police (France)," Wikipedia, http://en.wikipedia.org/wiki/Municipal _Police_(France). *See also* David T. Johnson, *The Japanese Way of Justice: Prosecuting Crime in Japan* (New York: Oxford University Press, 2002), 120.

64. E. R. Milner, *The Lives and Times of Bonnie and Clyde* (Carbondale, IL: Southern Illinois Press, 1996), 135. Barrow liked the V-8 Fords because they were "very fast" and could travel great distances without needing to be refueled.

65. *See* Chapter 6.

66. In addition to expense, training takes time; it can take a year to train an investigator to the point at which he or she can handle cybercrime investigations. Ulf Wolf, "Cyber-Crime: Law Enforcement Must Keep Pace with Tech-Savvy Criminals," *Digital Communities*, January 28, 2009, http://www.govtech.com/dc/ articles/575223?id=575223&full=1&story_pg=1. It is also difficult to find candidates who are qualified to be trained as digital investigators.

67. *See*, e.g., Jason Miller, "FBI, Secret Service Must Improve Cybercrime Training," *Federal Computer Week*, July 23, 2007, http://fcw.com/articles/2007/07/23/fbi-secret-service-must-improve-cybercrime-training.aspx.

68. *See* Joan M. Jensen, *The Price of Vigilance* (New York: Rand McNally, 1968), 18.

69. *See* Jensen, *Price of Vigilance*, *supra*.

70. *See* Jensen, *Price of Vigilance*, *supra*, 17–18.

71. Cynthia Morris and Brian Vila, *The Role of Police in American Society: A Documentary History* (Westport, CT: Greenwood Press, 1999), 84.

72. *See* Jensen, *Price of Vigilance*, *supra*, 20.

73. *See*, e.g., Clayton P. Gillette, "Courts, Covenants, and Communities," *University of Chicago Law Review* 61 (1994): 1375, 1392.

74. *See*, e.g., "Bay City Man Arrested in Internet Sex Sting," *WNEM.com*, April 16, 2009, http://www.wnem.com/news/19197983/detail.html; "John Atchison," Wikipedia, http://en.wikipedia.org/wiki/John_Atchison.

75. *See* "Bay City Man Arrested in Internet Sex Sting," *supra*; "John Atchison," Wikipedia, *supra*.

76. *See*, e.g., John Wagley, "McAfee Launches Cybercrime Unit," *Security Management*, April 8, 2009, http://www.securitymanagement.com/news/mcafee-launches-cybercrime-unit-005618 (cybercrime cost consumers $8.5 billion over the past two years).

CHAPTER 10. GLOBAL LAW ENFORCEMENT: FEW AGENCIES, EVEN MORE CHALLENGES

1. *See* Susan W. Brenner, "Toward a Criminal Law for Cyberspace: Distributed Security," *Boston University Journal of Science & Technology Law* 10 (2004): 2. The discussion that follows is taken from this article.

2. They may also have to deal with animal predators and/or environmental dangers.

3. *See* "The Failed States Index 2008," *Foreign Policy*, July/August 2008, http://www.foreignpolicy.com/story/cms.php?story_id=4350; U.S. Army Training and Doctrine Command, "A Military Guide to Terrorism in the Twenty-First Century," August 15, 2005, http://www.au.af.mil/au/awc/awcgate/army/guidterr/glossary.pdf (defining a failed state as a society with "no functioning governance.... If essential functions of government continue in areas controlled by the central authority, it has not failed").

4. J. Michael Olivero, Cyril D. Robinson, and Richard Scaglion, *Police in Contradiction: The Evolution of the Police Function in Society* (Westport, CT: Greenwood, 1994), 65.

5. *See* Olivero, Robinson, and Scaglion, *Police in Contradiction*, *supra*, 15.

6. *See* Olivero, Robinson and Scaglion, *Police in Contradiction*, *supra*, 19.

7. *See* London Metropolitan Police, *Brief Definition and History of Policing*, http://www.met.police.uk/history/definition.htm.

8. *See* Olivero, Robinson, and Scaglion, *Police in Contradiction, supra*, 19.

9. *See* Olivero, Robinson, and Scaglion, *Police in Contradiction, supra*, 20; David A. Sklansky, "The Private Police," *UCLA Law Review* 46 (1999): 1165, 1197.

10. *See* Olivero, Robinson, and Scaglion, *Police in Contradiction*, 20; Roger Roots, "Are Cops Constitutional?" *Seton Hall Constitutional Law Journal* 11 (2001): 685, 692–93.

11. *See* Olivero, Robinson, and Scaglion, *Police in Contradiction, supra*, 21.

12. *See* Olivero, Robinson, and Scaglion, *Police in Contradiction, supra*, 21.

13. *See The Role of Police in American Society: A Documentary History*, ed. Cynthia Morris and Bryan Vila (Westport, CT: Greenwood, 1999), 2–4.

14. *See* Douglas G. Browne, *The Rise of Scotland Yard: A History of the Metropolitan Police* (Westport, CT: Greenwood, 1973) (1956), 73–112; Sklansky, "Private Police," *supra*.

15. *See*, e.g., Sklansky, "Private Police," *supra*, 1202–3.

16. *Role of Police in American Society*, *supra*, 26. *See also* Bruce L. Berg, *Policing in Modern Society* (1999): 27–34.

17. *See* William D. Eggers and John O'Leary, "The Beat Generation: Community Policing at Its Best," *Policy Review* 74 (1995): 1 ("the public began to forget its role in controlling crime and grew increasingly dependent on the police").

18. The one-to-one nature of real-world crime is more a default than an absolute; exceptions can occur, especially as to the number of perpetrators. Many-to-one deviations from the one-to-one model have occurred for centuries, but one-to-many deviations were rare prior to the use of technology. *See* Brenner, "Toward a Criminal Law for Cyberspace," *supra*.

19. *See*, e.g., President's Working Group on Unlawful Conduct on the Internet, *The Electronic Frontier: The Challenge of Unlawful Conduct Involving the Use of the Internet*, § II(D)(2), March 2000, http://www.usdoj.gov/criminal/cybercrime/unlawful.htm#CHALLENGES.

20. *See* Chapter 6.

21. *See* Chapter 9.

22. It may be that cybercrime, unlike real-world crime, does not fall into identifiable patterns. *See* Brenner, "Toward a Criminal Law for Cyberspace," *supra*.

23. *See*, e.g., Graeme Wearden, "UK Fights Back against Cybercrime," *ZDNet UK*, May 14, 2002, http://news.zdnet.co.uk/internet/0,39020369,2110190,00.htm.

24. *See*, e.g., Andrew P. Snow and Mark Longworth, *The Greatest Information Survivability Threat: The Undetected Barbarian at the Gates*, CERT: Fourth Information Survivability Workshop, 2001, http://www.cert.org/research/isw/isw2001/papers/Snow-31-08.pdf.

25. *See*, e.g., Dan Raywood, "Call Made for More Cybercrime to Be Reported to Police," *SC Magazine*, December 9, 2008, http://www.scmagazineuk.com/Call-made-for-more-cybercrime-to-be-reported-to-police/article/122299/.

26. *See*, e.g., John Leyden, "Cybercrime Losses Tax UK Small Businesses," *Register*, February 19, 2009, http://www.theregister.co.uk/2009/02/19/cybercrime _small_business_survey/.

27. *See* Chapter 9.

28. The historical account of these efforts is taken from Marc D. Goodman and Susan W. Brenner, "The Emerging Consensus on Criminal Conduct in Cyberspace," *U.C.L.A. Journal of Law & Technology* (2002): 3.

29. *See* Organisation for Economic Co-operation and Development, About OECD, http://www.oecd.org/pages/0,3417,en_36734052_36734103_1_1_1 _1_1,00.html.

30. *See* Cybercrime Law, United Nations, http://www.cybercrimelaw.net/ content/Global/un.html.

31. *See* International Telecommunications Union, About ITU, http:// www.itu.int/net/about/index.aspx.

32. *See* Cybercrime Law, G-8, http://www.cybercrimelaw.net/content/Global/ g8.html. For a description of the G8, see "What Is the G8?" http://www.g7.utoronto .ca/what_is_g8.html.

33. *See* Cybercrime Law, The Global Legal Framework, http://www .cybercrimelaw.net/content/Global/framework.html.

34. *See* INTERPOL, About INTERPOL, http://www.interpol.int/public/icpo/ default.asp. In 1999, the European Union created Europol, the mission of which is similar to that of INTERPOL; it focuses on improving "the effectiveness and cooperation" between law enforcement agencies in the European Union. *See* Europol, Wikipedia, http://en.wikipedia.org/wiki/Europol.

35. *See* INTERPOL, INTERPOL's Four Core Functions, http://www .interpol.int/Public/icpo/about.asp.

36. *See* INTERPOL, Information Technology Crime, http://www.interpol.int/ Public/TechnologyCrime/default.asp.

37. *See* Chapter 9.

38. *See* "How Many Countries Are There in the World?" WikiAnswers.com, http://wiki.answers.com/Q/How_many_countries_are_there_in_the_world.

CHAPTER 11. PRIVACY VERSUS SECURITY: WHICH TRUMPS?

1. *See* Chapter 5.

2. *See* U.S. Census Bureau, U.S. POPClock Projection, http://www.census .gov/main/www/popclock.html.

3. *See* "United States," Wikipedia, http://en.wikipedia.org/wiki/United_States (Puerto Rico, the Virgin Islands, American Samoa, Guam, and the Northern Mariana Islands).

4. U.S. Constitution, Article VI § 2.

5. U.S. Constitution, Article IV § 1.

6. *See*, e.g., *Loving v. Virginia*, 388 U.S. 1, 6 (U.S. Supreme Court 1967).

7. U.S. Constitution, Article V.

8. Ronald D. Rotunda and John E. Nowak, *Treatise on Constitutional Law* § 10.10 (St. Paul, MN: Thomson West, 2007).

9. U.S. Constitution, Article V.

10. *See* Rotunda and Nowak, *Treatise on Constitutional Law, supra*, § 15.7.

11. *See* "Bill of Rights," Wikipedia, http://en.wikipedia.org/wiki/United _States_Bill_of_Rights.

12. *See*, e.g., William J. Cuddihy, *The Fourth Amendment: Origins and Original Meaning* (unpublished PhD dissertation, Claremont Graduate School), 31–75.

13. *See* Cuddihy, *Fourth Amendment, supra.*

14. *See* Cuddihy, *Fourth Amendment, supra.*

15. *See* Susan W. Brenner, "The Fourth Amendment in an Era of Ubiquitous Technology," *Mississippi Law Journal* 75 (2005): 1. *See also* Nelson B. Lasson, *The History and Development of the Fourth Amendment to the United States Constitution* (Baltimore, MD: Johns Hopkins Press, 1937), 23–24.

16. *See* Lasson, *History and Development of the Fourth Amendment to the United States Constitution, supra*, 24–25. The Stationers' Company was a guild of printers charged with enforcing the Star Chamber's restrictions on printing. *See* Susan W. Brenner, "Fourth Amendment in an Era of Ubiquitous Technology," *supra.*

17. *See* Lasson, *History and Development of the Fourth Amendment to the United States Constitution, supra*, note at 25–27.

18. *See* Lasson, *History and Development of the Fourth Amendment to the United States Constitution, supra*, 45 (quoting *Wilkes v. Wood*, 98 Eng. Rep. 489 [C.P. 1763]).

19. *See* Cuddihy, *Fourth Amendment, supra*, 128. *See also* Lasson, *History and Development of the Fourth Amendment to the United States Constitution, supra*, 30–45.

20. *See Money v. Leach*, 97 Eng. Rep. 1050 (K.B. 1765); *Entick v. Carrington*, 95 Eng. Rep. 807 (C.P. 1765); *Wilkes v. Wood*, 98 Eng. Rep. 489 (C.P. 1763); and *Huckle v. Money*, 95 Eng. Rep. 768 (C.P. 1763).

21. Seditious libel was essentially speech—written or oral—that incited contempt of the Crown or Parliament or otherwise brought the government into disrepute. *See* "Seditious Libel," Wikipedia, http://en.wikipedia.org/wiki/Seditious_libel.

22. *See* Cuddihy, *Fourth Amendment, supra*, 886–94. *See also* Lasson, *History and Development of the Fourth Amendment to the United States Constitution, supra*, 43–45.

23. *See* Lasson, *History and Development of the Fourth Amendment to the United States Constitution, supra*, 45.

24. Ibid.. *See also Entick v. Carrington*, 95 Eng. Rep. 807, 808 (C.P. 1765).

25. 95 Eng. Rep. at 818.

26. Book III, William Blackstone, *Commentaries on English Law 209*, Yale Law School Avalon Project, http://avalon.law.yale.edu/18th_century/blackstone _bk3ch12.asp.

27. *See Patcher v. Sprague*, 2 Johns 462, 1807 WL 931 (N.Y. Sup. 1807) (valid warrant is a defense to an action for trespass).

28. *See* Lasson, *History and Development of the Fourth Amendment to the United States Constitution, supra*, 53 (with a writ of assistance, one could "search any house, shop, warehouse, etc.; break open doors, chests, packages . . . and remove any prohibited or uncustomed goods or merchandise").

29. *See* Lasson, *History and Development of the Fourth Amendment to the United States Constitution, supra*, 51–61.

30. *See* Lasson, *History and Development of the Fourth Amendment to the United States Constitution, supra*, 51–61, 79–82.

31. *Jones v. Gibson*, 1 N.H. 266, 1818 WL 488 *5 (N.H. 1818).

32. *See Maryland v. Buie*, 494 U.S. 325, 331 (U.S. Supreme Court 1990).

33. 96 U.S. 727 (1877).

34. *See* 96 U.S. 727.

35. *See* Anisha S. Dasgupta, "Public Finance and the Fortunes of the Early American Lottery," *Quinnipiac Law Review* 24 (2006): 227; *United States v. Edge Broad. Co.*, 509 U.S. 418, 421–23 (U.S. Supreme Court 1993).

36. 96 U.S. 728 (emphasis added).

37. *See* Ronnie J. Phillips, "Digital Technology and Institutional Change from the Gilded Age to Modern Times: The Impact of the Telegraph and the Internet," *Journal of Economic Issues* 34 (June 2000): 267, 276–77, http://diglib.lib.utk.edu/utj/jei/34/jei-34-2-3.pdf.

38. *See* Herbert N. Casson, *The History of the Telephone* (Chicago: A.C. McClurg, 1922), 170–98.

39. *See* Daniel J. Solove, "Reconstructing Electronic Surveillance Law," *George Washington Law Review* 72 (2004): 1264, 1270.

40. *See* Andrew Ayers, "The Police Can Do What? Making Local Governmental Entities Pay for Unauthorized Wiretapping," *New York Law School Journal of Human Rights* 19 (2003): 651.

41. Ayers, "Police Can Do What?" *supra*.

42. "Police Espionage in a Democracy," *Outlook*, May 31, 1916, 235.

43. *See*, e.g., "Telephone Exchange," Wikipedia, http://en.wikipedia.org/wiki/Telephone_exchange.

44. *See* Robert Ellis Smith, *Ben Franklin's Web Site: Privacy and Curiosity from Plymouth Rock to the Internet* (Providence, RI: Privacy Journal, 2000), 155–56.

45. *See* "Prohibition in the United States," Wikipedia, http://en.wikipedia.org/wiki/Prohibition_in_the_United_States.

46. The account of Olmstead's career comes from "Olmstead, Roy—King of King County Bootleggers," *HistoryLink.org*, http://www.historylink.org/index.cfm?DisplayPage=output.cfm&file_id=4015.

47. "Olmstead, Roy—King of King County Bootleggers," *supra*.

48. *See Olmstead v. United States*, 277 U.S. 438, 455 (U.S. Supreme Court 1928).

49. Ibid.

50. *Olmstead v. United States, supra*.

51. *Olmstead v. United States, supra* (quoting *Carroll v. United States*, 267 U.S. 132, 149 [1925]).

52. *Olmstead v. United States, supra*, 473 (Brandeis, J., dissenting).

53. *See Katz v. United States*, 369 F.2d 130 (U.S. Court of Appeals for the Ninth Circuit 1966), reversed 389 U.S. 347 (1967). The facts leading to Katz's arrest all come from this opinion.

54. *Katz v. United States*, 389 U.S. 347–351 (U.S. Supreme Court 1967).

55. *Katz v. United States, supra* (Harlan, J. concurring).

56. *Smith v. Maryland*, 442 U.S. 735 (1979).

57. *Smith v. Maryland, supra.*

58. *Smith v. Maryland, supra.*

59. *United States v. Miller*, 425 U.S. 435, 442–43 (U.S. Supreme Court 1976).

60. *See* "Trap and Trace Device," Wikipedia, http://en.wikipedia.org/wiki/Trap_and_trace_device.

61. *Smith v. Maryland, supra* (Marshall, J. dissenting).

62. *Smith v. Maryland, supra* (Marshall, J. dissenting).

63. *See* Council of Europe, Convention on Cybercrime Article 1(d) (CETS No. 185) (traffic data are "computer data relating to a communication by means of a computer system"); Convention on Cybercrime—Explanatory Report ¶ 229 (content data are "the meaning or purport of the communication, or the message or information being conveyed").

64. *See*, e.g., Final Reply Brief for Defendant-Appellant United States of America, *Warshak v. United States*, 2007 WL 2085416 (U.S. Court of Appeals for the Sixth Circuit 2007) (Yahoo! and other ISPs screen e-mails).

65. *See*, e.g., Purdue University Information Technology: Electronic Mail Policy (V.3.1), http://www.purdue.edu/policies/pages/information_technology/v_3_1.html (university "reserves the right to inspect . . . or disclose the contents of electronic mail messages").

66. *See* The Case for Email Security, LuxSci FYI, http://luxsci.com/blog/the-case-for-email-security.html.

67. *Warshak v. United States*, 2006 WL 5230332 (U.S. District Court for the Southern District of Ohio 2006), affirmed 490 F.3d 455, opinion vacated 532 F.3d 521 (2008).

68. Encrypted email is presumably protected by the Fourth Amendment because it is directly analogous to a sealed letter.

69. A federal statute specifically authorizes this if the e-mail provider reads the e-mail(s) as part of providing e-mail service or protecting its rights or property. *See* 18 *U.S. Code* § 2511(2)(a)(i).

70. Officers do this with regular mail; federal regulations permit agents to obtain "any data appearing on the outside cover of any sealed or unsealed . . . mail." 39 *Code of Federal Regulations* § 233.3(c)(1). This apparently includes the contents of a postcard. *See United States v. Choate*, 576 F.2d 165 (U.S. Court of Appeals for the Ninth Circuit 1978).

71. For an account of the legislation that added Title III to the U.S. Code and the subsequent legislation that brought e-mail within its protections, *see* Maricela Segura, "Is Carnivore Devouring Your Privacy?" *Southern California Law Review* 75 (2001): 231.

72. *See* 18 *U.S. Code* § 2518.

73. It also does not require the suppression of e-mail obtained by violating the requirements of Title III. *See United States v. Jones*, 364 F.Supp.2d 1303 (U.S. District Court for the District of Utah 2005).

74. *See*, e.g., David Hricik and Amy Falkingham, "Lawyers Still Worry Too Much about Transmitting Email over the Internet," *Journal of Technology Law and Policy* 10 (2005): 265. A federal statute specifically authorizes this. *See* 18 *U.S. Code* § 2511(2)(a)(i).

75. *See Smith v. Maryland, supra* (Stewart, J., dissenting).

76. *See Warshak v. United States*, 490 F.3d 455 (U.S. Court of Appeals for the Sixth Circuit 2007), vacated in part 532 F.3d 521 (2008).

77. Voice mails and stored phone calls are analogous to stored e-mails and receive the same treatment under federal statutory law as stored e-mails. *See* James M. O'Neil, "The Impact of VOIP Technology on Fourth Amendment Protections against Electronic Surveillance," *Intellectual Property Law Bulletin* 12 (2007): 35.

78. *Warshak v. United States*, 490 F.3d 455, *supra*.

79. *See* 18 *U.S. Code* § 2703(d).

80. Ibid.

81. *Warshak v. United States*, 532 F.3d 521 (2008).

82. *Warshak v. United States, supra* (Boyce, J. dissenting).

83. *See* Email Tracking Tutorial, Visualware, http://www.visualware.com/resources/tutorials/email.html.

84. *See*, e.g., *United States v. Martin*, 2008 WL 5095986 (U.S. District Court for the District of Minnesota 2008).

85. 497 F.Supp.2d 117 (U.S. District Court for the District of Massachusetts 2007). The facts outlined in the text are all taken from this opinion.

86. *United States v. D'Andrea, supra* (citing Wayne R. LaFave, *1 Search and Seizure*, 4th ed. [St. Paul Paul, MN: Thomson West, 2006], 721).

87. 466 U.S. 109 (U.S. Supreme Court 1984).

88. *See* "Subpoena," Wikipedia, http://en.wikipedia.org/wiki/Subpoena.

89. *See United States v. R. Enterprises, Etc.*, 498 U.S. 292 (U.S. Supreme Court 1991)

90. 512 F.3d 500 (U.S. Court of Appeals for the Ninth Circuit 2008).

91. "IP address," Wikipedia, http://en.wikipedia.org/wiki/IP_address.

92. *See* "What Is Google's IP Address?" *Yahoo! Answers*, http://answers.yahoo.com/question/index?qid=20061120105411AAfT0I7.

93. *See* "What Is an IP Address?" *WiseGeek*, http://www.wisegeek.com/what-is-an-ip-address.htm.

94. *U.S. v Forrester, supra*.

95. *See* "Data Mining," Wikipedia, http://en.wikipedia.org/wiki/Data_mining.

96. *See* "Multistate Anti-Terrorism Information Exchange," Wikipedia, http://en.wikipedia.org/wiki/MATRIX.

97. *See*, e.g., "HTTP Secure," Wikipedia, http://en.wikipedia.org/wiki/Https; Anonymous Web Surfing, Secure NNTP, http://www.securenntp.com/; True Crypt, http://www.truecrypt.org/.

98. Mary Patricia Jones, "Proposed Rule 12.3: Prosecutorial Discovery and the Defense of Federal Authority," *Virginia Law Review* 72 (1986): 1299, 1316 note 93.

99. Trial of John Lilburne, 3 How. St. Tr. 1315, 1318 (1637).

100. *See United States v. Mandujano*, 425 U.S. 564 (U.S. Supreme Court 1976).

101. *See Hiibel v. Sixth Judicial District Court*, 542 U.S. 177 (U.S. Supreme Court 2004).

102. *See* In re Boucher, 2007 WL 4246473 (U.S. District Court for the District of Vermon 2007). The facts described in the text come from this opinion.

103. 425 U.S. 391 (U.S. Supreme Court 1976).

104. In re Boucher, 2007 WL 4246473, *supra*.

105. Federal magistrate judges work under federal district court judges. Their decisions can be reviewed by a federal district court judge, just as a district court judge's decisions can be reviewed by a federal court of appeals. *See* "United States Magistrate Judge," Wikipedia, http://en.wikipedia.org/wiki/United_States _magistrate_judge.

106. *United States v. Boucher*, 2009 WL 424718 (U.S. District Court for the District of Vermont 2009).

107. *Olmstead v. United States*, *supra*, 473 (Brandeis, J., dissenting).

CHAPTER 12. NEW WAYS TO FIGHT CYBERCRIME

1. *See* Council of Europe, Convention on Cybercrime (CETS No. 185), Article 36.

2. *See* Council of Europe, Convention on Cybercrime (CETS No. 185): Chart of Signatures and Ratifications.

3. *See* Chapter 10.

4. *See* Council of Europe, Convention on Cybercrime (CETS No. 185), Article 36.

5. *See* Council of Europe, Convention on Cybercrime (CETS No. 185).

6. *See* United Nations, ITU Toolkit for Cybercrime Legislation, http://www.itu.int/ITU-D/cyb/cybersecurity/projects/cyberlaw.html; Reducing Cyber Crime within the APEC Region through Knowledge Exchange and Capacity Building, COTCOMments, 2007, http://www.dot-com-alliance.org/newsletter/article.php?article_id=10.

7. *See* "Putin Defies Convention on Cybercrime," *Computer Crime Research Center*, March 28, 2008, http://www.crime-research.org/news/28.03.2008/3277/.

8. *See*, e.g., John Barham, "Russia's Cybercrime Haven," *Security Management*, November 2008, http://www.securitymanagement.com/article/russias-cybercrime-haven-004818.

9. *See* "Piracy in the Caribbean," Wikipedia, http://en.wikipedia.org/wiki/Piracy_in_the_Caribbean.

10. *See*, e.g., Bradley J.-M. Runyon, "Money Laundering: New Legislation and New Regulations, but Is it Enough?" *North Carolina Banking Institute* 3 (1999): 337.

11. *See*, e.g., G. Scott Dowling, "Fatal Broadside: The Demise of Caribbean Offshore Financial Confidentiality Post USA Patriot Act," *Transnational Lawyer* 17 (2004): 259.

12. The techniques are also known as "hack-back" techniques or "hacking back."

13. *See*, e.g., Richard E. Overill, "Reacting to Cyber-Intrusions: The Technical, Legal and Ethical Dimensions," *Journal of Financial Crime* 11 (2003): 163.

14. Joel R. Reidenberg, "States and Internet Enforcement," *University of Ottawa Law & Technology Journal* 1 (2004): 1.

15. *See* Reidenberg, "States and Internet Enforcement," *supra*.

16. Both conditions would be met if both countries had ratified the Convention on Cybercrime.

17. *See*, e.g., Curtis E. A. Karnow, "Strike and Counterstrike: The Law on Automated Intrusions and Striking Back," *Black Hat Windows Security*, February 27, 2003, http://www.blackhat.com/presentations/win-usa-03/bh-win-03-karnow-notes.pdf.

18. *See* Model Penal Code § 3.04 (Philadelphia, PA: American Law Institute, 1962).

19. *See* Model Penal Code § 3.06 (Philadelphia, PA: American Law Institute, 1962).

20. *See* Karnow, "Strike and Counterstrike," *supra*.

21. *See generally State v. B.J.V.M.*, 137 Wash. App. 1044, 2007 WL 806526 (Court of Appeals of Washington 2007).

22. *See*, e.g., *Brown v. State*, 2009 WL 866207 (Court of Appeals of Texas—Dallas 2009) (the defendant was mistaken as to the amount of force that could be used); *McIntyer v. State*, 1997 WL 732454 (Court of Appeals of Texas—Houston 1997) (the defendant was mistaken of the need to use force); *Stafford v. State*, 549 N.E.2d 377 (Supreme Court of Indiana 1990) (the defendant mistakenly used force against an innocent person).

23. *See*, e.g., *Brown v. State*, *supra*.

24. The DDoS attack is a property crime that can justify the use of force to repel the attack for either or both of two reasons. One is that the attack deprives the company of the use of its property, its computer system. Therefore, it can use force to regain the use of its property. The other reason is that the DDoS attack is depriving the company of some amount of potential revenues. Depriving

the victim of property can be theft, fraud, or extortion, any of which permits the use of defensive force to stop the crime in progress.

25. *See* Karnow, "Strike and Counterstrike," *supra*.

26. *See* Ruperto P. Majuca and Jay P. Kegan, "Hacking Back: Optimal Use of Self-Defense in Cyberspace," Social Science Research Network, March 18, 2009, http://papers.ssrn.com/sol3/papers.cfm?abstract_id=1363932.

27. *See* Testimony of Alan Paller before the U.S. Senate Committee on Governmental Affairs, Hearing on "Securing Our Infrastructure: Private/Public Information Sharing," May 8, 2002, http://chnm.gmu.edu/cipdigitalarchive/files/225 _useftp.cgi-2.pdf.

28. *See* Kevin Manson, *Robots, Wanderers, Spiders and Avatars: The Virtual Investigator and Community Policing behind the Thin Digital Blue Line*, Office of International Criminal Justice, 1997 ("Matters of comity, sovereignty and legal jurisdiction will . . . have to be resolved before intelligent agents begin coursing through servers").

29. Joan M. Jensen, *The Price of Vigilance* (New York: Rand McNally, 1968), 17–32.

30. *See* Jensen, *Price of Vigilance, supra*.

31. *See* Jensen, *Price of Vigilance, supra*.

32. Philippa Strum, "Brandeis: The Public Activist and Freedom of Speech," *Brandeis Law Journal* 45 (2007): 659, 664–65.

33. *See* "Blackout (Wartime)," Wikipedia, http://en.wikipedia.org/wiki/ Blackout_(wartime) (noting that a blackout was "the practice of collectively minimizing outdoor light" to make it difficult for enemy bombers to find their targets).

34. *See* Tom Standage, *The Victorian Internet* (New York, Walker & Company, 1998), 105–9. *See also People v. Carmen*, 9. N.E.2d 981, 986–987 (Ill. App. 1937). *Yeager v. State*, 106 Tex. Crim. 462, 294 S.W. 200 (Texas Court of Criminal Appeals 1927).

Index

About the Author

SUSAN W. BRENNER is the NCR Distinguished Professor of Law and Technology at the University of Dayton School of Law. She has published numerous articles on cybercrime and has spoken at cybercrime conferences around the world.